THE TOWNSEND MOVEMENT

THE TOWNSEND MOVEMENT

A POLITICAL STUDY

By

Abraham Holtzman

Introduction by Wilbur J. Cohen

With a New Preface by the Author

OCTAGON BOOKS

A DIVISION OF FARRAR, STRAUS AND GIROUX

New York   1975

Reprinted 1975
by special arrangement with Twayne Publishers, Inc.

OCTAGON BOOKS
A DIVISION OF FARRAR, STRAUS & GIROUX, INC.
19 Union Square West
New York, N. Y. 10003

Library of Congress Cataloging in Publication Data

Holtzman, Abraham.
    The Townsend movement.

    Reprint of the ed. published by Bookman Associates, New York.

    Bibliography: p.
    Includes index.
    1. Old age pensions—United States. 2. Townsend, Francis
Everett, 1867-1960. I. Title.
[HD7106.U5H6   1975]   368.4'3'00973   74-31007
ISBN 0-374-93934-9

Printed in USA by
Thomson-Shore, Inc.
Dexter, Michigan

To My Parents,
Rebecca and Morris

PREFACE TO THE OCTAGON EDITION

Despite the ravaging effects of inflation in the early 1970's upon the economic status of the elderly, old-age pension movements of the type epitomized by the Townsendites and associated with the politics of social security have not reemerged on the American scene; nor does their appearance seem likely. The campaign for Medicare, the latest public policy issue centering on old-age which convulsed American politics, was led primarily by Democratic Presidents John F. Kennedy and Lyndon B. Johnson. While a variety of interest groups involved themselves in this battle, the National Council of Senior Citizens was the one organization of the aged with sufficient resources and mass membership to engage extensively in lobbying and election-campaigning. It is noteworthy that this interest group of old people was formed with AFL-CIO financial support, and that the labor organization itself was *the* primary proponent among the interest groups.

The replacement of one set of political actors with that of another in the controversies over public policy for the aged, from those of the 1930–1950's to those in the 1960–1970's, was a prediction advanced in the first edition of *The Townsend Movement, A Political Study*. The major old age interest group of that earlier era, the Townsend Movement, remains relevant today for the study of interest groups in general in the United States. Group theory, relations between leaders and followers, political strategy—lobbying, candidate selection and election, the initiative and referenda—and the relationship between the internal decision-making of interest groups and their political effectiveness as they relate to the Townsend Movement are of concern to students of interest groups. This book contributes moreover to a better understanding of those aspects of United States history in the

1930–1950 period relevant to the development of social security policy in the Congress and the states, campaign politics of national as well as state Democratic and Republican parties as they struggled to adapt themselves to the policy demands of the organized aged, and third-party politics—the Union Party of 1936, the Progressive Party of 1948, and the California Townsend Party.

The book was published before the appearance of imaginative efforts by Mancur Olson, Jr. *(The Logic of Collective Action)* and Robert A. Salisbury ("An Exchange Theory of Interest Groups," v. 13, *Midwest Journal of Politics,* Feb., 1969, pp. 1–32) to develop a more systematic empirical theory of interest groups. Salisbury's theoretical formulation, emphasizing the entrepreneur-organizers, benefits (material, solidary, and expressive), group membership, and exchange, seem particularly appropriate for studying and understanding the Townsend Movement. The utility of much of Salisbury's conceptual orientation is, indeed, validated by the behavior of the Townsend leaders and aged followers.

A fascinating study of a state pension movement in California by Frank A. Pinner and associates *(Old Age Political Behavior)* also appeared subsequent to the publication of *The Townsend Movement, A Political Study*. Although the methodology of the two differ significantly, students of the political behavior of the aged, the politics of interest groups, and the social security policy area will find that the two books complement each other admirably.

ABRAHAM HOLTZMAN

July, 1974

ACKNOWLEDGMENTS

I wish to thank the leaders of the Townsend Movement who were more than generous in the assistance they afforded me in my research. In particular, I am indebted to Robert C. Townsend, who, as vice-president, made available to me the resources of the Townsend leadership, and who extended me the warmest personal welcome. Both he and the late Harrison N. Hiles, secretary to the Townsend corporations, provided me with the fullest opportunity to examine the records at Townsend National Headquarters while it was still located in Cleveland, Ohio. Many Townsendites, leaders and followers, ransacked their memories and personal files in their efforts to aid me. Among others I would like to thank John C. Cuneo, California State Organizer, Mrs. Edna L. Eaton, New England Regional Organizer, Mrs. J. A. Ford, Director of the Townsend Legislative Bureau in Washington, D. C., and, of course, the late Dr. Francis E. Townsend.

A brief note is in order regarding the period covered in this study. By 1953 the Townsend Movement had already contracted to a mere fraction of its former size and had ceased to be a significant force in pension politics. Hence, although I continued to follow its activities, I stopped conducting extensive research on the Townsend Movement after that date.

A number of my colleagues and friends have read the manuscript and given me the benefit of their advice: Professor V. O. Key, Jr., Harvard University; Professor Preston W. Edsall, North Carolina State College; Dr. Paul Tillett, Eagleton Institute of Politics; Helen Livingston, Legislative Reference Section, Library of Congress; Robert J. Meyers, Chief Actuary, Social Security Administration, Department of Health, Education and Welfare; Professor Wilbur J. Cohen, University of Michigan.

I would also like to express my appreciation to the Faculty Research and Development Fund of North Carolina State College for its generous financial assistance. My thanks also to the editors of the *Journal of Gerontology* for permitting me to draw upon an article of mine in the January, 1954, issue for use in this study.

To my wife, Sylvia, I owe an eternal debt of gratitude for her encouragement and patience as well as her critical editorial assistance; she was a true partner in the preparation of this study.

Abraham Holtzman

Raleigh, North Carolina
February, 1962

TABLE OF CONTENTS

LIST OF TABLES

11

INTRODUCTION

Professor Holtzman offers us an excellent documentary on the thirty-year-old Townsend Movement at a time when concern over the circumstances of the older population is finding a new surge of expression on the political stage, when methods of meeting some of the basic needs of older people have again become major controversial issues, and when there is renewed effort to organize them into pressure groups. The timeliness of its appearance should enhance the book's usefulness and popularity.

The Townsend Movement, which provides the basis for the author's extended observations, achieved a claimed membership of two million persons organized in 7,000 clubs during a period —the middle thirties—when the population 65 years of age and over stood at about seven and a half million. Had the organization grown parallel with the growth of the older population as a whole, the membership would have reached four or five million today, instead of falling to well under one hundred thousand as it has. That the movement did not continue to grow is perhaps largely due to its success in meeting its major objective. Contributing factors to the decline are also organizational problems in management and political maneuvering, competition of other organizations inspired by its popularity, and the passing of its founder.

Professor Holtzman arrives at the wholly tenable conclusion that the movement has nevertheless had unique and some permanent effects. It did much to make older people self-conscious and to begin to see themselves as a common-interest group. It dramatized their needs and made society aware of the existence of a new group in population. Certainly, anyone who lived through the period knows that *Townsend* became a household word. The movement also helped establish age as a basis for group identification and action as it had much earlier become the basis for establishment of behavior norms and action at the lower end of the age range. All these developments, along with the striking increase in their number, have brought recognition to older people as a new and forceful group in American society, as they had already become in other highly developed nations.

Beyond these consequences, the Townsend Movement was certainly one of several important factors behind the social security legislation and other measures taken on behalf of older people during the middle and late thirties. While Dr. Townsend failed to obtain recognition and support of economists for the soundness and financial feasibility of his "revolving-fund" proposal, he did amass such strength in the country that it appeared a majority of the Congress might be ready to support his plan and did become convinced of the need for specific action along some lines.

Much of the current significance of Professor Holtzman's analysis lies in the extent to which he has been able to develop generalizations concerning organization and political action by older people. To be successful, according to the author, an organization must reinforce or build up group consciousness; must create discontent, if it is not already existent; and must set up objectives or undertake to show how needs can be met. At the same time, the organization must maintain a respectability that will attract followers without forcing them to abandon long-held principles and group identifications. Immediate demands must be such as to arouse opposition, but long-range goals must be consistent with the values and objectives of the larger society.

The present study demonstrates once again that it is difficult to organize an effective third political party. The strength, experience, flexibility, and resources of established parties enable them to out-maneuver the would-be newcomer. Dissident groups develop among the newcomers as a result of differences in ideology or approach. At the same time, it is possible for new organizations to exert political influence through show of numerical strength, pressure on candidates, and maintenance of tenuous identification with or movement between established parties.

The Townsend Movement attained such strength and near success with what was widely held, and often derided, as an economically unsound and threatening (to taxpayers) plan, that fear of a large irresponsible, political organization of older people is still quite prevalent. This potential has obscured the fact that our American governmental system is a well-established and effective method for harmonizing and adjusting the interests and demands of numerous and frequently competitive groups.

The Townsend Movement provides a fascinating, almost play-by-play account of how Dr. Townsend helped older people achieve a new status in our society. Those who are fearful and those who hold for what we regard as more rational and socially responsible processes and progress will find satisfaction in Professor Holtzman's conclusion that there is not likely to be another large, generalized pressure movement of older people. The Townsend Movement developed and flourished in a particular vacuum—in an unusual situation characterized by sudden, rapid growth of the older population, large-scale unemployment and distress, and virtual absence of legislation or programs designed to provide lasting relief and security in retirement and old age. Since that time, interest in and measures to improve conditions for older people have developed widely and rapidly.

President Truman called for a National Conference on Aging in 1950 and the Congress, under the stimulus of Representative John E. Fogarty, called for a White House Conference on Aging that was held in 1961. Between these two dramatic meetings, the social security program became firmly established and now pays insurance benefits to fourteen million persons 62 years of age and over; there has been frequent legislation to provide health and rehabilitation facilities and housing for older persons; millions of dollars are being spent on research on the diseases of the later years; all of the states, dozens of communities, and scores of voluntary organizations, notably labor, civic, and religious groups, have developed activities and programs for older people; and the Congress, state legislatures, and the political parties have shown a rising interest in older persons and their needs. Thus, while many gaps and inadequacies remain to be corrected in the environment being created for our older citizens, the vacuum which nurtured the Townsend Movement has long ceased to exist.

Yet, there is today a resurgence of organizational activity by and on behalf of older people. In 1959, the U. S. Senate Subcommittee on Problems of the Aged and Aging reported an estimated total membership of two million in organizations composed of older persons. Currently, several organizations are campaigning for membership on a national scale with programs aimed at improving the financial, health, housing, and social status of the older population. While it is evident that most older people retain group loyalties developed earlier in life, there is, indeed, some indication of the appearance of a subculture—a self-identification among older people based on recognition of common problems of preserving income security without the indignity of means tests, of retaining the social status afforded to autonomous, participating members of the community, and seeking meaningful opportunities to use the retirement years. Dr. Holtzman's analysis should be helpful to all who are attempting to expand these opportunities for all our senior citizens.

Wilbur J. Cohen
Assistant Secretary of Health, Education, and Welfare, and Professor of Public Welfare Administration (on leave), The University of Michigan.

January, 1962.

CHAPTER I

THE AMERICAN AGED ENGAGE IN PENSION POLITICS

Old-age pension organizations, supported by an articulate, group-conscious segment among the aged population, have since 1933 constituted a new force on the American political scene. Prior to that time the aged had never formed a distinct entity within politics. A radical deterioration in the economic condition and status of older people, however, wrenched many from their positions within society. Exploiting the elements of discontent generated as a result of this disequilibrium, the Townsend Movement was able to create a powerful political force. Offering such slogans as "$200 a Month at Sixty," "Revolving Pensions and Prosperity," and "Honor Thy Father and Mother," its leaders succeeded in attracting millions of members and sympathizers. Such was the response evoked from the aged by the Townsend Movement that state legislatures, national and state parties, Congress and the President were compelled to adjust to its pressures.

An attempt to assess the factors—economic, political, social—responsible for the emergence of political consciousness among the aged poses a challenging question. Why have the aged in the United States undertaken independent political action in contrast to a conspicuous absence of such behavior in other countries? Faced with the grave problems arising out of old age insecurity, governments everywhere have been called upon to assume an increasingly greater role in providing for the older citizen. With one exception, the enactment of social legislation for the aged remained disassociated from special efforts by old people as a group. Only in the United States was the Social Security Act from its inception intimately affected by the politics of the aged. The significance of this behavioral pattern has been largely overlooked.

The Absence of a Separate Political Role for the Aged Outside the United States

Protection for the old was provided in varying degrees by most of the major countries of the world long before the United States Congress was compelled to deal with this problem in the depression decade of the 1930's. Toward the end of the nineteenth century, many governments had already begun to deal with old age insecurity on a systematic national scale. It might be surmised that a concern with the problem of old-age insecurity antedated the full development of popular democratic government, hence the absence of old-age pension movements. The reverse is true, however. National protection for the aged coincided with and benefited from the expansion of democratization. *Independent old-age politics failed to develop because citizens reaching advanced years were accommodated within major institutions, precluding thereby any autonomous role for the aged in politics.*

It is evident that socialist agitation and a rising labor movement in the late nineteenth and early twentieth centuries were directly responsible for modern national plans protecting the aged. In Germany a system of national compulsory old-age insurance, the first of its kind, was initiated as one of Chancellor Bismarck's measures to defeat an advancing socialist movement. In some countries Socialists and Labor enacted the initial legislation themselves. Helen F. Hohman credits the Social Democrats with being largely responsible for shaping social policy in Sweden, including old-age protection.[1] The nascent power of organized labor and the Socialists in alliance with political liberalism secured pension legislation in Great Britain. The Old Age Pension Law enacted in 1908, the first great reform since the Poor Laws of 1601, arose primarily from the massive defeat suffered by the Conservative Party in 1906 at the hands of a coalition of labor and the middle class.[2] True, the previous propaganda efforts of Canon William Blackley, the careful reports of Charles Booth, and Joseph Chamberlain's espousal of pension legislation had contributed to a growing political concern with the problem. But it was the support provided by the Cooperative

Unions, the Trade Union Congress and the Fabians which furnished the political stimulus that made old-age pensions mandatory legislation for Lloyd George, the Liberal Prime Minister.

Across the world in New Zealand, the Old Age Pension Law of 1896 was enacted under the auspices of a Liberal Party which united a politically conscious trade-union movement with small farmers as well as land-hungry city and farm laborers. Leslie L. Lipson points to the Old Age Pension Law as a successful political maneuver to regain for the Liberals the votes lost in urban districts in previous elections.[3] And to cite one example from South America's experience, the Compulsory Old Age and Sickness Insurance Act passed in Argentina in 1923 is attributed by Abraham Epstein to agitation on the part of organized labor.[4]

The participation of Labor and Socialists in the development of old-age pension insurance programs eliminated any grounds for a self-conscious political effort on the part of the aged. Aggressive, social-security minded, and politically potent organizations advanced the interests of old people as an integral part of their general program of reform. Ideologically, the programs of socialism and of labor unions precluded the conception of an independent aged pressing separate demands upon society. In addition, the serious divisions—social, economic, political and/or religious—which characterized the populations of most countries, foreclosed the emergence of any new division on the basis of age alone.

The acceptance of a positive role for the state in many countries facilitated an early national approach to old-age protection. And major political parties other than those of the labor-socialist left also promoted old-age pensions. In Denmark, one of the few countries where pension legislation was not directly related to fear of socialism or to labor agitation, the progressive Left Party of the farmers was chiefly responsible for the first national, noncontributory pension law.[5] The operation of the parliamentary system in these countries also helped prevent the development of independent pension groups. The special-interest group is at a disadvantage in attempting to maneuver between voter and candidate, between party leadership and legislator, and between executive and legislature in a parliamentary system.

The nature of the family and the general status of old people in European cultures combined to inhibit independent old-age politics. Greater respect and social status are granted the aged in European cultures than in our own.[6] Sociologists have stressed the extraordinary emphasis upon youth in contemporary American culture and the isolated position of the aged from ". . . participation in the most important social structures and interests."[7] The extreme conjugal type of family and the isolated role it forces upon old people failed to develop as extensively in Europe as was the case in the United States. The European aged retained vital social and psychological ties with basic institutions from which they derived status and respect.

Factors Leading to Old-Age Politics in the United States

The forces creating old-age insecurity in the United States were similar in many respects to those prevailing in other countries. Industrialization and urbanization precipitated a devaluation in the position of older people. In contrast to conditions of 1880 when the vast majority of our population was a rural one centering primarily around agriculture, by 1920 a majority was engaged in industrial and non-agricultural occupations, and over 50 per cent of the population resided in urban centers. The aged, too, were encompassed in this trend; by 1930, over 50 per cent of those sixty-five years of age and over lived in urban communities.

The sustaining and comforting support for the aged found in the rural community and the strong family disappeared for many individuals. The rural family, in contrast to the urban one, is a more cohesive unit with firm ties, and one wherein aged parents and grandparents can contribute to its solvency.[8] As has been pointed out with reference to the aged in European countries, the emphasis upon youth in our culture and the predominance of the extreme type of conjugal family robbed many older people of a vital stabilizing force. Talcott Parsons has suggested that this "structural isolation from kinship, occupational, and community ties is the fundamental basis of . . . political agitation," on the part of aged in America.[9]

In the transition from a land economy to a money industrial economy, the contribution which old people could make lost its former value. The average city family no longer lived in dwellings adequate for the sheltering of aging parents and relatives. Nor were there large families, gardens or kitchens in which the aged could be of assistance. Indeed, the smaller size of the family contributed to the precariousness of old age. There were fewer children to provide for their parents, and the burden upon younger people was consequently a greater one. Home ties and family solidarity were also weakened by the high geographic mobility which has characterized the population of the United States.

Changes in technology and a lowering of the hiring age weakened the position of old people within the labor force. A long-term decline in farm employment and the expansion of occupations wherein fewer older people were utilized greatly limited employment opportunities. In 1890, about two-thirds of all men sixty-five years of age and over were in the labor force; by 1930, this rate had declined to slightly over one-half.[10]

As the American economy began to affect adversely the position of the aged, the proportion of older people within the population was increasing. Those sixty-five and over had constituted approximately 3 per cent of the total population in 1870, numbering 1,153,649; in 1930 this group comprised 5.4 per cent or 6,633,805. The total population by 1930 had increased threefold since 1870, but the number of those sixty-five and over was nearly six times as large as before. On the average, men and women reaching sixty-five in 1930 could anticipate more than eleven additional years of life.

Another factor, the maldistribution of income, played a role in equating old age with insecurity. According to a study of family incomes and savings by The Brookings Institution for the year 1929, three-fifths of the families in the United States earned $2,000 or less and could save little or nothing.[11] Not only were families of industrial and agricultural workers unable to save, but many in the so-called middle class found themselves in a similar predicament. As late as 1940, the Director of the Bureau of Employment Security, Social Security Board, characterized as fairly liberal, estimates of 10 or 20 per cent for the number of persons reaching an independent old age through savings.[12]

The movement for old-age security up to the time of the depression was almost completely divorced from economic or political expression. Conversely, efforts that were made in the interests of such security stemmed from forces which were politically impotent. Only in the 1920's did organized groups begin a concerted drive to secure pension legislation. It is a revealing commentary on the nature of this endeavor that the Fraternal Order of Eagles deserves primary credit for the few state pension laws that were in existence. For years the leaders of the American trade-union movement opposed any form of social insurance legislation. Not until 1922 did a national convention of the

American Federation of Labor endorse the principle of federal old-age pensions; that year the American Association for Labor Legislation first became active in the area. The A. F. of L. was primarily concerned with wages, hours, and working conditions. It was not comparable in size, influence, or political maturity with the extensive labor movements in Europe nor did it incorporate their basic political approach or possess a similar link with socialism. And it was not until 1927 that the American Association for Old Age Security was first organized under the leadership of Abraham Epstein to unite community leaders and social workers in a campaign for the protection of the aged.

Even before the onset of the depression, Abraham Epstein had estimated in 1928 that 30 per cent of the aged sixty-five years and over were dependent upon others for support, the majority being assisted by relatives and children.[13] In view of known data on low incomes and the inability of three-fifths of the nation's families to save, the strain upon family resources even at that time must have been burdensome. Only six of the forty-eight states provided old-age assistance; less than 1,000 persons were being cared for. A few private pension plans and government retirement plans were in operation, but the number of persons covered was extremely small, and many of the plans were poorly constructed and badly financed. The remainder of the dependent aged was compelled to seek the meager aid offered by private charity or that furnished by local communities through outdoor relief or almshouse confinement.

An acute deterioration in the situation of the aged, resulting from the depression of the 1930's and the inadequacies of ameliorative measures, created the conditions from which old-age pension movements arose. Estimates for 1930 placed the number of dependent aged at 40 per cent of those sixty-five and over, or about 2.7 million; by 1935 the dependency rate had risen to 50 per cent.[14] The precipitous and widespread decline in employment was more severely felt by the old people than by any other group except for the Negro. Labor force participation among men sixty-five and over dropped sharply from 54 per cent in 1930 to 42.2 per cent by 1940.[15] The number of aged sixty-five and over increased at this time from 6.6 million and 5.4 per cent of the population in 1930 to an estimated 7.5 million and 6 per cent in 1935. With unemployment well over the twelve million mark in the depth of the depression, the support of aged relatives became impossible for many families. Private charity and pension plans proved useless in the face of the magnitude of the task; many of the plans collapsed entirely.

State governments were unable to cope adequately with a problem that was national in scope. By the end of 1934, only 180,000 persons were receiving old-age assistance. Twenty-eight states had enacted pension laws, but three of these were inoperative. The elderly population in twenty-three states was not even protected by old-age assistance!

From 1910, when the initial national old-age pension bill was introduced, until 1930, Congress had refused to consider such legislation. Committee hearings were held for the first time in 1930 and 1931, but no bill was reported to the floor of Congress. Favorable recommendations were granted pension bills in the next Congress, but none was submitted to a vote. In 1934, the fifth year of the depression, a national old-age pension bill (S. 493) was approved by the Senate which immediately rescinded its action in deference to President Franklin D. Roosevelt's call for a special study on economic insecurity. Not until late 1934 was a special presidential committee even appointed to study problems of economic insecurity. Although a retirement system for railroad labor was authorized that year, no provision was made for a general old-age pension system for the nation. In this failure of the national government to act during the five gravest years of the depression lay a major responsibility for the subsequent rise of pension movements.

A significant change had occurred, meanwhile, in the composition and character of the dependent aged. Their jobs eliminated, businesses ruined and savings wiped out, an influx of despoiled professional men, retired farmers, skilled workers and small businessmen entered the ranks of dependent aged. These were the people who had attained a degree of independence and economic security. The *laissez-faire* philosophy which had predominated during their lifetime taught that the virtues of hard work and steady thrift were rewarded by an old age of comfort and security. Indeed, these newly depressed groups occupied a special position: they had exemplified the rewards of and beliefs in the prevailing system; they had proved it and therefore trusted and believed in it. Yet they were as helplessly broken on the economic wheel as were their less fortunate brethren. These new accretions to the ranks of dependent aged represented a particularly sensitive force receptive to protest politics.

Political leaders and parties were certainly aware of the plight of the aged. The 1932 Democratic platform called for old-age pension legislation, although through state action. Up to 1934, however, the politicians remained unaware of the extent to which the depressed condition of the aged might generate a threat to their political futures.

The American constitutional framework places a premium upon pressure politics—political action by special-interest groups independent of the major parties. The viability of this form of political action stems primarily from the separation of powers principle incorporated in our governmental organization and from the nature of our major parties, each of which is a loose coalition of state parties and groups with divergent interests. Party leadership and responsibility, both within our bicameral legislatures and between executive and legislature, are fragmented and party discipline negligible. Legislatures are characterized by fluid majorities, constantly changing and cutting across party and sectional lines. Individual legislators may defy with impunity the party or administration leadership. Their party nomination and generally their election to office are autonomous local affairs in which the national party organization and the national platform frequently play little or no role. Under such circumstances well-organized, vociferous special-interest groups entrenched in local communities may intervene advantageously in both the electoral and legislative processes.

Major parties, moreover, generally avoid the championship of new or unorthodox causes until their political attractiveness has been assured. Special-interest groups which are dissatisfied or ignored in representation by parties may initiate independent action on all levels of the political process in the local, state, or national arenas. If, therefore, the major parties would not or could not incorporate protection for the aged within their politics, it was inevitable that such a large, unstable element in the population would find its expression in pressure politics or in the third party. A separate division on the basis of old age alone was possible in the United States in the absence of fixed antagonistic elements within our population.

A number of the new depression messiahs, principally Upton Sinclair and Huey Long, sought to capitalize upon old-age discontent. Not only were their political operations limited geographically, but their appeals to the aged—promises of $30- and $50-a-month pensions to all over sixty years of age—were merely incidental to the programs which they espoused. One minor pension promoter, Dr. J. E. Pope, a chiropodist, tapped for a brief time in 1932-34 the rich potential inherent in a specialized appeal to the aged.[16] His National Old Age Pension Association proposed $30-a-month pensions for citizens sixty-five years and older who retired and surrendered their estates to the national government. On the basis of ten-cent membership fees alone, his organization had accumulated over $60,000 from August, 1932 to February, 1934. In proportion to the small size of his organization and the limited locale of its operations, the response he evoked among the old people in the Southwest was astonishing; the aged were ripe for organization and politics! However, Dr. Pope was exposed in 1934 by a congressional committee as being a fraudulent promoter with a long criminal record, and the limited scope of his program was completely eclipsed by the tremendous dramatic appeal of the Townsend Plan.

The full articulation of the aged came about through the efforts of Dr. Francis E. Townsend and the Townsend Movement which brought their interests into the highest political refinement and expressed them in indigenous American fashion: money radicalism, the pressure group, and the third party. Only when despair among the aged assumed a threatening political form did the major parties and political leaders weigh its strength and future in conjunction with their own.

The concentration of a large and very sensitive group of older people in a state characterized by weak political parties and a tradition of independent political action provided a fertile environment for the growth of the Townsend Movement. In 1930, California, the nation's fifth most populous state, contained the fifth largest number of aged—366,125—sixty-five years and over in the United States. While seven states outranked California in the proportion of aged within their population, none of these states contained more than a fifth of California's old people except for Washington, with less than a third.

A great number of the aged in California were recent migrants who were highly concentrated within one area of the state. From 1920 to 1930 the population of the state had increased over 65 per cent. At the same time, its aged population, sixty-five and over, increased over 80 per cent. No other state had approximated this rate of growth. And in the nation as a whole during this decade, the number of aged had increased only by about 14 per cent. These figures indicate an extremely high influx into California of older people from the rest of the nation. An even greater concentration occurred within the state, principally in Southern California; the number of people sixty-five and over increased by 100 per cent or more in Los Angeles and Long Beach and by over 90 per cent in San Diego and Pasadena.

Consequently few of the older people in the state had resided there for any great length of time, most of them having arrived in the decade prior to the depression. For many, important primary group ties had been severed, and for all, an abrupt transition had occurred at a stage in life when readjustment was most difficult. At this unstable transitional period, the depression caught the aged of California in a particularly exposed position. Many of the elderly had sought semi-retirement and easy living, bringing incomes with them rather than appearing as job seekers.[17] During the depression, pensions and savings were wiped out or frozen through the mass of bank failures. Small marginal businesses failed, and the collapse of the stock market and the California real estate boom carried away the economic security of thousands of these new Californians.

The state itself provided a political atmosphere conducive to the rise of old-age reform movements. In California, political parties had traditionally been relegated to a meager and nominal role—impotent, ill-organized, and dishonored.[18] As a consequence, well-organized and well-financed pressure groups occupied an influential position, benefiting greatly from the availability of the initiative, referendum, and the recall. In terms of new political and economic revivals—Utopianism, Technocracy, End Poverty in California—this state had become a western "burned-over" area.

The Townsend Plan which appealed directly to the aged originated in the Southern California community of Long Beach. Rapid initial expansion of the Townsend Movement was facilitated by the very large number of elderly people residing in this locale. Aged Townsendites and their brethren were able to see immediate concrete results in terms of increasing membership, financial contributions, publicity, and political recognition.

Without this concentration of a particularly unstable group of aged in a politically atomized community, the Townsend Movement might never have attained that initial impetus which fired it across California and into the other states of the nation. This is not to suggest that independent old-age politics could not have been promoted elsewhere. Dr. Pope's Old Age Pension Association had been active when the Townsend Plan was initiated. However, special conditions in California launched a pension movement which succeeded in covering the entire country. The success of the Townsend Movement compelled an immediate consideration of old-age security legislation and stimulated the organization of other pension movements.

CHAPTER II

THE TOWNSEND PLAN

The Townsend Plan was probably the most popular economic panacea in the depression decade of the 1930's. Its promises of $200-a-month pensions for the aged, full employment, and permanent recovery evoked the enthusiastic endorsement of millions of aged and middle-aged Americans, many of whom flocked to the Townsend clubs. Their fellow citizens were confronted with a problem that had long been ignored—the plight of the older person—and one that was new and could not be disregarded—the crystallization of the aged into a political force.

The Townsend Plan was also a bitterly divisive issue. For many of its aged adherents, the Townsend Plan became a matter of faith, a new version of the millennium. Virtually all the economists who commented upon it mocked the plan as the epitome of naïveté. For once, Liberty Leaguers, Socialists and Communists, the National Association of Manufacturers, and the American Federation of Labor found themselves in accord—all opposed the plan. From the politicians it elicited diverse reactions. Some, searching for a means to greater political power, saw it in the memorable words of Chicago's "Big Bill" Thompson as ". . . the most Christ-like plan that has been conceived since the crucifixion. . . ."[1] Others damned it as a utopian pipe dream.

The Plan in Its Environmental Context

A brief examination of the factors entering into the salability and acceptability of unorthodox reforms which are offered for mass consumption might profitably precede an analysis of the

Townsend Plan itself. Groups which address themselves in this fashion to the American public must conform to certain imperatives peculiar to our political patterns.

I THE CONSERVATIVE NATURE OF AMERICAN RADICALISM

Within the American experience of politically significant protest movements, money radicalism has played a vital role. Its tenets have revolved around the demand for cheap, abundant money and for governmental rather than Wall Street control of the banking and credit systems. Faith in the simple manipulation of currency and the monetary system as the solution to difficult socio-economic problems lies at the heart of money radicalism.

Waves of popular discontent which have swept the American political scene—Townsendism, Coughlinism, Populism and Greenbackism—reveal the tremendous appeal money radicalism has possessed. To a large extent this reliance on monetary reform has stemmed from the everyday experiences of people with money and from their respect for its power. Difficulties inherent in understanding the nature and operation of a complex economic system helped foster a conceptualization of major problems in terms of currency or banking crises. At the same time, this attitude has been encouraged by the political necessity of sharpening and simplifying issues in order to secure mass support.

Underlying this close affinity of protest politics for money panaceas is *the conservative nature of American radicalism* which has conditioned our major expressions of politico-economic protest—money nostrums, the regulation of business, and the welfare state.[2] Operating within the framework of the existing system, these reforms have sought to enhance rather than attack its fundamental tenets.[3] Paradoxically, this conservative trait has enabled American radicalism to become a viable force.

Those groups most consistently disturbed in America—agrarian, small business, labor—have believed in free enterprise, competition, and private property. Such groups have proposed adjustments within the existing economic system and machinery of government to ameliorate their own plight or to place themselves in a better position vis-à-vis other groups. They have not sought to repudiate the accepted fundamentals on which they felt assured of well-being once their position was secured. Since conservatism plays a vital role in the American radical tradition, any

program competing for widespread political support must conform to this ideological heritage.

II THE INTERRELATIONSHIP OF PLAN (OR
PROGRAM) AND ORGANIZED GROUP

For this brief discussion, a distinction may be drawn between
a plan and a program, the former constituting a single concept
to which all other proposals are intrinsically related and subordinate, and the latter being composed of a number of independent proposals. A central idea around which an integrated
plan is developed affords many advantages to a new group which
offers a radical solution and appeals to a mass base. For purposes
of propaganda, the plan possesses virtues of simplicity and concreteness, easy political digestibility and salability. Furthermore,
it is more susceptible to being transformed into a faith than is a
program incorporating many proposals.

On the other hand, this course has its implicit dangers. Subsequent modifications in the features of a plan may engender a
significant loss of allegiance from component elements within
the group. An ideological straitjacket, moreover, can cripple a
pressure organization in its efforts to operate within legislative
halls. By offering a number of proposals, the organization which
advocates a program may shift points of emphasis with greater
facility and organizational safety. Whether a plan or a program,
what is proposed is shaped by or affects the following considerations.

(A) *A search for respectability.*—A new organization offering
an unorthodox solution is handicapped from the beginning by
its newness. As Thurman Arnold has pointed out, there is often
no previous or logical place in the mythology of society to which
such solutions may be assigned.[4] Denied a respectable position,
they must engage in a battle for recognition. It is imperative
therefore that the plan incorporate symbols and concepts which
will overcome the stigma of unorthodoxy and provide the plan
with the necessary respectability By infusing therein accepted,
established symbols of recognition, however, the pressure organization, of necessity, de-radicalizes the very nature of its proposals.

(B) *Moral righteousness as a factor.*—Emotional trappings enhance the attractiveness of a plan, especially if the plan can be
identified with immediate self-interest, religion, or patriotism.
For a new organization, this additional coloration represents, in
part, at least, an attempt to gain the respectability that permits

acceptance. In the main, however, it engenders faith in one's cause, a vital attribute for a new organization with unorthodox ideas. Belief in the moral righteousness of one's cause is a spur to activity as well as an inducement to financial contributions. Deep-rooted feelings that theirs was a crusade characterized the prohibition, suffrage and pension movements and imbued their members with an evangelical zeal.

(C) *Creating and reinforcing group consciousness.*—The plan [or program] must aim specifically at the creation of group consciousness on the part of individuals. The relationship should be such that if other sources of strength disappear, group allegiance will provide a base for continued existence in terms of financial and membership support, bargaining power, self-justification. Not to achieve this identification and support is to risk remaining politically impotent.

Individuals who already possess group consciousness due to the pressure of events, personal beliefs, or tradition can readily organize to exert political pressure. The existence of functioning economic and social units—unions, businesses, women's clubs, patriotic societies—provides established bases for group intervention in politics. Even here organizational stability demands a continuous emphasis upon group consciousness.

That organization which advocates a radical politico-economic solution and seeks to become a popular mass movement must be identified with an extensive discontented group. Those persons to whom it appeals may not as yet be sufficiently aware of a common set of interests distinct from those of others in society. Consequently the pressure organization may be compelled to fashion and accelerate the process of group differentiation.

In this endeavor the organization is confronted with a curious paradox. To create a sense of separateness, its proposals must crystallize discontent and capitalize upon broken lines of allegiance to old symbols and authorities. To secure popular acceptance, however, the new and radical proposal must also conform to the criteria of respectability and appeal to accepted symbols and values within the culture. A synthesis of conservatism and radicalism is imperative if a significant group is to be attracted and retained.

(D) *Organizational structure.*—The plan [or program] is related also to the structure and leadership within the pressure organization. This relationship may play a crucial role in determining the degree of success by which the plan is adapted to varying circumstances. In organizations combining pre-existing units, such as churches in the Anti-Saloon League or manufacturing concerns in the National Association of Manufacturers, strikingly different factors enter into the development and modifications of their proposals from those operating in an organization built upon single individuals and specially created units. If policy is formulated through consultation, debate, and vote, the effects upon a plan or program will be markedly different from those decisions which are concluded in an organization characterized by autocratic leadership.

(E) *The question of responsibility.*—It is worth reemphasizing that a solution ". . . around which a political movement is rallied need not be, for effectiveness, a workable remedy."[5] All groups contend that theirs is a responsible program or plan; they cannot do otherwise. But the nature of the pressure process does not necessarily lead to responsibleness. On the contrary, what is irresponsible may be politically attractive. The pressure organization which seeks to mobilize popular strength in order to translate it into political action confronts a tendency, difficult to resist, to stress that which will elicit the widest degree of support.

A Political Analysis of the Townsend Plan

In contrast with the different versions of the Townsend Plan which have appeared since 1935, the original plans possessed two outstanding advantages. They were advanced at a propitious time, the United States being engulfed in the depths of a depression, and they were unrestrained in content. Spectacular claims and glittering promises were rarely, if ever, reduced to sober specifics. Neither internal nor external coercions impelled such a course. Only when confronted with the task of obtaining congressional approval was the Townsend Plan deflated.

I ORIGIN OF THE TOWNSEND PLAN

The official explanation of the Townsend Plan's genesis is that in a moment of horror at the degradation to which human beings had been reduced by the depression, Dr. Francis E. Townsend conceived of the entire plan. As assistant medical officer in Long Beach, California, he had been oppressed by the hopeless condition of aged men and women who, as he, had in their youth pushed forward the frontiers of America. At sixty years of age he faced a similar hopelessness, his own medical position having terminated in a change of administrations.

One morning from his window, so the story goes, Dr. Townsend was startled to see three old women rummaging for edibles in garbage cans. Was this to be the end of the bright American dream?

A torrent of invectives tore out of me, the big blast of all the bitterness that had been building in me for years. I swore and I ranted, and I let my voice bellow with wild hatred I had for things as they were.
My wife came a-running.
"Doctor! Doctor!" She's always called me doctor, ". . . Oh, you mustn't shout like that. All the neighbors will hear you!"
"I want all the neighbors to hear me!" I roared defiantly. "I want God Almighty to hear me! I'm going to shout till the whole country hears!"[6]

The account of the three old women and Dr. Townsend's reaction presents a stirring picture. However, in 1934, Dr. Townsend reported that he had pondered for three years over the means for permanent relief of the aged before devising his plan.[7] In an interview with a New York *Times* correspondent, in December, 1935, Dr. Townsend emphasized that he had initially talked with businessmen, bankers, and economists.[8] In neither of these press interviews did he mention the "old-women-garbage-can" incident, although it was being widely exploited in current Townsend literature.

More conclusive circumstantial evidence that the story lacked veracity is Dr. Townsend's failure to cite this pivotal incident in his autobiography written many years later.[9] The plan was originally conceived, explained Dr. Townsend in 1943, as an idea which might restore hope. While working for the Health Department he had already formulated his conclusions and discussed them with his colleagues. In fact, he explained his continued preoccupation with the plan as due to his state of idleness—he had little else to do!

Dr. Townsend's "inspiration" was essentially an excellent propaganda device, part of the myth element embroidered to sustain the faith of his followers. The legend contained an element of sympathy with the aged, equated the Townsend Plan with the means for preventing such a brutal fate, and identified Dr. Townsend as the champion of the old people. To his followers Dr. Townsend was a savior and the plan a product of his genius.

Two very critical studies of the Townsend Movement have impugned the doctor's claims of originality. Richard L. Neu-

berger and Kelley Loe, in their book, *An Army of the Aged,*
contended that the plan was based upon the premise that "prosperity would come slipping in on a banana peel," an argument
elaborated by Bruce Barton in the August, 1931, issue of *Vanity
Fair.*[10] If the vendors of depression apples sold bananas instead,
a reporter had suggested, prosperity could easily be restored.
Citizens slipping on banana peels would stimulate the economy
by reinvigorating hospitals and clothing businesses which, in turn,
would activate agriculture and industry. In a similar mocking
style, Barton had urged the less dangerous method of retiring
persons at the age of forty-five at a rate of one-half their average
earnings in the previous five-year period. This special class of
spenders would insure perpetual prosperity.

Neuberger and Loe purported to find a remarkable similarity
between the Barton and the Townsend plans in that both called
for a retired pensioned class and urged their followers to organize
and to write Congress. And the Townsend slogan, "Age for
leisure; youth for work," was compared to Barton's "Let young
men do the work, and old men loaf."

According to a second set of critics, Luther Whiteman and
Samuel L. Lewis, Dr. Townsend probably obtained his main
ideas from a plan advanced by a Stuart McCord in 1931.[11] Entitled "A Lecture—Mercy Death for Surplus Labor," it employed
ideas and terminology very similar to the original Townsend
Plan. McCord contended that the aged who were responsible for
America's past production and progress should be removed from
the competitive labor market. Their retirement (at ages fifty to
fifty-five) upon an annuity insurance of fifty to eighty dollars a
month would eliminate permanently the excess labor displaced
by an advanced economy.

Old-age relief was condemned by the McCord "lecture" as un-
just and cruel; annuities were to be paid as a matter of right, not
charity. The sales tax was advocated as being particularly
adapted to the insurance principle, a simple tax which would
prove popular. In spending money each person would contribute through this tax to the purchase of his own insurance.
Maximum benefits were required to insure the full realization of
the plan's objectives.

McCord's plan attacked hoarding and stagnant money. It
promised to increase currency circulation by millions of insurance dollars each month. Aged recipients would spend freely from
the knowledge that their annuities would be continuous. Con-

stant circulation of this vast amount would augment purchasing power and achieve permanent employment and prosperity.

The only important differences from the original Townsend Plan, as will be seen, were the specified amounts of the annuity and the absence of a compulsory spending provision. Implicit, however, in McCord's rejection of the value of thrift and saving and in his emphasis upon continuous circulation of money is the revolving feature of the Townsend Plan premised upon compulsory spending.

In an interview with this writer in 1952, Dr. Townsend denied categorically having extracted anything from the McCord "lecture." He insisted, as he had always, that he was the sole author of all the features of the Townsend Plan. And, indeed, this is quite possible for many of the basic assumptions underlying the Townsend and McCord theses were currently popular in the 1930's. But whatever the possible relationship between the two, it was, after all, Dr. Townsend who carried his plan to national prominence.

II   THE DEVELOPMENT OF THE PLAN:
A STUDY IN IRRESPONSIBILITY

Careful scrutiny of successive versions of the Townsend Plan reveals a mixture of economic naïveté and irresponsibility coupled with a shrewd insight into the dynamics of political psychology. Though there is little doubt that Dr. Townsend believed in the plan's feasibility, crucial features were apparently employed more for their political appeal than for their economic soundness.

(A) *A letter to the editor.*—A letter in the Long Beach *Press-Telegram* of September 30, 1933, marked the first appearance of the Townsend Plan. Entitled "Cure for Depressions" and signed by one F. E. Townsend, it incorporated most of the basic concepts of the plan, although on a relatively unsophisticated level. If money were plentiful, asserted the writer, business would be prosperous. Our technological system had created a surplus of workers which had to be removed from competitive economic life. Retirement by the national government of everyone sixty years of age and over on a pension of $150 a month, on condition that the sums be spent immediately, would insure a distribution of two to three billions of fresh money each month.[12] Pension costs would be offset by a decrease in the taxes necessary for the support of poor farms, insane asylums, and prisons, since the number of inmates would greatly decrease once old-age security was assured.

Money for the pensions was to be raised through a national sales tax set at a sufficiently high rate to insure adequate pensions for maintaining a healthy business community. A sales tax, F. E. Townsend contended, would be the easiest tax to collect as all would realize that their tax payments would stimulate business prosperity and provide for their own futures. Inheritance and income taxes would provide more revenue, and property taxes could be greatly reduced. The letter concluded with an admonition to the citizen to contemplate his government in a new light. The federal government had to assume the positive function of regulating business activity through control of the circulating medium.

In a few weeks an entire page of the Long Beach *Press-Telegram* was devoted daily to letters debating Dr. Townsend's suggestion. To the doctor's astonishment—his autobiography reveals that he had contemplated no program of action whatsoever—people invaded his home to inquire about concrete proposals for achieving his plan.[13] By November, only one month later, he had decided to devote his entire time to the plan, such were the possibilities inherent in it.

The first congressional petitions which circulated soon thereafter in Long Beach incorporated important revisions and called for the enactment of two laws. One was to grant pensions of $200 a month to all citizens without criminal records who retired at age sixty or over and who promised to spend the money within thirty days. The second was to provide a national sales tax to finance the pensions. The response to the petitions was so encouraging that Dr. Townsend was able to convince his former employer, real estate promoter Robert Earl Clements, to enter into a partnership with him to promote the plan. On January 24, 1934, they incorporated as Old Age Revolving Pensions, Ltd.

Although minor changes were made in the form of the plan, it remained at this stage for over a year.[14] Justification for the plan became increasingly sophisticated, however, and by the middle of 1934 an elaborate economic foundation was appended. The $150 pension was so rapidly superseded by the $200 figure that this transition escaped the attention of virtually all students of the Townsend Movement. Confusion was compounded upon confusion by the substitution of the sum $200 for that of

$150 in reprinting the original letter in Dr. Townsend's auto-
biography.[15]

(B) *Two hundred dollars a month pensions.*—The $200 pen-
sion was indirectly justified in early leaflets by emphasizing the
necessity for purchasing power which would exhaust supplies and
reinvigorate business. By the fall of 1934, a more systematic
attempt was made to explain the need for the $200 sum. Any-
thing less, it was asserted, would constitute a dole and prove incapable of stimulating the economy. Pensions had to be sufficient to establish the recipients as envied individuals in society
and to insure an abundant supply of money. As explained to the
nation:

> We set this figure because a standard of living measured by any-
> thing less than $200 per month does not permit the enjoyment of
> enough of the spiritual, educational and artistic features of life to
> bring out the really valuable traits of human character and make the
> most of our citizenship.[16]

The major justification remained basically economic. According to Dr. Townsend, actuarial figures indicated that an annual
investment of $2,000 to $2,500 in commercial production was
required to provide permanent employment for one worker.
Two hundred dollars a month spent by one pensioner would
create employment for one man. What if eight million of those
sixty years and over spent this sum monthly? Not only would
eight million new jobs materialize, but two to three million additional jobs would be available for younger workers since all
pensioners would retire.

The first economic adviser to the Old Age Recovery Plan,
Ltd., Dr. Samuel M. Dick, warned that $200 was the minimum
required to insure "Perpetual Prosperity."[17] One new job would
develop from each $200 additional money introduced into cir-
culation over and above the existing supply. This shift from
investing $200 in production to spending a sum of $200 in excess
of the existing money supply culminated in the flat assertion by
Townsend leaders that each $200 spent would in itself insure
one job.

So central was this provision that all Townsend speeches and
literature identified the $200 pension with the plan. As late as
December, 1935, Dr. Townsend stated categorically:

> . . . a fundamental on which I shall never give way, is that a re-
> volving fund be created sufficient to pay $200 to all American citizens

over 60 who can qualify. Social dividends must be started and maintained at $200 a month—not one cent less.[18]

Inadvertently, however, the political nature of the $200 provision was divulged. "The main reason," replied Dr. Townsend to the query why he had selected this figure, "was so that nobody would come along and offer more. The country couldn't stand more. But also that amount spent every month would provide somebody else with a job."[19] An admission that the pension sum was designed to prevent effective competition is disclosed in a sympathetic biography of Dr. Townsend, published by the privately owned company of Dr. Townsend and Robert E. Clements. Dr. Townsend was quoted on how he had persuaded Clements to join in promoting the plan. " 'But the amount of money!' argued Mr. Clements. 'How are you going to convince the country at large that $200 per month is not unsound?' "[20] The sum had to be large enough, Dr. Townsend replied, to create prosperity through a high volume of purchasing power.

"There are two other points we must bear in mind," Doc told Clements. "First, the glamor of a two-hundred-dollar pension. It will compel attention, and has great psychological value. Second, with our figure set as high as $200 we can feel reasonably sure that no one will bring out a pension plan with a higher amount."[21]

So strong was its appeal and so integral a part of the plan did the $200 pension become that when it was jettisoned from Townsend bills for political expediency, official Townsend literature persisted in espousing that amount. And when it was totally abandoned by the Townsendites, their opponents continued to utilize it as an effective weapon against the plan. The $200 figure ultimately became such a liability that the pension leaders sought to expunge it from Townsend history, contending that the plan had never called for $200-a-month pensions![22]

(C) *The Townsend tax.*—An analysis of the transformation of the sales tax into the transaction tax furnishes additional insight into the nature of the Townsend Plan and its promoters. The original letter and the congressional petitions of 1933 called for a federal sales tax to finance the pensions. Aside from one official reference to a 10 per cent sales tax early in 1934,[23] the OARP, Ltd., did not designate a rate. This hesitancy to espouse publicly an official tax rate must have stemmed from a realization that nothing short of an astronomical sales tax could approximate the sums promised.

Official Townsend literature reveals little consistency with regard to the amount of money to be raised. The original letter called for from two to three billion dollars a month based upon the retirement of from fifteen to twenty million old folks on $150 a month. More modest figures in the first leaflet describing the plan suggested slightly more than one billion dollars a month for one-half this number of aged at $200 a month pensions. Estimates jumped again in the fall of 1934 to approximately two billion dollars a month for eight million pensioners.

The most frequently quoted figures in Townsend speeches and in official literature were twenty to twenty-four billions a year, sums which would have required a tax rate of approximately 80 to 90 per cent since retail sales in 1933 approximated $25.7 billion. It would have been courting political suicide for the plan to have incorporated a tax of this magnitude! Yet from September 30, 1933, through fall, 1934, it was premised upon a federal retail sales tax. It is true that until the transaction tax completely replaced the sales tax, the Townsend Plan called for a higher rate upon luxuries and a lower one upon necessities. This differential, however, served merely as a sop to pacify anyone doubting the beneficial aspects of a retail sales tax. Until its elimination from Townsend literature, the retail sales tax was proclaimed to be the best conceivable tax, and one certain to meet with universal approval. Since all citizens would enjoy its benefits, it was pointed out, all should be compelled to carry a just share in proportion to an ability to pay.

The pension leaders must have become aware of the political and economic shortcomings of their financing device for in mid-year, 1934, a decision seems to have been made to replace the retail sales tax. On the other hand, Townsend Club members and sympathizers were never advised of its "evil" nature until after it had been officially discarded. Without any publicity, the word "transaction" began to be coupled with the term "sales tax." A 2 per cent "transaction sales tax" was first employed in late spring, 1934, although until November a "retail sales tax" continued to be cited by Clements as well as other writers in official publications. The two terms were used interchangeably, almost as if to leave the impression that the difference between them was a semantic one. After "transaction sales tax" had become sufficiently familiar, the term "sales" disappeared entirely.

By January, 1935, the transaction tax had been officially substituted as the financing device which was to be levied upon business transactions in the United States. The figure $1,200 billion appeared as the base of total transactions from which a 2 per cent tax would abstract twenty-four billions of dollars annually. This tax was proclaimed to be the best and only equitable method for raising revenue for the Townsend Plan since it placed no hardship on any class of citizens. As the tax was to be paid in relation to transactions only, the largest taxes would be paid by the largest income group, the smallest by the smallest income group. The sales tax was denounced as unjust since it was not applicable to all sales, but only to the final ones; therefore, the poorer groups carried the chief burden. The official *Speaker's Manual* issued by the Townsend National Headquarters to its organizers in the field admonished that: "All speakers are requested not to use the term 'Sales Tax.' . . . It is a TRANSACTION TAX ONLY and NO OTHER TERM should be used."[24]

Both the transaction tax and the $1,200 billion base were in time modified or eliminated from the Townsend Plan as were the $150–$200 pensions and the sales tax. Reference to $1,200 billion as the total transactions for any normal year constituted misrepresentation, for the figure had been taken from an estimate of 1929 transactions, and the sums for the depression years were obviously much lower.[25] The $1,200 billion figure was attractive, however, in producing twenty-four billions for pensions if multiplied by 2 per cent.

An examination of only two of the principal features of the initial plan reveals that they were inherently political, involving popular appeals to attract mass support. The question of economic practicability and responsibility was a secondary one. The plan could and did extend any promise in the absence of legislative restraint and in the search for as wide a popular base as possible.

III   THE APPEAL OF THE TOWNSEND PLAN

What in the plan made it so attractive as to appeal to millions of Americans, particularly the aged? Specifically, what were the elements of success underlying its assumptions and features? The Townsend Plan's attractiveness was based upon the following factors: (A) a similarity of ideas with the existing socio-ideological climate; (B) its simplicity and concreteness; (C) its promise of hope and optimism; (D) a radical-conservative synthesis; (E) a direct appeal to the aged.[26]

(A) *A similarity of ideas with the existing socio-ideological climate.*—The widespread acceptance of the Townsend Plan can be traced in part to a favorable ideological framework, to the high degree of receptivity in America at that time to new ideas. It was not necessary for the Townsend Plan to overcome the handicap of a world of orthodoxy and respectability. The inertia of prosperous times with its complacency, its hostility and resistance to innovation is a strong barrier to the acceptance of new, unorthodox ideas.[27] Four long years of severe depression had badly shaken the authority and reliability of old beliefs and the trust in conservative leaders. The public was receptive to new ideas and was prepared to advance in new directions under the auspices of new leaders.

In the general dissatisfaction with the status quo, powerful forces had already stirred up an emotional and intellectual ferment. Concepts similar to those embodied in the plan pervaded the American scene and possessed a degree of legitimacy and respectability because of their espousal by recognized leaders and organizations: an economy of abundance; an emphasis on consumer purchasing power; an attack on the evils of excessive savings; the importance of enforced circulation of money and money velocity; reliance upon the national government as the only instrument capable of effecting economic recovery.

The assumptions of an economy of abundance were widely accepted in the economic and political thought of the 1930's. Stuart Chase had asserted that Americans could produce enough to maintain everyone on a living standard of $5,000 a year.[28] John Maynard Keynes, the British economist, had emphasized that ours was not a crisis of poverty, but a crisis of abundance, and the efforts of the New Deal in restricting production underlined this ability to overproduce.[29] Popular attention had been captured briefly by the Technocrats' doctrine that this country was potentially and actually the richest on earth.

The consumer-purchasing power theory of recovery and the attack on idle money found expression both in the practices of the New Deal and in the theories of many economists. Vast public works programs were initiated to increase purchasing power by placing public funds at the disposal of groups which would spend dollars immediately for goods and services. Keynesianism stressed the anti-social character of withholding money from circulation, a philosophy reflected in President Franklin D. Roosevelt's letter of instruction to the Temporary National Economic

Committee: ". . . I take it that a major problem of your committee will be to ascertain why a large part of our vast reservoir of money and savings have remained idle in stagnant pools. . . ."[30]

The forced spending of money was advocated by Professor Irving Fisher of Yale. Fisher's stamped money scheme postulated that the chief cause of the depression lay in the failure of money to circulate. His plan favored enforced spending and penalized hoarding.[31]

Reliance upon the national government as the major instrument for coping with the depression was a logical consequence of the inadequacies of state governments in the face of a national crisis. Bold federal action was stressed not only in the programs of the New Deal, but in the attractive panaceas of popular movements such as Share-Our-Wealth, Technocracy, and Father Coughlin's Union for Social Justice.

(B) *Simplicity and concreteness.*—". . . the greatest value of our plan is its simplicity," Dr. Townsend was quoted as saying in 1935. ". . . I don't want to depart from that. People can understand it."[32] The plan was characterized by a brevity, directness and immediacy that enhanced its salability. Its features were few in number and easy to grasp. One operation, revolving pensions, provided a cure-all for America's ills. The only step necessary was the provision of $200-a-month pensions for the aged. Eligibility requirements appeared reasonable and attainable—retirement at age sixty or over from active economic pursuit and no criminal record. Agreement to spend the money within the month received was the only qualification imposed upon recipients.

The 2 per cent transaction tax appeared to impose an infinitesimally small burden upon individuals. Two per cent of $1,200 billion annual transactions would yield twenty-four billion dollars, sufficient to pay $200 a month to ten million pensioners. If eight million applied, surplus revenues could be used to retire the national debt. "This is simple mathematics which everyone should be able to understand," proclaimed Dr. Townsend before a congressional committee in 1935.[33] Four million aged citizens who had jobs would retire, their positions becoming available to the middle-aged and younger workers. The remaining unemployment would be abolished by the "$200-a-month-spent-equals-one-job" formula. The plan was to become effective immediately upon its enactment, and benefits would be realizable in the present, not at some distant future.

Certain details remained indefinite such as the administrative procedures for raising revenue, disbursing pensions, and enforcing the act as well as the provision for a financial outlay to initiate the plan. But these, it was asserted, were matters of ordinary common sense on which Congress could easily legislate. The appeal to "common sense" in explaining away any vagueness provided an important supplement to the plan's simplicity.

Mathematical exactitude, simplicity, and an appeal to common sense enhanced the competitive position of the Townsend Plan vis-à-vis other radical proposals. Utopianism, Technocracy, Share-Our-Wealth, Social Justice, and End Poverty in California comprised a complex of solutions and a plethora of devices. In contrast, the Townsend Plan offered neither socialism, mysticism, ergs and technate facts nor the promise to make "Every Man a King." It was phrased in terms of everyday hopes and ambitions for jobs, higher wages and profits, comfort in old age.

(C) *A positive program of hope, an earthly salvation for all.*— The Townsend Plan first appeared in 1933 at the end of four years of widespread unemployment, disillusionment, and insecurity. The crisis was all the more overwhelming in that it confronted the individual with vast impersonal forces over which he possessed no control. As never before in the twentieth century, this shook his confidence in himself and in the American ideal of continuous progress.

In place of confusion the plan offered order and direction; for despair it substituted faith and certainty. It relieved the individual of any sense of personal guilt by placing the responsibility for the depression upon the complexity of the economic system. Accepting the machine economy and glorying in its productivity, the Townsend Plan proposed to establish man as its master, never again to fall victim to technological unemployment and business cycles. Farmers were assured higher prices, workers the benefits of a tight labor market, and business an everlasting brisk trade. The unemployed were guaranteed ten to fourteen million job openings, while the aged could retire on the comforts of $200 a month. The Townsend Plan fostered optimism at a time when Americans needed faith and confidence.

(D) *A conservative-radical synthesis.*—Essential features of the plan corresponded to conservative elements in the American heritage. Its objectives were to be achieved legally through the familiar patterns of pressure politics and legislation. It was to be financed through a pay-as-you-go tax program in contrast with New Deal financing. Hence, the plan affirmed a fundamental of the sound money, stable credit tradition of American conservatism.

Diverging sharply from the progressive-radical tradition, the plan made no attempt to "soak the rich." The sales tax or the 2 per cent transaction tax was to be paid equally by all regardless of income. With regard to this aspect of the plan, Townsendites contended that Americans *wanted* to be taxed to provide for old age security. In the plan's repudiation of a dole and its espousal of individual responsibility for financing pensions lay an important appeal to a middle-class morality ashamed of relief. The term "annuity" replaced "pension" in Townsend bills and literature largely because a pension smacked of support by the government. An annuity connoted a reward for individual initiative and reliance.

Nor was the Townsend Plan to be a new device for breeding alphabetical agencies. To the consternation of many Americans the New Deal seemed to be transforming the national government into a conglomeration of strange-sounding bureaucratic agencies. Dr. Townsend endeavored to capitalize upon this sentiment: "The Townsend Plan will serve the . . . purpose of checking the alarming growth of Federal bureaucracy which, in my opinion, is a short cut to Fascism. . . ."[34] The plan proposed operating through familiar departments of government—Treasury and Post Office—and did not contemplate any "new-fangled," triple-lettered agency. Its proponents proclaimed that:

The Townsend Plan interferes in no way with our present form of government; contemplates no change in the profit system of business nor change of specie in our economic set-up. It is a simple American plan dedicated to the cause of prosperity and the abolition of poverty.[35]

While the conservative aspects of the plan reinforced existing values and respected norms, its radical features fired the imagination. The plan promised an immediate and painless economic recovery which many Americans hoped would be "just around the corner." Promises had to be spectacular if only because the crisis and disillusionment were correspondingly extensive. Anything less dramatic would have lacked "shock" value and been lost in the glitter of competing programs.

The magnitude of the pension sum, $200 a month for individuals and $400 for couples over sixty years of age, aroused great excitement. The attractiveness of this amount can be understood only when contrasted with the income figures for 1935, an estimated 87 per cent of families receiving less than $2,500 annually.[36] However, the vistas of security evoked by the $200–$400 a month pensions were fully in accord with the beliefs of aged Americans and their children that they were entitled to a just share in the richness of their country.

The concept of revolving pensions possessed an intriguing appeal in itself. Once pensions were paid, compulsory spending would propel the national income successively to greater heights. At each level more money would revolve back to the Treasury through a tax on business activity, and out again to restimulate an ever-growing prosperity.

In the early 1930's, sums of eighteen to twenty-four billions of dollars as envisaged by the Townsend Plan were awesome amounts which, with only one exception, had never been spent in any single year in the history of the Republic. They exceeded by two or three times the expenditures of the national government in 1935, and dwarfed the total national debt up to that year. Yet the billions of dollars to be spent appeared meaningful in terms of the vast untapped sources of tax revenue purportedly uncovered by the plan. And if the plan extended the power of the national government, the latter alone appeared capable of overcoming the crisis. Nor was any difficulty anticipated in the spending of $200 a month pensions by old people. That anyone would fail to spend the money seemed absurd; especially as it was free and more would follow.

In contrast with its pay-as-you-go features and its refusal to "soak the rich," the plan lay within the tradition of radical protest in its espousal of a monetary panacea as the corrective for the country's ills.[37] The depression was to be conquered by accelerating money velocity, distributing dollars in a manner calculated to guarantee a successful rate of turnover. Moreover, the plan represented an advance over traditional money radicalism in its emphasis upon the welfare state. The national government was to be responsible not only for the operation of the economic system through the continuous turnover of currency, but for the care of a special group within the population. Furthermore, the older citizen was to be provided this security as a matter of right. In offering every citizen of the United States upon reaching "old age" a security which would make him an envied member of the community, the plan broke sharply with traditional practices and philosophies.

(E) *An appeal to the aged.*—Centering upon a new conception
of the role of aged individuals, the Townsend Plan offered to
halt the deterioration of their socio-economic condition and to
restore them to a respected, vital position within society. Consequently, the plan identified itself with the interests of an unstable and potentially dynamic group, one whose numbers were
rapidly increasing. In 1935 more than eleven and one-half million people had already reached or passed sixty years of age, the
period wherein the plan promised immediate personal benefits.

The plan exploited the humanitarian feelings of people in
general toward the aged. The simple fact that people had parents and grandparents made them sympathetic toward attempts
at ameliorating the plight of their elders. Moreover, the plan
embodied a precept of the Judaic-Christian tradition which per-
meates the American culture. "Honor Thy Father and Mother"
represented more than a Townsend slogan; it constituted an
ethical commandment familiar to most Americans.

The plan embodied, moreover, a penetrating insight into the
psychology and role of old age. Affection, prestige, security,
power, and participation are fundamental goals for individuals,
attainment of which depend in the late years of life more upon
society and others and less upon what one can do oneself.[38]
The Townsend Plan promised to attain these goals, whereas
society appeared to be assigning the aged a role of uselessness
tempered with pity and charity. Hence, moral righteousness kin-
dled even higher the indignation and resentment of many older
persons. Not only did they deserve a better life, but if the rest
of America would merely recognize the importance of enacting
this simple law, older men and women could restore prosperity
for all. The spending of billions of dollars necessary to restimulate the economy was entrusted to their hands. They were not
to be pensioners but "Distributor Custodians," trustees of the
nation, under obligation to spend for the common welfare. They
would provide the younger generation with employment, a bal-
anced budget and reduced taxes.

In a society placing a high premium upon youth, the Townsend Plan offered to elevate "old age" to an equal if not more
exalted position. It bolstered the ego of individuals who because
of advanced years had lost self-esteem, status and self-sufficiency.
And it maintained that the wisdom and abilities of the aged
were still required by society to solve its problems. Little wonder
that the Townsend Plan evoked enthusiasm among the aged.

CHAPTER III

STRUCTURE AND CONTROL

Two distinct levels of participation, interdependent but one superimposed upon the other, have characterized the Townsend Movement: the Townsend clubs and the various Townsend corporations. Within the first the aged played the predominant role, although under close supervision and control from the corporations. Power to define the plan, ownership of corporations, and direction of the organizational bureaucracy remained concentrated at a second level. Here leadership and control were vested initially in a private partnership and subsequently in a single family.

The Aged Followers

In terms of the goals embodied in its plan and the composition of its rank and file, the Townsend Movement was primarily identified with the aged members of society. So spontaneous was their response that within two years after the initial Townsend Club had been chartered, seven thousand clubs with a membership of approximately 1.5 million aged people had been organized throughout the United States. In the early days of the Movement the promotion of new membership posed no problems; on the contrary, difficulties were encountered in establishing an organizational apparatus that could absorb the vast influx of old people.

I THE COMPOSITION, NUMBER AND DISTRIBUTION OF THE AGED CLUB MEMBERS

Who were these aged who flocked to the banners of the plan? Observers at Townsend Club meetings and national conventions in the early years reported a predominantly middle-class participation: small businessmen and farmers, retired and otherwise, skilled independent workers and housewives.[1] "Just folks ... Methodist picnic people," is one description of delegates at the First National Convention of Townsend Clubs in 1935.

In 1953, long past the heyday of the Townsend Movement, the following composite picture was said to characterize the typical Townsend Club member.[2] He resided in a small town or on a farm (45.2 per cent lived in communities of less than 10,000 population; 20 per cent in cities between 10,000 and 50,000). He was Protestant (86.4 per cent). He owned his own home (52.5 per cent). He was in his seventies (48 per cent; 26 per cent below 70; 74 per cent above 70). He was retired (54.6 per cent) and received either old-age assistance (31.8 per cent) or old-age insurance (55.7 per cent) or both. His retirement income ranged between $25 and $75 a month ($25–$50: 34.1 per cent; $50–$75: 35.8 per cent). If he were employed (13.2 per cent were employed; 26.5 per cent were unemployed), his earnings were less than $1,000 per year (68 per cent). By occupation he had been either a farmer (29 per cent) or a small businessman or a member of a profession (34.2 per cent).

A high percentage of husbands and wives has belonged to Townsend clubs. Occasionally entire families from grandparents to the smallest grandchild were enrolled as members. While some Negro clubs as well as mixed racial clubs were organized, on the whole the aged Negro population did not participate in the Townsend movement.

Exact membership figures for the early years of the Movement's ascendency are not available, for accurate records were never compiled. Although the leaders boasted of ten to thirty million Townsendites, such figures reflected inflated claims of signatures on a petition to Congress and never represented paid club membership. A more reasonable estimate was advanced by Robert E. Clements, the co-founder of the Townsend Movement and its initial organizational director, who testified before a congressional committee on April 2, 1936, that a total of 7,000 clubs were functioning at the time with a probable average membership of three hundred each or around two million members.[3] Figures released by Congressman John H. Tolan, (Calif., D) later that year indicated that 4,450 clubs representing 1,456,-000 members had forwarded affidavits of loyalty to the Townsend leadership.[4] Assuming that the other 2,550 clubs were active at the time of the original estimate of 7,000 clubs and that they had contained the same proportion of members, a total membership of 2.2 million can be estimated for that period. Discounting a third as young and middle-aged people, a very liberal deduction, about 1.5 million or over 10 per cent of the total aged sixty years and older in the United States had probably belonged to the Townsend Movement in 1936. A nadir for membership occurred in 1953 when only 22,101 paid regular members were recorded.

While precise membership figures were never compiled for the period 1934–37, records of paid membership are available for subsequent years. In contrast with exaggerated boasts by Townsend leaders of millions of members, their club membership figures (which were never publicly disclosed) reveal a much different picture.

TABLE I

PAID TOWNSEND CLUB MEMBERSHIP, 1938–1953*

1938	612,577	1946	173,566
1939	761,624	1947	134,297
1940	646,864	1948	92,687
1941	468,699	1949	52,803
1942	297,610	1950	33,500 (7 months)
1943	271,783	1951	56,656
1944	269,633	1952	31,125
1945	234,754	1953	22,101

* Financial statements submitted annually by the Townsend corporations' accountants listed membership figures. This practice was discontinued in 1947, but from financial returns from sale of membership cards sold for twenty-five cents in 1947 and part of 1948, and one dollar thereafter, the approximate totals can be ascertained. In 1948, 31,298 one-dollar memberships were sold and 61,389 were purchased at the rate of twenty-five cents each. The figures from 1951 on represent a twelve-month year ending July 31. From June, 1950 to January, 1954, 230 life memberships at twenty-five dollars each were also sold.

Although the Townsend Plan was national in scope, appealing to the self-interest of all the aged throughout the country, the distribution of Townsend clubs reveals that old people everywhere did not respond in a uniform manner.

TABLE II

TOWNSEND CLUBS BY REGION AND STATE, 1934–1953

Regions/States	Total Number of Clubs Organized 1934–1950*	Active Clubs 1951–1953**
Far West		
Arizona	80	2
California	1,073	87
Colorado	336	31
Idaho	115	
Montana	128	1
Nevada	11	
New Mexico	68	
Oregon	414	29
Utah	41	
Washington	454	36
Wyoming	78	3
Total	2,798	Total 189
Midwest		
Illinois	547	22
Indiana	604	7
Iowa	362	14
Kansas	312	16
Michigan	864	43
Minnesota	535	35
Missouri	334	14
Nebraska	191	2
North Dakota	105	1 } includes all
Ohio	842	65 } clubs in state
South Dakota	153	15
Wisconsin	487	14
Total	5,336	Total 248

* Data on Townsend clubs obtained from a list of all clubs by states as of August, 1950, contained in a letter to this writer dated August 23, 1950, from Harrison N. Hiles, Secretary, The Townsend Plan, Inc. Alaska (6 clubs) and District of Columbia (3 clubs) have been omitted from this Table.

** With minor exceptions, the Active Clubs ("Banner Winners") represent those ordering 30 or more prepaid membership application blanks in a contest extending for the period of September 9, 1951 to June 27, 1953. See *Townsend National Weekly*, June 27, 1953. Thirty-eight active clubs constitute those "Busy Bee Clubs" (representing another membership drive) not included among the Banner Clubs.

TABLE II (cont.)

TOWNSEND CLUBS BY REGION AND STATE, 1934–1953

Regions/States	Total Number of Clubs Organized 1934–1950*	Active Clubs 1951–1953**
Northeast		
Connecticut	72	1
Delaware	11	
Maine	187	8
Maryland	92	1
Massachusetts	297	21
New Hampshire	97	1
New Jersey	157	
New York	832	34
Pennsylvania	946	32
Rhode Island	6	
Vermont	60	
West Virginia	139	
Total	2,896	Total 98
South		
Alabama	56	
Arkansas	116	2
Florida	410	15
Georgia	61	2
Kentucky	109	
Louisiana	26	
Mississippi	23	
North Carolina	34	
Oklahoma	159	
South Carolina	11	
Tennessee	56	
Texas	190	3
Virginia	21	
Total	1,272	Total 22

Total in U.S. 12,302 Total in U.S. 557

With the existing data, no membership figures being available by states, the relationship between region, aged population and the clubs can be explored only in the most tentative fashion.

TABLE III

GEOGRAPHICAL REGIONS, TOWNSEND CLUBS AND AGED POPULATION,

SIXTY YEARS AND OVER, 1934–1950

Region	Number of Townsend Clubs	1930		1940		1950	
		Total aged population	No. of states whose % of aged was less than national average (8.5%)	Total aged population	No. of states whose % of aged was less than national average (10.5%)	Total aged population	No. of states whose % of aged was less than national average (12.1%)
Northeast	2,896	3,353,866	3	4,373,876	2	5,713,777	2
Midwest	5,336	3,668,121	3	4,631,390	3	5,929,855	2
South	1,272	2,195,974	13	3,070,287	13	4,193,516	11
Far West	2,798	1,122,854	6	1,607,147	7	2,405,352	6

It is immediately clear from Table III that the number of old people within a region was totally unrelated to the response to the plan when measured by the number of clubs that were established. The aged in the Far West were over-represented in the Townsend Movement and those of the South grossly under-represented. The South, with almost twice the number of aged residing in the Far West, contained less than one-half the clubs organized in the Far West. In the Midwest where there resided one-third more aged than in the South and 300 per cent more than in the Far West, three times as many clubs were organized than in the South, but less than twice the number in the Far West. The aged population of the Northeast and Midwest approximated each other, but the latter region contained almost twice as many clubs. The Northeast contained nearly three times as many aged as the Far West, but about the same number of clubs.

The concentration of aged as a percentage of total population within states in the different regions also bore no meaningful relationship to the response of the aged measured by the number of clubs. It is true that the one region, the South, where all the states ranked below the national percentage of aged, also contained the smallest number of clubs. On the other hand, the Northeast possessed a higher percentage and gross number of aged, sixty years and older, than the Far West. And yet the number of clubs in the two regions was virtually identical. A comparison of states between and within regions fails to disclose a correlation between percentage of aged population and the number of clubs. To cite but one example, Iowa in the Midwest contained a higher number and percentage of aged than Minnesota, Oregon or Washington, but also fewer Townsend clubs.

A more acceptable explanation for the geographical distribution of clubs is to be found in the fact that the plan was first propagated in California. The initial organization which coincided with the greatest activity and receptivity to the plan, 1933–36, occurred primarily in the Western states;[5] the first Townsend National Headquarters was in fact located in Southern California. Not until the middle of 1935 were special efforts devoted toward expanding the clubs into the eastern half of the country. Thereafter large gains were achieved among the aged living east of the Mississippi. But the first flush of enthusiasm for the plan had passed, and the momentum of the Townsend Movement was already slackening by the middle of 1936.

The Far West was characterized by a tradition of political independence and direct democratic action on the part of its citizens: cross-filing, recall, referendum, initiative, direct primary, non-partisan local elections. The extensive system of strong party organizations buttressed by tradition and prestige which were found in Eastern states was not prevalent in the Far West. In conjunction with a tremendous influx of population in the Far West, the prevalence of relatively less conventional attitudes and the existence of greater social mobility, the Western political environment was conducive to the initiation of independent popular action at the grass roots level of politics.

In the South only five states, including two border states, contained more than one hundred Townsend clubs in the period 1933–50: Florida—410; Texas—190; Oklahoma—159; Arkansas—116; Kentucky—109. The greatest response among the southern aged occurred principally in those states characterized by a more independent political tradition and a greater contact with other sections of the country. Failure of the Townsend Movement to activate the aged population in the South may be attributable, in part, to the absence of a dominant tradition of direct participation in political affairs by the general population. Dr. Townsend's attacks upon the national Democratic leadership in 1936–40 and his identification with the presidential ticket of the Republican Party must also be considered (See Chapter VIII). Moreover the Townsend Movement was not an indigenous Southern phenomenon, a decided handicap in a region with strong parochial attitudes.

Whether a pressure group operates more effectively within a two-party system and is intrinsically retarded in a one-party system requires further study before it can be advanced as an explanation for the lack of club organization in the South. Comparison with so-called single-party states during this period, such as Maine or North Dakota, does not resolve this question since both had strong Townsend representation in Congress, a higher concentration of aged, and a tradition of local political activity.

Another explanation for the regional pattern of clubs may lie in the impact of the depression upon the socio-economic status of the aged. Figures for 1930 reveal a higher gainful employment among aged persons in the South than in any other area.[6] It is reasonable to assume, therefore, that if the aged elsewhere were more disastrously affected by the depression, they would be more receptive to the Townsend Plan. The greater security of the aged within a rural society may also be suggested as one relevant factor in the lack of response on the part of the aged in the South; except for Florida, the Southern states remained predominantly rural in population in the period 1930–40. And yet strong club concentrations were found in such rural non-Southern states as Idaho, Iowa, Nebraska, North and South Dakota.

One additional factor might account in part for Southern apathy toward the plan. As V. O. Key, Jr., has pointed out, ". . . in the last analysis, the major peculiarities of southern politics go back to the Negro."[7] The plan offered $200 a month to every citizen sixty years of age and older, Negro as well as white. Having little experience in independent political action and residing in an environment where it had not been encouraged, Southern Negroes did not respond to the plan's appeal. On the other hand, the plan was looked upon with suspicion by many whites as a threat to the South's supply of cheap labor. And within the South, the states with the smallest response in terms of number of clubs were not unexpectedly those with the largest number of "black-belt" counties. While undoubtedly arising from many sources, Southern hostility or apathy and its effect upon the growth of clubs had important consequences in the political battles for the plan in Congress.

II THE AGED AND THEIR IDENTIFICATION WITH THE MOVEMENT

The Townsend Plan was initially the primary attraction of the clubs. It opened up for older people a promising future in contrast with what was for many a bleak, lonely present. Placing the aged at the heart of the American recovery program, the plan appealed greatly to the emotional, economic and psychological needs of the older person.

Outstanding among its promises was the $200 pension which was called for in the first Townsend bill. Although this feature of the plan was diluted in later versions of Townsend bills, the aged were encouraged to believe that Townsend legislation would produce $200-a-month pensions. The Townsend press and official speakers stressed the sum of $200 a month until its realization seemed virtually imminent.

Townsend leaders fostered discussions within the clubs of pension budgets which could be employed by the aged—a psychological luxuriating with the money that was soon to be theirs. Two examples illustrate the desperate eagerness and faith of many of the Townsendites with regard to the impending $200 pensions. In February, 1935, the Immigration and Naturalization supervisor for San Francisco cited the plan and a desire to become eligible for its $200 pensions as one of the factors responsible for a record-breaking rush of aged foreigners seeking naturalization. About the same time, large numbers of aged in San Diego endeavored to purchase goods from merchants with deferred payments pledged upon receipt of their first Townsend Plan checks.[8]

While the plan remained a primary inducement for membership, other incentives played an increasingly significant role in attracting the aged and in securing their adherence. Old age brings with it many grievous, psychologically sapping experiences—loss of friends and relatives, subordination by a young and aggressive world, and often physical isolation within a lonely room. Townsend clubs furnished the warmth, friendship and color that no longer existed for many older people. Extensive social activities such as community sings, dances, bazaars and picnics were undertaken by the clubs. The numerous notices of weddings among club members which appeared in the Townsend press revealed that many old people discovered their new life partners at these affairs. As the plan itself declined in appeal, the social character of the clubs which was always a strong attraction assumed greater importance.

Moreover, the clubs afforded old people opportunities for securing respect and admiration from their fellows and from the community through the assumption of leadership positions. Responsibility was not preempted by younger individuals as for the most part the latter did not participate within the Townsend Movement on the club level. Furthermore, as the Movement developed, a hierarchy of positions involving greater status became accessible: congressional district boards or councils, state and regional councils and at the apex, the "citizens maximi" or the national advisory council.

Clubs demanded of their members personal participation in politics and community affairs in contrast with the lack of such participation generally characteristic of the period of old age. Soliciting signatures on petitions, securing new memberships, selling official literature, campaigning for endorsed candidates represented immediate and meaningful activity. Within the clubs, aged members shared in a personal sense of power as the press and community recognized the significance of their plan, and politicians appealed to them on their terms for votes and support.

Premised upon a predominantly aged membership, the Movement manifested a highly religious character. Notwithstanding the large number of ministers active in the Movement, identification of the Townsend Plan with religion was a concomitant of the religious upbringing of the older generation of Americans. In thousands of American communities during the plan's heyday, Townsend ideas were sanctified by being delivered in churches where many club meetings were initially conducted. Every Townsend meeting of whatever size opened with a prayer, and the songs and hymns at the national conventions of Townsend clubs reflected this strong religious influence.

"Our Plan Is Marching On," sung to "The Battle Hymn of the Republic," a popular song at the 1936 Townsend convention, is representative of this identification.

> The Townsend Plan is marching——
> It will never know defeat——
> It will vanish want and sorrow
> And will make our years more sweet;
> Heal the dread of our tomorrows——
> It will make our lives complete——
> God's Plan is marching on!
>
> Chorus
>
> Glory, glory, Hallelujah!
> Glory, glory, Hallelujah!
> Glory, glory, Hallelujah!
> God's Plan is marching on.
>
> The Townsend Plan is marching——
> It will cause all fear to cease——
> It will give us larger freedom.
> And a greater sense of peace.
> Let us praise our God in heaven,
> And give glory to His name——
> His Plan is marching on.

The belief that theirs was a crusade sanctified by Christian principles reinforced allegiance to the plan as well as to its spokesmen, and provided the Movement with an initial evangelical character.[9] Similarly, it colored the attitude of Townsendites toward their opponents who were viewed with an animosity and distrust believers exhibit toward infidels. The organizational leadership played upon this note to solidify group consciousness and identification. "God is on our side, and with God all things are possible," the Reverend Clinton Wunder assured the First National Convention of Townsend clubs in 1935.

Leadership

Leadership in the Townsend Movement revolved principally around one individual, Dr. Francis E. Townsend. While he shared power with a partner in the inception of the pension crusade from 1934 to 1936, the latter was never more than a "co-founder"; to Dr. Townsend was always reserved the primary title of "founder." Control of the Movement appeared to have slipped out of his hands for a brief period in the 1940's, but he quickly succeeded in reestablishing his dominance. In effect the Townsend Movement was the personal creation and possession of Dr. Francis E. Townsend, and his virtues as well as his weaknesses were "writ large" in the plan which it advocated, the nature of its organization, and the politics it employed.

I DR. FRANCIS E. TOWNSEND

Dr. Francis E. Townsend embodied to a striking degree characteristics common to the depressed aged of his time and locale. Like many of the old people in Southern California, he, too, was a migrant having arrived from the Midwest late in 1919. When he first proposed his plan, he was already sixty-six years of age. He had just lost a temporary job as an assistant county health officer, and his prospects for the immediate future were almost as bleak as those of the thousands of old people who were destitute and without hope. It is true that unlike many of the depressed aged, he and his wife possessed a small bank account into which they could dip. Nevertheless, his health was very poor, and he had abandoned all hope for a fresh start in private medical practice. In 1933 the Townsends could see no way out for the future; both were past sixty years of age, alone, and without any income.[10]

Descendent from old American stock, Francis E. Townsend was born in a log cabin on a farm in 1867 in northern Illinois. His formal education was obtained in a small rural school with admittedly poor teachers and in a Congregational Academy.

From childhood, however, he had been an inveterate reader which helped him compensate for some of the gaps in his education. The first fifty years of his life were spent largely on the Middle Border and in the Far West—as a farmer's son in Illinois, a hay speculator in California, an itinerant ranch hand and farm laborer in the West, a mucker in the Colorado mines, a homesteader, teacher and a salesman of iron cook ranges in Kansas, and a medical doctor in South Dakota. Life was hard from the early days of his youth and economic success was elusive. Ten years of roaming the West, of failure and uncertainty antedated his decision to study medicine. At one point in this decade of his twenties, Dr. Townsend reported feeling as if he were "a lost soul, without aim or purpose of existence."[11]

At the age of thirty-one, the oldest member of his class, Townsend enrolled in the Omaha Medical School in 1899. He was compelled to work throughout his training in order to pay tuition and upkeep. And even after he graduated, his medical practice never brought him economic security and comfort. Until the age of fifty when he enlisted in the army in World War I, Townsend spent a very hard life as a country doctor in the Black Hills of South Dakota ministering to farmers and ranchers, cowboys and saloon hostesses. His only prosperous days were confined to a very short period spent as a doctor in the town where he had served as medical officer for an army training camp. Bad health, however, compelled him to move to a more temperate climate than that of the Dakotas.

In 1919, Francis E. Townsend moved to Long Beach, California with his wife and son. Throughout the 1920's recurrent periods of ill health kept him from becoming financially secure. His practice was a meager one. But for a few investments in real estate which, he claimed, brought in a "dribble of cash," the Townsends would have found themselves in more desperate straits. A medical job with the county health department for nearly three years carried him through the first years of the Great Depression. It was while he worked with the indigent of Long Beach as a medical officer that the tragic consequences of the depression were deeply impressed upon him. Here he made a dramatic acquaintance with the distress, poverty and loss of hope characteristic of the needy population and particularly its aged members. This, in brief, was the history of Francis E. Townsend before he penned his famous letter to a Long Beach newspaper which led to the inception of his pension movement.

As a pension leader, Dr. Townsend never cut a dramatic figure in contrast to the other depression messiahs of the 1930's. In appearance he was rather inconspicuous except for a long, gaunt face. His manner of speaking—a dry marshalling of arguments mixed with familiar homilies and delivered in a flat voice—was anything but electrifying. Here were the facts, take them, they are obvious, his speeches seemed to say. No histrionics accompanied his addresses as did those of the Reverend Gerald L. K. Smith or Father Charles E. Coughlin, his temporary associates in 1936. And yet there can be little doubt that with regard to the aged in the pension movement, Dr. Townsend possessed that special quality of leadership which is referred to as charisma.

In the tumultuous struggles for power that characterized the early and even some of the later years of the Movement, Dr. Townsend alone survived; his rivals all disappeared. In part this is attributable to his strategic position in the corporations which controlled the Movement. It stemmed also from the trust and faith of the aged in him personally. His life history was not sufficiently successful so as to induce envy, but it could inspire confidence. While he had failed in terms of accumulating wealth, as a member of the medical profession he was deeply respected. He, too, was an old man, but one who, when faced with economic insecurity and moral despondency brought about by the depression, had refused to admit defeat. By ingenuity and inspiration, he alone had conceived the Townsend Plan for the salvation of old people and all of America. To the realization of this goal he was dedicating his life in leading the old-age pension movement. He had provided the aged with hope where none had existed before; he had articulated their needs when they were voiceless and unrecognized. In the evangelical spirit of the Townsend Movement, this plain, bespectacled man with a dry, uninspiring manner was transformed into a Messiah.

The strong religious influences which pervaded the Movement in its early days contributed also to a reverence and respect for Dr. Townsend. The official publications of the Movement reflected this attitude. Letters by old people and featured columns in the Townsend press identified the doctor and his plan with Christianity and God's work. Some of this writing concealed no doubt the hand of the organization endeavoring to shape a set of prescribed images for the aged membership. But much of it was genuine, a deeply sensed conviction of a generation which had grown up in intimate contact with the Bible and whose members suddenly discovered among them a leader who revealed that they could realize an earthly promised land.

The "founder" was himself an individual of great faith. Whatever his faults as a leader, which were both numerous and critical, Dr. Townsend believed wholeheartedly in the merits of his plan. Its features may have been altered from time to time in order to enhance its political attractiveness, but its premises were fundamentals to which Dr. Townsend remained committed until his death in 1960. Associated with this commitment were a set of attitudes and experiences of the doctor's which may be said to have shaped the nature of his leadership.

Early in his life Dr. Townsend had been attracted to socialism. He had first been exposed to its appeal as a ranch hand and itinerant farm laborer in the Far West at the age of twenty-one. His sympathetic response represented less an intellectual acceptance of its premises and analysis than a strong personal reaction against the harshness of his life and that of his associates. The idealism of socialism captured his imagination for it promised, as he saw it, a world free from poverty, vice, and disease.[12] Medical school reinforced this identification, for his most treasured teacher was a Socialist with whom Townsend discussed controversial issues and whose generosity enabled the new doctor to establish his first practice.

As a pension leader, Dr. Townsend never identified his plan with socialism; indeed, he attacked EPIC and Upton Sinclair for socialistic bias while pointing to his pension plan as continuing and strengthening the capitalistic system. But his sympathetic experience with socialism influenced, if it did not shape, his idealistic approach to human misery and suffering, his diagnosis that something was wrong with the economic system, his reliance upon the national government's assuming a positive responsibility for welfare and recovery.

The doctor was, moreover, a fighter prepared to battle for "right" and against "wrong" despite the consequences. This quality had been tested long before he was identified with a pension plan. In Belle Fourche, South Dakota, the town where he had initiated his medical practice, Dr. Townsend undertook a public fight against boss rule and corruption.[13] At first the new doctor confined his civic activities to a weekly column in the town's newspaper in which he called for justice and clean government. He had been, at that time, he declared with some pride in his autobiography, a "fiery writer in the cause of what I be-

lieved to be right and humanity."[14] In the hope of silencing their
critics, the town bosses conceived the plan of electing the doctor and a fellow reformer, a lawyer, to public office. The two
refused to be bought off, however, and continued to protest,
only now from within the city council. When Dr. Townsend
and his ally became too great a threat to the bosses, a boycott
was organized against them and the two were, in effect, driven
out of town.

Neither politics nor fighting publicly for a cause were un-
familiar to Townsend, the pension leader. Nor was Dr. Townsend devoid of any experience with or feel for promotional or
risk ventures. In his early twenties, he had come to California
to speculate in hay in order to exploit the real estate boom of
1885–87. In 1899 he obtained his first selling job—inducing Kansas farmers to purchase iron cook ranges. He credits this experience with providing him with excellent training and rich insight into the psychology of salesmanship. Summer vacations
from medical school he spent as a traveling salesman.

His acquaintanceship with the psychology of the promoter
also bore the imprint of a more recent and different experience.
Among his close friends in Long Beach were those who sold
real estate in the boom days of the 1920's. In 1927–28 the doctor,
himself, had participated in a real estate venture in Southern
California called Midway City. And after his county medical
job disappeared in 1933, he tried his hand again at selling real
estate. He was never a successful real estate operator and he
met absolute failure in these efforts in the midst of the depression. But it is not irrelevant that the first national organizational
drive on behalf of the Townsend Plan was born "in November
of 1933, in a little eight-by-ten room in the rear of a real estate
office."[15]

In his plan and his movement, Dr. Townsend tasted for the
first time in his life the heady wine of success. The aged responded enthusiastically, at least in the beginning years. Numerous politicians paid public homage to the plan and to Townsend's political prowess, and the national press did not ignore
his contribution. As a result of the pension movement Dr.
Townsend now commanded a national force! He, himself,
marched across the political stage of the nation in the company of the giants of the day, a number of whom solicited his
advice and cooperation.

The old pension leader could not help but be affected by this sudden transformation in his fortune, one which he attributed to his own inspiration and endeavors. Not only did it instil in him a sense of pride in his creation, but it hardened the conviction that he was absolutely right in his course of action. He became very sensitive to criticism, confident that his role was crucial to the entire venture, and somewhat authoritarian in his relations with others. From his associates and political allies in Congress, he expected total compliance with his decisions. Any deviation was interpreted as a repudiation of his leadership which could not be tolerated. Hence the tremendous attrition in the ranks of the senior and intermediary executives within the Townsend corporations and clubs, the unnecessary and often costly conflicts with a number of his legislative leaders as well as members of the Townsend bloc in Congress. Even his bitter opposition to President Franklin D. Roosevelt may be traced largely to his hurt pride; Dr. Townsend considered it a personal affront that he had not been requested by the President to confer with him in the White House, whereas other national leaders had received such invitations. In the doctor's eyes the Townsend Movement was his creation. He had originated it, it bore his name, it proposed his plan. Therefore it should respond as he alone directed.

The fact that the Movement represented Dr. Townsend's sole remaining source of livelihood must also have affected the excessive proprietary attitude which he adopted. When he began to devote himself entirely to the crusade in behalf of his plan, he was already sixty-six years of age, unemployed, and unable to resume the practice of his profession. It must be emphasized that the doctor never grew rich at the expense of the aged despite the sensational charges and allegations leveled by many of his opponents. What money he received as a result of the Movement, he ploughed back into it. He drew a modest salary when compared to those received by leaders of other organized groups; although as compared to the pittances upon which many of the aged relied for their support, it may have appeared overgenerous.

II THE NATURE OF THE LEADERSHIP

A common denominator united the three types of leaders attracted to the Townsend Movement in its initial period of expansion. The majority of national leaders were promoters by profession—real estate operators, ministers, and politicians. Evangelizing the plan was essentially a promotional venture, the sale of a panacea to millions of prospective customers, and their organization into clubs for financial support and political activity.

The director of organization for the Townsend Movement from 1934 to 1936 was the co-founder, Robert E. Clements, an experienced real estate promoter. Clements was thirty-nine years old when Dr. Townsend first proposed that they join forces to promote the plan. From 1920 until he entered into partnership with the doctor, Clements had concerned himself with his real estate firm. He had employed Dr. Townsend in 1927–28 in one of his promotional enterprises, and he had again offered him the opportunity to sell real estate after the doctor had lost his county medical position in 1933. As a broker Clements had dealt with numerous agents, and as a promoter in the California real estate boom he was experienced in organizational and business activities.

The partners divided their responsibilities, Clements assuming the role of organizer and Townsend that of public leader and spokesman. Hence, the leaders and owners of the Townsend corporation which advanced the plan and organized the aged were well acquainted with the tactics, style, and psychology peculiar to the field of real estate promotion. Since Clements frankly considered the pension movement a business venture, and Dr. Townsend viewed it in much more idealistic and personal terms, a clash between the two was inevitable. Clements left the Movement much richer than when he had entered it, having profited considerably from his association with it. Dr. Townsend bought out Clement's share in the partnership in 1936 by employing most of the profits he had accrued from the corporations.

Their immediate subordinates divided largely into ministers and politicians. The eastern regional director, subsequently a member of the Board of Directors, OARP, Ltd., was the Reverend Clinton Wunder, a nationally prominent Baptist clergyman. A central regional director, later a national lecturer, was another clergyman, Dr. Frank Dyer. A third minister, the Reverend A. J. Wright, served both as state manager of Ohio and member of the Board of Directors in 1936. Who better to preach the virtues of the plan and spread its tenets than ministers of the gospel?

A number of aspiring politicians sought ascendency to public office through the Movement. In 1936, some of the principal Townsend leaders campaigned for election under its auspices.

The then vice-president and director of the OARP, Ltd., Gomer Smith, was defeated by a narrow margin for the Democratic nomination as United States senator from Oklahoma. He was subsequently elected to the House of Representatives. Democrat Sheridan Downey, one of Dr. Townsend's most intimate advisers in 1935–36, lost in the California congressional primaries as did Republican ex-State Senator F. A. Arbuckle, western regional director and member of the Board of Directors, OARP, Ltd. Two years later Sheridan Downey won the Democratic nomination and the election for the United States Senate. Townsend Board of Directors D. O. Potts (Kansas) and Otto Case (State Treasurer of Washington) were defeated in 1936 in their attempts to secure the Democratic nomination for United States senator and governor, respectively.

A second characteristic of the senior leadership in the initial era was the relative impermanency of its personnel. As ownership and control resided in the two partners and ultimately in one individual, a ruthless rivalry developed among subordinates to occupy the position of chief adviser and confidant. Because of this competition as well as Dr. Townsend's personal animosities, by the end of 1937 not one top leader who had been active in the preceding years remained with the Movement except the doctor. After 1937, with one or two exceptions, leadership was monopolized by Dr. Townsend and his son.

Leadership became ultimately dynastic in nature, important positions of ownership and control being occupied by Dr. Townsend, his wife, two brothers, and his son. Robert C. Townsend, groomed to take over when his father retired, assumed an active executive role in 1937 at the age of twenty-three as a result of a serious revolt that year: "The doctor wanted one man he could trust and be sure of."[16] After serving in World War II he became part owner and director or executive officer in all the Townsend corporations, in effect, the real operating head of the Movement.[17] Young, likeable, a persuasive speaker and an experienced leader, Robert C. Townsend constituted the instrument through which continuity of leadership was assured. There was to be no abrupt break, no crisis or struggle for domination when the doctor died. Since 1939 the clubs were prepared for this transition, each of their conventions enacting a special resolution designating Dr. Townsend the leader and his son his successor. "Captain Bob" was looked upon by members of the clubs as their own, a product of their Movement, and a

Townsend, which name evoked allegiance and loyalty. Outside the ranks of the rapidly contracting membership, however, the younger Townsend never projected that image among the aged which his father had achieved.

Internal Organization

Structurally the Movement was divided into a national corporation responsible for leadership and the conduct of pressure politics, an official publication to advance the cause, and clubs which encompassed the aged membership. Functionally, the national corporation constituted the legal entity around which the Movement was organized and from which clubs derived their permits to operate. Ownership and direction of the corporation and, therefore, domination of the clubs rested initially in the partnership of Robert E. Clements and Dr. Townsend, and subsequently entirely in the hands of the latter and his family. In spite of the elaborate national conventions of Townsend clubs, the aged were for the most part excluded from the choice of national officers as well as the determination of policy.

The official newspaper was originally owned by a private corporation consisting of the aforementioned partners who monopolized its profits. Only for a short time in 1945–46, and after 1948, did representatives of clubs participate in the direction of their official publication. In 1938 a fourth organ was created, the Townsend Foundation, an unincorporated trust, organized to perpetuate the plan and to function primarily as a money-raising device. It was established by Dr. Townsend who appointed its Board of Trustees; the doctor, his son, and their trusted secretary consistently served as members of the board and as its sole officers. The Townsend Foundation owned the United Publishing Company which included the Townsend printing plant and the building housing the Townsend National Headquarters while it was still located in Cleveland, Ohio, in 1953–54.

I THE TOWNSEND CORPORATIONS

The nature of the organization of the Townsend Movement derived from its initial conception as a personal venture to promote the plan. Once Dr. Townsend had convinced his former employer in the winter, 1933, of the virtues of his plan, the favorable public response to its appeal, and the possibilities inherent in its promotion, a partnership was created.[18] On January 24, 1934, articles of incorporation were filed with the Secretary of State of California creating a nonprofit corporation, Old Age Revolving Pensions, Ltd. (OARP, Ltd.).

"Membership" or ownership of the corporation could not be altered except by vote of its existing "members" who were its incorporators. They were empowered to choose the Board of Directors who in turn appointed the executive officers. The articles of incorporation listed as "members," Dr. Townsend, his brother, Walter Townsend, and Robert E. Clements who served as president, vice-president and secretary-treasurer, respectively.[19] Since Walter Townsend was a silent third partner, Dr. Townsend and Clements comprised, in effect, the Townsend Movement. A corporate apparatus and an attractive plan were their initial assets.

By December 1, 1934, the Movement's expansion had required the establishment of a national headquarters and its transfer from Long Beach to Los Angeles. At the end of the first year's operation, approximately twenty employees worked at National Headquarters; over 1,000 clubs had been organized and more than $84,000 had been contributed. By summer 1936, an elaborate apparatus of regional directors, state managers, and congressional district organizers had been established, a national convention of Townsend clubs had been convened, and close to one million dollars had been contributed to promote the plan.

On September 21, 1936, after the original partnership had been dissolved, Dr. Townsend replaced the OARP, Ltd., with a new corporation, the Townsend National Recovery Plan, Inc. (TNRP, Inc.). A subsequent corporation functioned thereafter under the title, The Townsend Plan, Inc. In contrast with the OARP, Ltd., whose assets upon liquidation could be divided among its "members," articles of incorporation of the latter corporations required, in the event of dissolution, the transfer of all assets to the government of the United States. Except for a brief period 1945–46, "membership" in the corporations remained in the hands of the Townsend family.

II THE TOWNSEND CLUBS

The clubs were unplanned additions to the corporation. It is difficult today to comprehend the enthusiasm with which the plan was greeted in its early years. In fact, the two partners were themselves unprepared for the avalanche of volunteers and letters offering money and assistance and pleading for leadership to secure the enactment of the plan. Hundreds of volunteers evangelized for the plan and Townsend coffers began to fill at an astonishing rate. As explained by Clements: "Enthusiasm grew, and it seemed feasible, and almost a necessity, to . . . keep the people enthusiastic."[20] By July, 1934, steps had been taken to establish Townsend clubs, the first club permit being granted to a group in Huntington Park, California, on August 23, 1934.

Initially, clubs could organize with a minimum of fifty members, each paying twenty-five cents for a booklet describing the plan. To facilitate the organization of new clubs in the first half of 1937, the required number of charter members was lowered to five. Subsequently it was raised to thirty and it continued at twenty after 1941. Similarly, the money transmitted to the parent corporation varied with the dues. Dues payments fluctuated throughout 1937–47 from two dollars to twenty-five cents a year. In the period of 1948–53, Townsendites paid one dollar a year, and beginning with July, 1953, dues were increased to two dollars a year. In return for their membership dues, Townsendites received a permit to operate as a club, a subscription to the official publication, and guidance from the national organization.

In official Townsend literature and through speakers and organizers employed by the national corporation, clubs were led to believe that they determined policy, that their Movement was thoroughly democratic. Before a congressional investigating committee, however, Clements admitted that the founders had not intended the clubs to have any voice in the parent organization. The following held true for every Townsend Club, 1934–54: the permit did not include the club as an integral part of the corporation, and membership of the aged was limited to the club solely. In other words, the OARP, Ltd., TNRP, Inc., or the Townsend Plan, Inc., remained closed corporations, clubs acting merely as service units to provide the mass base upon which the former operated.

The formal relationship between clubs and the national organization was codified in the *Townsend Club Manuals* which were published by the corporation and which described the obligations of the permit and the government of the clubs. The corporations' leadership always reserved the right to amend at will the rules and regulations even though the first *Manuals* granted it no such authority. Up to 1937 the *Manuals* vested in a majority of all members of each club the right to discontinue individual memberships. Club permits could not be revoked except by a majority vote of all members of the State Advisory Board, composed of representatives of the clubs. In spite of these rules, Dr. Townsend personally revoked memberships and club permits. Commencing in 1938, National Headquarters was officially empowered to suspend permits and individual memberships at any time, with or without cause.

Clubs were permitted to direct their own activities "democratically" through successively higher and more responsible levels: district, state, and later regional and national bodies. Two major points characterized this type of self-government. Clubs were represented in higher units through a series of indirect elections only. Initially, 1935–36, the clubs elected representatives to Congressional District Conventions which in turn chose District Boards, the latter selecting the members of the State Boards. All the boards were abolished in 1938, however, by the national leadership. Commencing in 1940 and operating again through indirect elections, District Club Councils were chosen which elected representatives to State Councils, the latter sending three of their members to Regional Councils of twelve. Each of the twelve Regional Councils selected one member to a National Advisory Council. Although the selection process for the National Council was altered slightly in the early 1950's, all of the councils served solely in an advisory capacity; control and ownership of the corporations resided in Dr. Townsend, except for a brief period, 1945–46.

As the clubs through indirect elections extended successively to higher levels of organizational activity, they were directed by a parallel organization of employees personally responsible to the president and secretary of the corporation. These area officers exercised the actual authority, direction, and control over the clubs in their jurisdiction. In 1935–36, congressional district organizers, state managers, and regional directors were appointed by Townsend National Headquarters. By 1937 the entire apparatus was dismantled, but National Headquarters subsequently reintroduced state organizers who were empowered to choose deputies for district work.

With the resurrection of the various levels of council government in 1940, regional directors were also reinstated, although they were abandoned shortly after the collapse of the 1945–46 experiment in democracy. Regional supervisors were operating again by 1952 and a western division supervisor was

established that year. In 1936, virtually every state contained
at least one state area manager and a number of district organizers; some states had from two to five state area managers.
In January, 1954, however, only sixteen state organizers and a
small number of deputies were active in twenty-one states. The
aged in more than one-half of the states were not in contact
with any Townsend organizers.

On two occasions, policy-making powers were conferred upon
the councils by the national organization. In 1942, sole authority
to recommend congressional candidates was transferred to District and State Councils; in 1952, the Townsend newspaper was
also empowered to recommend candidates. The National Advisory Council was also granted some voice in the leadership of
the Movement.

III   CONVENTIONS

Beginning in 1935, and except for 1937 and the war years,
1942–45, when regional conventions were held, the clubs were
assembled annually in national conventions. In theory the delegates in convention constituted a deliberative body, determining policy and reviewing the operation of the leadership. The
gap between theory and practice, however, was always a wide
one. At fault was the composition of the conventions as well as
the leadership and the structure of the parent corporation. In
view of the thousands of delegates, conventions were transformed into mass demonstrations rather than deliberative assem-
blies.[21] Numerous, often important, resolutions were submitted
to the delegates concerning such matters as youth clubs, financial
contributions, revisions of the club manuals, authorization of
additional powers to the leadership and political decisions. Since
the conventions were convened for a period of approximately
four days, most of which was devoted to speeches, reports and
demonstrations, they remained, with one or two exceptions, mass
ratifying bodies, approving whatever was submitted.

National conventions served a useful purpose. The club members believed that they participated in the management and
policies of the Movement. At the same time, the leadership was
considerably strengthened, for whatever policies were adopted
advanced to the clubs with the approval of their own representatives. Ultimately, in terms of internal management and control, the conventions were inconsequential, for the articles of
incorporation of the chartering organizations did not provide for

their existence. Decisions of conventions were not binding on those responsible for conducting pressure politics or for organizing and supervising the clubs, since they served not the clubs but the president and general manager of the corporation. Legally, the leadership could have dispensed with the conventions had it so desired.

IV   THE OFFICIAL TOWNSEND NEWSPAPER

So popular had the Townsend Plan become by summer, 1934, that Clements and Dr. Townsend decided to establish their own publication. Their original venture, a weekly magazine, *The Modern Crusader,* was replaced in 1935 by a sixteen-page tabloid weekly newspaper, the *Official Townsend Weekly.* Circumstances surrounding the origin and use of the Townsend press are such as to suggest that Clements and Dr. Townsend sought to conceal from their followers that the Movement's "official organ" was privately owned.

According to the minutes of the OARP, Ltd., for December 4, 1934, Dr. Townsend and Clements personally decided upon the publication of the newspaper and designated a publisher to work " '. . . solely in a fiduciary capacity *although appearing as the nominal owner of the Townsend Weekly.'* "[22]

The Prosperity Publishing Company which owned the *Official Townsend Weekly* was organized by three incorporators in fall, 1934: Dr. Townsend, Clements and a third member required by California law.[23] The clubs held no share or voice in the Prosperity Publishing Company or in the direction of the *Weekly,* Dr. Townsend and Clements constituted its chief officers and two of its three member Board of Directors. Although 25,000 shares of stock were authorized, only twenty were issued, ten each to Clements and Dr. Townsend. No money was invested in the company other than incorporation and legal fees; it possessed neither printing plant nor capital. An official announcement five weeks prior to the publication of the *Weekly* had elicited sufficient cash subscriptions from Townsend clubs to provide the partners with funds to operate.

Clubs were warned by Townsend National Headquarters against the purchase of unauthorized leaflets or papers published for personal enrichment, since the OARP, Ltd., did not benefit financially from such publications and money would be diverted from the Townsend Movement. Consequently, it was reasonable to assume that if money from such publications did not enter the Movement's treasury, revenue from the *Weekly* did.

Four months after the *Weekly* first appeared in January, 1935, its editor defiantly proclaimed on the front page: "So you want to know who owns the Townsend *Weekly?* Well, Dr. Townsend and Mr. Clements own it. What of it?"[24] A rebellion had broken out in the Movement and the partners were accused of owning the paper. Not one cent of OARP, Ltd., money was used for the paper, asserted the editor, yet all had benefited from it and neither leader "... ever got a thin dime from the paper."[25]

In April, 1936, Clements sold his half interest in the Prosperity Publishing Company and retired with a profit of $50,000 in addition to previous dividends. The purchase sum consisted of dividends of $25,000 each, the doctor using his share to buy out his partner. When the OARP, Ltd., was replaced by the TNRP, Inc., the Prosperity Publishing Company was also replaced by the Townsend National Weekly, Inc.; shares in both corporations were owned by the Townsend family, but the two corporations remained completely separate from each other.

With the inception of the Townsend National Weekly, Inc., all revenue from the *Weekly*, except salaries and a small dividend which the doctor received in 1937, was devoted to financing the promotional and political activities of the Townsend National Recovery Plan, Inc. In fact, during 1937–38, the Townsend National Weekly, Inc., served as the principal financing tool for the TNRP, Inc., and prevented its financial collapse. Dr. Townsend retained ownership and control, and the corporation owning the *Weekly* remained free from club influence until 1945. Beginning in 1948, ownership in the corporation was transferred to The Townsend Plan, Inc.

V   CLUBS AND "DEMOCRATIC" GOVERNMENT

The relationship between the internal components of the Movement is best exemplified in an analysis of the three abortive steps toward democratization that were undertaken. Coincident with the defeat of the plan in the House of Representatives in 1935, there erupted within the clubs a series of revolts sufficiently widespread to indicate that rank and file were responding to charges of dictatorship, inefficiency, and corruption which had been raised by important club leaders. Assured in the past that their Movement was democratic, the clubs were now suddenly informed by Clements that the time had come to establish a democratic organization, long contemplated by the leaders.[26] Congressional and state area boards were instituted whereby clubs could elect their leaders and make the Movement democratic. Democracy represented, of course, little more than window dressing, for the boards were advisory in nature, and ownership and control remained firmly in the grip of the two partners. Nevertheless, the leaders weathered the rebellion.

With a congressional committee in 1936 probing the charges raised by the rebels of 1935, Dr. Townsend offered a new program of democratic self-government. To do away with one-man control, he announced, the Board of Directors of the OARP, Ltd., had been expanded to include seven members of the Movement. Since all seven were actually hired employees of the OARP, Ltd., appointed by and personally responsible to the doctor who was empowered to appoint the board at will, the extent of club participation in the management of the Movement is obvious. Secondly, clubs were instructed to elect an outstanding Townsendite from each state to serve on a National Advisory Board of "Citizens Maximi" to counsel the Board of Directors on national policy.

One of the most controversial resolutions before the delegates at the Second National Convention of Townsend Clubs in 1936 concerned the replacement of the Old Age Revolving Pensions, Ltd., with a new corporation, Townsend National Recovery Plan, Inc., and the transfer of its ownership and that of the *Weekly* to the "Citizens Maximi."[27] The doctor succeeded in having this resolution recommitted to committee. A similar proposal was offered as a compromise, excluding all reference to the *Weekly* and entrusting the "membership" shares in the TNRP, Inc., to the "Citizens Maximi," to be held in trust for one year before that group exercised full control. At one point the doctor urged its adoption, but at the crucial moment he helped engineer its defeat. Whether he would actually have transferred his shares in the face of an adverse vote remains doubtful.

Within a short time both democratic reforms were nullified. Once the convention had dissolved, the "Citizens Maximi" disappeared as an organized body; they were never summoned to advise on policy. A somewhat similar fate befell the new Board of Directors. Of the seven appointed when the doctor announced his new reform, four were dismissed by Dr. Townsend within a few months for political and organizational differences and one resigned in protest.

Ownership and control of the TNRP, Inc., was voluntarily transferred by Dr. Townsend, in 1945, to representatives of the clubs. A year later, upon his insistent demand, and under threat of a civil war that might have destroyed the Movement, the club representatives restored to him complete authority. What occurred in the interval is an interesting commentary on the character of the old pension leader and on the relationship of clubs, organizational structure, and demcratic leadership.

A revolt of intermediary Townsend leaders in 1937, which led to the establishment of a competing pension organization, and the defeat of the Townsend bill on a record vote in the House of Representatives in 1939 set the background for the advancement of this new form of self-government. From the outset, Dr. Townsend encouraged the fulfillment of the club-council form of government similar to the advisory boards of 1935–36. Through a series of indirect elections, club representatives were chosen to serve on congressional, state and regional councils and ultimately on a National Advisory Council, each composed of twelve club presidents. While this organization was evolving from 1940 to 1945, Dr. Townsend publicly proclaimed his intention to place the Movement completely within the hands of the clubs through their National Advisory Council.[28]

Ironically, the first meeting of the National Council with Dr. Townsend, in May, 1945, represented the apex rather than the beginning of mutual trust and cooperation between the two.[29] Dr. Townsend, as president, expressed his deep joy and satisfaction with the completion of club-representative government. He had maintained an almost autocratic control over the organization since its inception, he informed the council, and he now wished to see control and guidance placed in their hands. Dr. Townsend included the councilmen as "members" and directors of the TNRP, Inc., and they voted unanimously to retain him as president and leader, his son to be his successor. Since the council now constituted a majority of the owners and directors of the TNRP, Inc., the Townsend corporation responsible for chartering and directing the clubs and for conducting political activities on behalf of the plan belonged legally to representatives of the Movement's rank and file.

Although the doctor had announced his intention to transfer ownership of the Townsend National Weekly, Inc., to the council, this step was not accomplished at the initial meetings. Structurally the Movement remained divided instead of being unified under the new leadership. The Townsend Foundation, a principal money-raising branch, and the *Weekly*, the propaganda medium, were still controlled, and the latter owned, by the council's executive employee, Dr. Townsend. To protect itself and to insure the development of a unified, harmonious policy, the National Council demanded that complete authority over all the organs of the movement be integrated under its direction and supervision. In spite of his speech at the first meeting, Dr. Townsend had contemplated that the council would turn to him for guidance and leadership.[30] Once the council assumed an independent position in deciding policy and a clash developed between the two, it was inevitable that Dr. Townsend would resort to the use of his personal organizations, thereby creating a division in leadership as well as confusion within the Movement.

At the second meeting of the National Council, Dr. Townsend and his employers clashed repeatedly over his proposals to reinforce his position. The council refused to accede to his demands and the atmosphere of mutual trust which had characterized the earlier meeting disappeared in a welter of charges and countercharges. The session was ultimately brought to a peaceful conclusion, however, and Dr. Townsend arranged for the councilmen to become directors of the Townsend National Weekly, Inc.

The relationship between the council and its president deteriorated completely when the *Weekly* announced in September, 1945, that it reserved the right to comment critically upon the actions of the council and its members; otherwise, the doctor editorialized, Townsendites would have little opportunity to learn whether their representatives were misleading them.[31] This proposal constituted a direct challenge to the council as owner and director of the pressure organization as well as majority director of the Townsend National Weekly, Inc. That its policies and actions should be subject to criticism and attack by hired employees responsible for carrying out such policies was intolerable. At an increasingly rapid rate, thereafter, the council undertook to isolate Dr. Townsend within the Movement in so far as it was possible; he was shorn of his executive powers, retaining merely the title of president. A position of executive vice-president, responsible solely to the council, was created to which were transferred the powers previously held by the president.

A counterattack emphasizing the importance of continued loyalty to Dr. Townsend was undertaken by the *Weekly*, the clubs being advised that opportunists were attempting to usurp the doctor's position. The rank and file of the Townsend clubs had never been informed through the *Weekly* that Dr. Townsend had been divested of his powers or that their own representatives had found it necessary to do so. The conflict came to a climax in a bitter session of the council in May, 1946. Dr. Townsend charged the council and its executive vice-president with inefficiency and incompetency, and demanded restoration of full executive powers, threatening, otherwise, to resign and carry civil war to the clubs.[32]

At first adamant in refusing to accede to Dr. Townsend's demands, the council finally surrendered. The club representatives had determined to retain full governing power, but adroit maneuvering on the part of the leader's son frustrated their plans. According to Robert C. Townsend, as treasurer of the Townsend Foundation and one of its trustees, he had withdrawn all of its funds and entrusted them to his wife.[33] Since this sum constituted the available funds in Townsend National Headquarters, the National Council capitulated, realizing that it could not meet the payroll of the TNRP, Inc.

By the end of the year, most councilmen had resigned as corporation directors and "members," and Dr. Townsend had regained legal ownership as well as operative control of the TNRP, Inc. Councilmen had sought to reassert their primacy within the corporation, but the secretary of the corporation, a loyal supporter of Dr. Townsend, thwarted all their attempts to secure the meeting of a quorum of directors and "members."[34] In the absence of a quorum, they were legally precluded from acting. As a direct consequence of this controversy, a new and competing pension organization, the American Pension Committee, Inc., was established by a number of the dissident Townsendites.

At the 1947 National Convention of Townsend Clubs, a resolution to restore full control to the National Council was defeated at Dr. Townsend's insistence: "I personally object to giving control of this organization to any elected group."[35] National council members continued to be elected to the Board of Directors of both The Townsend Plan, Inc., and the Townsend National Weekly, Inc., but "membership" or ownership remained vested in Dr. Townsend, Robert C. Townsend and H. N. Hiles, the secretary of The Townsend Plan, Inc.

VI GROUP LOYALTY AND CONTROL

Organizations attempt to instil in their membership an identification with and an adherence to the organization and its
ideals. The more successful are these efforts to develop separateness from and a priority over other group allegiances, the greater
is internal cohesion, loyalty, and obedience. A group belief system and established behavior patterns were primary objectives
of the leaders from the very inception of the Movement.

Townsend propaganda employed a twofold approach to this
problem. It stressed the existence of a separate old-age group in
the population with peculiar problems and interests, and it attempted to identify the well-being of this group with the Townsend Movement. Similarly, it sought to create "Townsendites,"
loyal to the Townsend leadership, plan, clubs, and congressmen.

Club members were encouraged to identify themselves and
their movement with one central symbol, Dr. Townsend. The
organs of the Movement bore his name: Townsend Plan, Townsend Club, Townsend *Weekly*, Townsend National Recovery
Plan, Inc., Townsend Plan, Inc. Club meetings closed with the
Townsend Pledge, carefully phrased to associate success of the
plan with loyalty to the Movement's leadership.

The Townsend Plan WILL succeed. I therefore pledge my allegiance to its principles, to its Founder, Dr. Francis E. Townsend, to
its leaders, and to all loyal members. . . .

And in their oath of office, club council officers promised to "promote the Townsend Plan as defined and explained by the
Founder-Leader of the Townsend Movement, Dr. Francis E.
Townsend."[36] Any violation of this oath constituted sufficient
grounds for removal from office.

Two national celebrations were instituted to focus upon the
pension leader. Beginning in 1938, conventions annually decreed
that the clubs celebrate Dr. Townsend's birthday. It provided
an occasion for festivity and for the raising of funds. The annual
homecoming or Founder's Day Rally involved a pilgrimage of
the faithful to the Illinois birthplace of their leader. Before it
was discontinued in the late forties, thousands of followers had
flocked annually to Fairbury, Illinois, where the old Townsend
farm had been located.

To isolate Townsendites from exposure to "undesirable" influences, National Headquarters at all times insisted that unauthorized speakers and literature be excluded from club meetings.

The *Weekly,* the *Townsend Flash,* the official newsletter of the Washington Legislative Office, and club bulletins served as instruments for conveying official attitudes. The nation's press, largely antagonistic to the plan, was characterized as a "kept" press dominated by financial interests. To negate adverse testimony by economists, Townsendites were assured that their plan was a "common sense" proposal which anyone could understand; those condemning it were deliberately distorting the facts. Theirs was no "crack-pot" panacea; rather it was the Social Security Act which was unsound, un-Christian and a fraud upon the nation!

VII FINANCES

In 1936, Dr. Townsend seriously contemplated raising one hundred million dollars from his followers, and, in 1937, he proposed a personal loan from them of five million dollars.[37] Although funds of such magnitude never materialized, enthusiasm for the Townsend Plan, a constant campaign for funds, and the development of devices particularly suitable to an old-age organization provided the necessary finances for the Movement.

TABLE IV

TOTAL GROSS RECEIPTS FROM PRINCIPAL ORGANS OF THE
MOVEMENT, 1934–1953*

Year	Income
1934–1936	$1,684,613
1936–1937	368,743
1938	452,709
1939	621,793
1940	689,440
1941	636,139
1942	485,521
1943	424,084 (TW, Inc., ¾ yr.)
1944	627,862
1945	511,595
1946	518,512
1947	418,488
1948	352,855
1949	328,291
1950	228,190 (7 mos.)
1951	406,532
1952	381,234
1953	306,209

Total Receipts: $9,442,810

* The figures for 1934 through the first part of 1936 are somewhat over-inflated. Actual receipts for the period 1939 to 1953 were larger than is indicated in this table. Gifts from the Townsend Foundation are included in the income of the pressure organization and its press, but the Foundation usually received more donations than it distributed. Since the financial year of the Foundation did not coincide with that of the two corporations, it is impossible to estimate the surplus and add it to the annual total gross receipts. From its surpluses, for example, the Foundation made an initial payment of $50,000 for the purchase of the United Publishing Co. and undertook the payment of the remaining mortgage which was $34,500 on August 31, 1953. In addition, from January, 1950 through August, 1953, the United Publishing Co. earned gross receipts of $425,320 (sales from newspaper and other printing) derived from Townsend and non-Townsend sources. Therefore, total receipts are even larger for the years commencing with 1950.

TABLE V

REVENUE FROM PRINCIPAL TOWNSEND CORPORATIONS, 1934–1953

Year	Old Age Revolving Pensions, Ltd., Townsend National Recovery Plan, Inc. Townsend Plan, Inc.	Prosperity Pub. Co. Townsend National Weekly, Inc.	Year
1934 Jan.			1934
1935 thru	$983,131* (approx.)	$193,106**	1935
1936 June Oct.	121,185†	508,376	1936
1937 Dec.		247,558	1937
1938	204,686	248,023	1938
1939	314,084	307,712	1939
1940	349,253	340,187	1940
1941	365,206	270,933	1941
1942	247,620	237,901	1942
1943	255,681	168,403††	1943
1944	373,695	254,167	1944
1945	300,415	211,180	1945
1946	233,148	285,364	1946
1947	141,962	276,526	1947
1948	160,588	191,270	1948
1949	160,466	167,825	1949
1950 (7 mos)	83,960	144,230 (7 mos.)	1950
1951	167,320	239,212	1951
1952	202,062	179,172	1952
1953	150,817	155,392	1953

* See *National Townsend Weekly,* July 20, 1936. This sum approximates closely that estimated by Robert E. Clements for the same period in *Hearing Before the Select Committee to Investigate Old Age Pension Organizations, Pursuant to H. Res. 443,* U. S. House of Representatives, 74th Cong., 2nd Sess. (Washington, 1936), vol. 1, pp. 81–83.

** Figures abstracted from a financial statement on the Prosperity Publishing Company, 1935–36, by the accounting firm of William Costenholtz, Chicago, Illinois. Another financial report on this corporation by a different acounting firm lists $476,477 for the year 1936. Both reports are found in Townsend National Headquarters.

† No membership fees were paid to TNRP, Inc., for January–August, 1937, since each subscription to the *Weekly* for one year was equivalent to membership.

†† Financial records available to this writer for the first three quarters of 1943 only. Except as indicated above, all data was abstracted from the financial statements of the different Townsend corporations.

TABLE VI

THE TOWNSEND FOUNDATION

GENERAL INCOME AND DONATIONS TO OTHER TOWNSEND CORPORATIONS*

Year (ending Mar. 31)	Total Income	Donations to TNW, Inc.	Donations to TNRP, Inc. TP, Inc.
1939	$28,336	$ ——	} $23,838
1940	?	?	
1941	68,105	10,000	52,775
1942	25,226	——	24,000
1943	44,611	——	28,000
1944	37,797	——	34,000
1945	32,454	15,000	22,000
1946	63,858	25,000	5,000
1947	130,780	47,000	62,930
1948	62,942	29,683	——
1949	43,845	25,717	6,028
1950	17,163	3,942 ?	19,018
1951	13,625	——	——
1952	1,860	——	——

* Figures for years ending March 31, 1941 to 1949, were abstracted from the financial reports of the Townsend Foundation. Total income for 1939 was abstracted from *Townsend National Weekly*, July 14, 1939. Complete data for year ending March 31, 1940, was unavailable to this writer. The financial statement for the TNRP, Inc., 1939, listed a gift of $23,838 from the Foundation.

Approximately nine and one-half million dollars, for the period 1934 through 1953, from a segment of the population, the aged, whose economic position was never a favorable one, must be construed as generous support. Aside from subscriptions to the *Weekly*, the great bulk of this money came from small contributions and dues. While many clubs voluntarily forwarded substantial quotas to National Headquarters, individuals contributed significantly large sums only for the purchase of the United Publishing Company with its printing presses and building.[38]

Among the numerous financing devices which were employed, two showed promise of developing into excellent sources of revenue. The Townsend Foundation encouraged gifts of property and stock as well as cash donations. It also undertook an aggressive campaign to solicit bequests in wills. "A monument

to your name that will live forever. Make a will now," constituted a frequent Townsend advertisement in the *Weekly*. Up
to 1954, bequests from wills totalled approximately $57,412, of
which only a portion had been realized because of litigation.

The sale of products catering to the declining physical condition of old people opened a more immediate as well as an
excellent source of income. The *Weekly* had always attracted
numerous advertisements purporting to rejuvenate health and
youth. Beginning in 1943, however, the Movement, itself, undertook to capitalize upon the preoccupation of the aged with their
health. A number of medicinal products were offered for sale
by the *Weekly*, of which two, Dr. Townsend's 4-Star Vitamin
Pills (later referred to as Dr. Townsend's Own Formula) and
Dr. Townsend's Zoadal Stomach Tablets, were sold as the doctor's own prescription. The results, in terms of financing the
Movement, were very encouraging.

TABLE VII

INCOME FROM VITAMIN PILL SALES, 1946–1953*

Year	Cost	Income
1946	$11,808	$41,502
1947	24,455	60,490
1948	13,161	48,517
1949	19,467	53,660
1950 (7 mos.)	22,164	40,453
1951	46,514	83,978
1952	48,426	88,204
1953	34,660	90,835

* Abstracted from financial reports of the Townsend National Weekly, Inc.,
for the years 1946–53.

Club members were assured by Dr. Townsend that the vita-
mins represented a personal formula which he had developed
during his medical practice. Before this official story was adopted,
the doctor had explained in a special editorial introducing the
vitamin pills that the formula had been given him by a refugee
intern at Johns Hopkins hospital. The success of this financing device is indicated by the fact that income from the sale of
vitamin pills eventually surpassed that derived from the *Weekly*.

VIII   AUXILIARY ORGANIZATIONS AND OTHER INTEREST GROUPS

The Townsend leadership organized a variety of auxiliary agencies to reinforce identification with the Movement, to strengthen its financial base, and to expand its popular base through the incorporation of groups other than the aged. For these purposes four subsidiary organizations were created: the Townsend Legion, the Townsend Millions Clubs, the Townsend Women's Organization, and the Townsend Youth Association. Two additional organs, the Townsend National Voters League and the Townsend Trailblazers League, are more properly discussed in their political context in Chapter VI.

In 1935, Townsendites contributing one dollar per month were enrolled in the Townsend Legion and designated Minutemen of the Movement responsible for protecting the plan. Although 11,000 members had joined by 1936, the Legion disintegrated rapidly thereafter. It was never more than a revenue raising device and never developed a defined purpose of its own. Attempts to revive it proved futile although the Townsend Legion was subsequently assigned such functions as reporting un-American activities, helping the aged before relief agencies, contacting fraternal organizations to support the plan, and enlisting business and professional people in the Townsend Movement.

The Townsend Millions Clubs served as a financing device only; membership fees were collected, but no separate units were established. A Townsend women's group was organized in 1935, which continued as the "Women's Drill Corps" whose complicated marches and striking uniforms contributed color to the annual national conventions

The Townsend Plan was promulgated as a recovery measure which would benefit all age groups. At various times appeals were directed toward attracting the support of young people, workers, businessmen, and farmers. Public opinion polls provide one index for measuring the success of Townsendites in securing approval from the rest of the population. A Gallup Poll published January 12, 1936, revealed that only 3.8 per cent of the population favored $200 pensions.[39] In the three west coast states as well as in Maine and Michigan, a wider approval was registered, ranging from a low of 6.2 per cent to a high of 25.2 per cent. The Townsend eligibility age of sixty years was endorsed by a majority of those polled. A subsequent Gallup Poll in

January, 1939, revealed a considerably higher percentage expressing belief in the plan.[40] Ninety-five per cent of those polled had
heard of the Townsend Plan, of whom 35 per cent favored it,
12 per cent had no opinion, and 53 per cent responded un-
favorably. Older and poorer people were reported more favorably disposed; individuals in lower economic brackets tended to
be more disposed toward the plan than those in higher income
groups irrespective of age.

"Youth for Work—Age for Leisure," was the official Townsend
Slogan. A few youth clubs were organized in 1934–35, and in
1936 a more ambitious campaign to set up Townsend youth
groups was contemplated. With the departure from the Townsend Movement of the Reverend Gerald L. K. Smith, the leader
assigned by Dr. Townsend to this task, the project never materialized. Interest in attracting youth continued to grow, however, and the Townsend Youth Association was organized in
1939. Estimates in 1941 by its national youth director of 50,000
members constituted typical Townsend exaggeration; very few
youth clubs were chartered: 1940—17; 1941—19; 1942—5; 1943—
3; 1944—2.[41] On the whole, young people were disinterested in
or unaware of the Townsend Movement.

Special appeals were also directed toward businessmen, as-
suring them that the plan guaranteed greater purchasing power,
lower taxes, and increased profits.[42] In addition to the Townsend Legion's efforts, "Business and Professional" Townsend
clubs were organized to cater especially to these groups. Nevertheless, the chief opponents to the plan whenever it appeared
on state ballots were business organizations. And never more
than a handful of "Business and Professional" clubs was ever
organized.

Appeals to farmers and union labor elicited somewhat better
results. Arkansas and Alabama branches of the Farmers' Union
endorsed the plan in 1939; in 1942, the Townsend state organizer in Arkansas was the president of the Farmers' Union in that
state. It is significant that support for the plan came from the
less prosperous of the organized groups of farmers, and never
from the Grange or the Farm Bureau Federation. Nevertheless,
Grange leaders who campaigned against the plan within their
own organization were reported in 1939 to have aroused such
outspoken hostility on the part of many of their members that
they contemplated forbidding further discussion of the subject
in order not to disrupt Grange meetings.[43]

In spite of the opposition expressed by leaders of the two largest labor organizations in the country during the congressional debates on the Townsend bill in 1939, many labor leaders and hundreds of union locals endorsed the plan. Commencing in 1938, the Townsend leaders initiated a concerted drive to win over union labor. The formation of Union-Townsend clubs was encouraged, and "Labor Issues" of the *Weekly* as well as special Townsend literature were published. Townsend leaders never succeeded, however, in organizing many Union-Townsend clubs or in obtaining labor's consent for Townsend clubs to amalgamate with the labor movement! In 1942, Dr. Townsend failed to interest the labor unions in his plan to have their members affiliate as associate members of Townsend clubs. Both A. F. of L. and C. I. O leaders also rejected his proposal to affiliate 10,000 (sic) Townsend clubs as locals of their organizations.[44] Nevertheless, Townsend leaders continued to solicit labor's cooperation for joint political action and eventually achieved some success on the state level.

CHAPTER IV

THE TOWNSEND PLAN
IN CONGRESS

From its inception as a letter to a newspaper in 1933, the Townsend Plan stressed the national character of an old-age pension system. Before a formal organization was even created to propagandize the plan, petitions had been circulated in Southern California which called upon Congress to provide the $200-a-month pensions. Since the national government alone could finance the required sums and insure the adequate circulation of currency to effect economic recovery, political activities centered upon congressional rather than state action.

The politics on behalf of the Townsend Plan in Congress divides into three phases. In 1934–35[1] the Townsendites were unprepared, politically and organizationally, for their legislative battle. At the same time their plan was phrased in its most radical version. During 1937–39 a more experienced pressure organization and a bill modified to attract maximum congressional support were elevated to political importance by Democratic-Republican rivalry at the polls and as a result of inadequacies in the Social Security Act. Both periods culminated in votes on the Townsend bills. From 1940 on, the Townsend influence in Congress receded rapidly. Despite a constant refinement and expansion of the plan to maximize its appeal, no Townsend bill ever again was afforded a vote in Congress.

The following questions seem especially pertinent in exploring the relationship between the Townsend Plan and Congress: To what degree is the formulation of public policy influenced

86

by the pressure group, particularly in view of strong majority party discipline and hostility? To what extent is the plan of the pressure group affected by the imperatives involved in obtaining a congressional majority? Specifically, what was the impact of Congress upon the Townsend Plan? What relationship exists between the nature of the lobbying activities of the pressure organization and the prospects for its legislative goals? Did the acts of the Townsend leadership and those of its congressional supporters aid or hinder the progress of their cause?

Period I: 1934–1935

I THE TOWNSEND PLAN AND THE SOCIAL SECURITY ACT

The Townsend Plan and the Social Security Act are inextricably linked together, the inclusion of an old-age insurance provision within the Act representing a direct response to Townsend pressure. The Townsend Movement must be credited with having crystallized tremendous popular sentiment in favor of old-age security.[2] And the threat posed by the plan weakened conservative opposition to the more moderate proposals encompassed in the Social Security Act.

Although President Franklin D. Roosevelt had agreed before his inauguration to explore methods for establishing old-age insurance, the Wagner-Lewis bill of 1934 which he encouraged dealt only with unemployment insurance. Apparently the President had not contemplated asking for old-age insurance at that time. But Townsend pressure developing in 1934, an election year, forced its inclusion as a political necessity. As recalled by his Secretary of Labor, Frances Perkins:

. . . there was a great demand for old age insurance also. It was easy to add this feature—and politically almost essential. One hardly realizes nowadays how strong was the sentiment in favor of the Townsend Plan and other exotic schemes for giving the aged a weekly income. . . . The pressure from its [the Townsend Plan's] advocates was intense. The President began telling people he was in favor of adding old-age insurance clauses to the bill and putting it through as one program.[3]

A cabinet-level Committee on Economic Security was established in June, 1934, to recommend social security legislation. Difficulties in devising an old-age insurance system may have caused the President to reconsider its inclusion, for in a major speech in November he remarked: "I do not know whether this is the time for any Federal legislation on old-age security."[4] Nevertheless, the urgency of the issue, reflected in the election of Townsend congressmen and the mounting public demand which the Townsend Plan spearheaded, could not be ignored. In warning his committee to solve its problems relating to the financing of old-age insurance, he stated:

> We have to have it. . . . The Congress can't stand the pressure of the Townsend Plan unless we have a real old-age insurance system, nor can I face the country without having devised at this time . . . a solid plan which will give some assurance to old people of systematic assistance upon retirement.[5]

This political response on the part of the President was, in reality, grossly disproportionate to the actual strength of the pension forces among the aged in 1934. The apprehension which the pension movement generated among politicians, however, was not incommensurate with the great threat that the Townsendites *appeared* to pose. Boasts by Townsend leaders of an enormous membership were provided national publicity and were further exaggerated by the press.

Membership figures as reported by the press during 1934 oscillated between 300,000 and 4,000,000, both extremes unrealistically high. Rumors were widespread that hundreds of thousands of dollars were flowing into Townsend coffers. Yet the financial report for the OARP, Ltd., reveals only $84,957.78 in revenue for its initial eleven months' operation ending December 31, 1934.[6] In December, 1934, Dr. Townsend proclaimed the existence of 2,000 clubs with a minimum membership of 100 each; *Time Magazine* reported 25,000 clubs in January, 1935![7] In fact, only 1,200 Townsend clubs had been organized through 1934, although 2,000 more were formed in the first five months of 1935. The momentum of the Townsend Movement was, therefore, clearly evident, for the initial club had been organized as late as August, 1934!

As the plan gained national attention, signatures on petitions urging its enactment mounted by the hundreds of thousands. Arriving in Washington late in 1934, Townsend leaders boosted their alleged totals from one and two million to fifteen, twenty, even thirty million! The inflationary nature of such claims was not apparent when the Movement seemed to be mushrooming everywhere.

The pension leadership was indeed cognizant of the tremendous political advantages accruing from this exaggeration. Writing from the nation's capitol in January, 1935, the Townsend national publicity director boasted to Co-Founder Clements that "the newspapers are sold on our strength; and as long as that continues everything is O. K. here. Our big job is to get that strength before our strength is actually measured."[8]

Although President Roosevelt over-assessed Townsend claims of popular support, he perceived that the response to the Townsend Plan reflected a fundamental in the depression psychology of the American people. He countered the political threat inherent in the mushrooming pension movement by utilizing this public clamor for old-age pensions to justify the enactment of a moderate social security program of his own.

The President offered the new Congress in 1935 an attractive, unified approach to the problem of social insecurity: unemployment insurance, old-age insurance and assistance, federal grants-in-aid to states for dependent children, the blind, etc.[9] Compulsory old-age insurance for all employees was to be financed through joint employer-employee contributions; benefits were payable upon retirement at age sixty-five. For old people in immediate need, assistance was to be furnished through the states with federal grants up to $15 per person aided. Voluntary insurance was to be provided for the self-employed.

Identification of the Social Security Act with the Democratic leadership cannot be overstressed as the significant factor in blocking any opportunity for the Townsend Plan in Congress. President Roosevelt's promise of an extensive program of social security in June, 1934, had captured national attention. The issue had also served the Democrats well in the campaign for Congress that November. The Roosevelt stamp upon such legislation carried great weight in a Democratic Congress that had just been strengthened under the auspices of his popularity and despite the usual political "law" that the "ins" invariably suffer losses in non-presidential years.

The President placed social security upon his "must" list; this was to be *his* program.[10] With the leadership making available proposals for their support, congressmen were able to oppose the Townsend Plan without being driven into a position against old-age pensions. Other provisions of the Administration's bill furnished additional political security in that they were favored by organized labor, enlightened businessmen and

others. The cutting edge of the Townsend force was dulled per-
ceptibly by the availability of a respectable alternative which
commanded the highest degrees of political support.

While President Roosevelt never attacked the Townsend Plan
publicly,[11] by indirection he clearly indicated his disapproval.
Congress was warned against discrediting the social security system by attempting to apply it on too ambitious a scale; the recommendations of his Committee on Economic Security, the
President pointed out, did not attempt to achieve the millennium at a single bound.[12] His lieutenants, on the other hand,
engaged in a frontal assault. The Secretary of Labor, the Senate
Majority Leader, and other Administration spokesmen publicly
attacked the plan as an impracticable, fantastic scheme leading
to unbearable tax burdens and destructive inflation.

II   THE TOWNSENDITES WIN A HEARING IN CONGRESS

Consideration of the Townsend Plan by the House Committee on Ways and Means and the Senate Committee on Finance,
especially the former, represented a substantial victory for the
Townsend Movement. Congressional machinery is so constructed
as to confront bills and their sponsors with innumerable ob-
stacles. For a controversial measure to receive a public hearing
by a substantive committee is a major accomplishment, especially
if the committee chairman is not favorably disposed thereto, no
outstanding legislative leader sponsors it, and the Administration opposes the bill.

The first day that the Ways and Means Committee opened
public hearings on the President's social security bill, its chairman flatly rejected any consideration of the Townsend Plan.
Asked by committee member Harold Knutson (Minn., R)
whether he intended to have Dr. Townsend appear, Chairman
Robert L. Doughton (N. C., D) replied: "It is not the purpose
of the chairman to do so. We are not considering the Townsend
bill."[13] Yet eleven days later, committee members Jere Cooper
(Tenn., D) and Fred M. Vinson (Ky., D) assured a pro-Townsend witness, Congressman James W. Mott (Ore., R), that the
bill was pending and that Dr. Townsend would testify. Not only
did Dr. Townsend appear on three different occasions, but virtually every important witness was queried about the plan. Moreover the hearings were especially reopened to admit additional
Townsend testimony.

This reversal on the part of the committee stemmed from a

growing realization on the part of its members that the Townsend Plan was too important politically to be disregarded with impunity. Congressman Knutson, who ignored his chairman's initial remarks, elicited responses from leading governmental and private authorities which demonstrated their concern with the Townsend Plan and a profound conviction that it possessed great popularity. Their testimony was underscored by a flood of mail which demanded that the committee not disregard Dr. Townsend and his bill. At the conclusion of the hearings, the chairman referred to entire "carloads" of letters inundating Congress. There can be little doubt that herein lay a primary factor in the decision to consider the plan.

H. R. 3977, the "Townsend Old Age Revolving Pension Plan," introduced by Congressman John S. McGroarty (Calif., D) on January 16, 1935, appeared to be a paragon of simplicity, directness, and clarity.[14] It proposed to promote the general welfare, assure permanent employment and security for all, and to stabilize business conditions. Upon their application and qualification, citizens sixty years of age and over were entitled to $200-a-month pensions for life. Pensioners had to refrain from gainful competitive pursuits or salaried positions and to agree to spend the entire pension in the United States within thirty days of receipt. Only 15 per cent of each month's pension could be donated for charitable purposes or to churches and fraternal organizations. Except for disabled war veterans, pensioners were forbidden to receive other pensions from any level of government. Inmates of jails, insane asylums, or eleemosynary institutions were excluded from the benefits of the act.

The bill levied a 2 per cent tax on the gross dollar value of each "business, commercial and/or financial transaction done within the United States," the President being empowered to raise or lower the rate by 50 per cent. Only salaries for individual services were specifically exempt from the tax which was to be paid each month upon gross sales; a license was required of "all sellers of goods, commodities and commercial things of value."

Full discretion in collecting the tax and administering pension payments was entrusted to the Secretary of the Treasury. Upon enactment of the law, he was to authorize all national and state banks to credit $200 to each pensioner on the first day of each calendar month; banks were to be reimbursed from the

United States Treasury. To decrease operating costs, the Secretary of the Treasury was to appoint three-member pension boards for each county and for each metropolitan ward to help administer the act. For a pensioner or seller to misrepresent or falsely respond to any provision under the act with intent to defraud the government constituted a felony. Pensioners forfeited benefits for ten years upon conviction of a felony or for a violation of the compulsory spending or retirement provisions of the proposed law.

The hearings conducted by a hostile Ways and Means Committee provided a sounding board for discrediting the Townsend Plan before Congress and the country. Although none of the non-Townsend witnesses volunteered to discuss the plan, each was carefully queried as to his view. As the responses were in almost every instance unfavorable, committee members were able to pose leading questions designed to emphasize the defects in the plan and the dangers it posed. And the national press which followed the proceedings with great interest gave widespread dissemination to the more flamboyant charges.

An impressive opposition to the Townsend Plan was marshalled in this manner. Spokesmen for the Administration characterized the Townsend bill as "a fantastic dole" (Secretary of Labor Perkins), a "cock-eyed" proposal depending upon miracles (Federal Relief Administrator Harry Hopkins), and as "not within the structure of our present economic or governmental system" (Dr. E. E. Witte, executive director of the President's Committee on Economic Security). Dr. Witte subsequently submitted a detailed analysis which demonstrated that the term "transactions" was so vague as to render the Townsend tax unworkable, that the base figure for taxation was over-exaggerated, and that, at the maximum, only one-third of the revenue called for would be produced. In his opinion the tax was certain to increase prices, thereby restricting purchasing power rather than stimulating business. The administrative features of the bill involving compulsory spending, licensing and reporting were also severely condemned.

The committee succeeded in recording opposition to the plan from a wide gamut of organizations. Representatives of respectable, established groups included a Princeton economist, an insurance executive, officials of the Fraternal Order of Eagles and of the American Association for Social Security. They were joined by leaders of such liberal and radical groups as The People's Lobby, the National Council for Unemployment Insurance, and the Workers' Unemployed Union of New York. In addition, one congressman, Samuel B. Pettingale (Ind., Indep.), submitted evidence to demonstrate the fallacious nature of the plan.

Townsendites were unable to muster a single important independent witness in favor of their bill. Despite Dr. Townsend's assurance to the committee that labor had endorsed his plan, no union leader testified in its behalf, nor did representatives from any other organized group. The few independent witnesses who appeared would not accept the bill as drafted. One claimed to represent the Association of Drainage and Levee Districts of Illinois. But it was ascertained that his organization had never acted officially on the Townsend Plan, and he, moreover found the $200 provision unacceptable. The others were two California congressmen, one of whom, Sam Collins (R), admitted that he knew nothing about the plan, but that 85,000 constituents in his district were alleged to have signed Townsend congressional petitions. George Burnham (D) asserted that 50,000 of his constituents had also signed the petition and that he had cooperated with Townsend leaders. Nevertheless, he avoided a direct endorsement of the plan. When finally compelled to state his endorsement, he qualified it so broadly as to render his support meaningless.

The brief for the Townsend bill was undertaken principally by Dr. Townsend, Glen Hudson, the Townsend actuary, and O. Otto Moore, a representative of the Denver Townsend clubs. In his statement, Dr. Townsend sought to counter the unfavorable testimony and to impress upon committee members that the tremendous support behind the plan posed a threat to them should they act upon it adversely.[15] He dismissed a great deal of previous testimony as false and misleading. Millions had endorsed his plan, he claimed, and newcomers flocked to his banners in the hundreds of thousands. After five years of starvation in the midst of plenty, the nation needed a new experiment which did not have the "blessing of the so-called 'economists.'" The Townsend Plan sought to establish that high standard of living which Stuart Chase and Professor Mordecai Ezekial claimed the country could easily provide. Instead of interfering with "the economic laws of God" in repressing production, his plan would painlessly adjust man to the machine and make available twelve million jobs.

When the Townsend leaders were cross-examined by the committee, their case for the bill disintegrated completely. The pension proponents neither understood nor defended their bill adequately; they contradicted themselves, each other, and provisions of the bill. It immediately became apparent through their own testimony that H. R. 3977 was poorly drafted and that its premises and consequences had not been carefully considered. Almost every Townsend witness repudiated it.

The definition of a "transaction" plagued both the committee and the Townsend witnesses. Dr. Townsend and Hudson could offer no clear definition which did not conflict directly with the bill's provisions. They contended that bank deposits and withdrawals were not transactions, but, as was pointed out to them, all financial as well as business and commercial transactions were taxable under their bill. Asked why sellers of services had been omitted from the licensing requirement while all others were included, Hudson could find no justification; they should be licensed, he asserted. After explaining that wages and salaries had been exempted from the tax in order to free workers from double taxation—payment of direct taxes on income and indirect taxes through higher prices—he reversed himself and his bill; wages and salaries should also be taxed! O. Otto Moore noted that the bill failed to authorize any appropriation for pension funds without which no appropriation committee could provide the money to pay the banks.

A number of damaging statements by Dr. Townsend and his assistants exposed the bill to considerable criticism. Glen Hudson admitted that Townsend literature had cited false sources for its $1,200 billion base tax figure. To an economy-conscious committee, Dr. Townsend remarked, "I say we are not interested the least in the cost of it." Asked if the pensioner could squander his money, he retorted: "Why not? We do not care what he does with it. . . . Let him buy whiskey with it if he wants to kill himself off as quickly as he chooses."

The greatest blow to H. R. 3977 was its repudiation by its chief proponents. Hudson admitted to so many defects that he finally disclaimed all responsibility for the bill. If he had to vote to report the bill as it was written, he would not do so. Moore arrived at a similar conclusion; he could not support the bill unless it was drastically revised. Dr. Townsend equivocated, contending he would vote for it if certain amendments were added. But when queried as to what amendments he would suggest, he conceded that he had none in mind nor did he particularly favor any that had been suggested.

Committee members charged that none of the witnesses had demonstrated that sufficient revenue could be raised to pay one-third of the $200 pensions. The congressmen also attacked provisions for licensing virtually everyone concluding a transaction and for taxing gross incomes irrespective of net profit or loss. And that people not in need should receive $200 pensions, even before tax revenues were collected, was patently anathema to the committee.

Although Dr. Townsend had ridiculed the idea that economists could judge the validity of his plan, the hearings were reopened so that he could present Dr. Robert R. Doane, director of research for American Business Associates. Dr. Doane had never read the bill, however, and he refused to endorse either the Townsend Plan or H. R. 3977. He indicated that the plan was worthy of consideration, but he equivocated as to its possible effects, committing himself only to the statement: ". . . *if* through the collection of these taxes we *could* stimulate additional purchasing ability, it would have a favorable effect."[16] Mathematically the plan was possible on a limited basis, he asserted, but as an economist he wanted at least six months to study it before assessing its soundness.

Dr. Doane informed the committee that $200 pensions for all those eligible were financially impossible. His estimates of tax revenues were also revealing. The maximum theoretical revenue which could be raised through a 2 per cent transaction tax in 1935 varied between 4 and 9.6 billion dollars, and prices could be expected to increase from 12 to 24 per cent. This contradicted Dr. Townsend's assurances that prices would not be materially affected and that a sufficient tax base existed to pay $200 to at least eight million pensioners. Moreover, Dr. Doane's figures were based upon transactions which included wages and salaries (specifically exempt in H. R. 3977), and revenue from interest on government bonds, which was constitutionally free from taxation.

Dr. Townsend immediately assured the committee that no one had been "fool enough" to consider paying from the outset $200 pensions to all eligible aged. He now favored initiating pensions at age seventy-five and registering the rest of the old people until business was sufficiently stimulated before paying $200 to all.

In so doing, he repudiated the bill, his testimony, and the entire literature of the Townsend Movement.

In the Senate, the Committee on Finance, which also considered social security legislation, evidenced little concern with the Townsend Plan. Nevertheless, both Dr. Townsend and Dr. Doane appeared in behalf of the plan, the economist testifying more favorably this time.[17] The comments and questions of two senators at these hearings led to modifications in the subsequent Townsend bills. Senator Pat Harrison (Miss., D) expressed a Southerner's fear that Negroes would desert their jobs to aid grandparents in the spending of pensions. Whereas Dr. Townsend had previously contended that it did not matter how the money was spent, he now reversed himself: "We will not permit the elderly people to hand them the money." H. R. 3977 contained no such provision however. Under Senator Hugo L. Black's (Ala., D) sharp questioning, Dr. Townsend was forced to concede that the transaction tax was a sales tax and a burden upon the poor. In addition, the doctor could not cope with the objection that a transaction tax discriminated against small businesses in favor of vertical trusts and chain stores.

No campaign on behalf of a Townsend bill was initiated on the floor of the Senate. Such was the lack of enthusiasm among its supporters in the House that only four proponents spoke for H. R. 3977 in the four months following its introduction.[18] One argued for a completely different version of the plan, another admitted indirectly that $200 pensions were unnecessary to the plan's success, and a third contradicted Townsend literature as well as Dr. Townsend's testimony by conceding that the cost of living would increase by 10 per cent. Yet on this bill, which had been repudiated in whole or in part by all Townsend witnesses at the committee hearings, a discharge petition was sponsored which was signed by 57 representatives.[19]

III   THE HOUSE VOTES ON A NEW TOWNSEND BILL

To obtain a favorable vote on the plan in the House, Townsend congressmen relied upon a new bill, H. R. 7154. They endeavored to preserve the popular flavor of the original plan within a framework designed to overcome the objections raised against the initial bill. While H. R. 7154 retained the compulsory spending and retirement provisions as well as the sixty-year pension age, it represented a drastic revision in both approach and substance.[20]

A careful effort had been made to eliminate the contradictions, omissions and vagueness revealed in the committee's hearings. The term "transaction," defined in minute detail, now specifically included services of all kinds, including wages and salaries. Loans, deposits, withdrawals from deposits and pledges of property or money were excluded from the definition as were single transfers of property less than $100 in value which did not occur in the usual course of business.

The mandatory district pension boards were eliminated in the new bill, and administrative responsibility was divided between the Secretary of the Treasury, who was charged with collecting tax payments, and the Administrator of Veterans' Affairs. Disbursement of annuities was entrusted to the latter who was empowered to create boards of review, to issue and enforce rules regarding registration of applicants, and to insure the proper spending of the annuities. The bill now authorized the payment of annuities and provided for a separate fund in the Treasury for the deposit of Townsend taxes.

Annuitants were restricted in the use of their money. The new bill prohibited them from any unreasonable and unnecessary employment of persons. The retired aged were also forbidden to maintain any able-bodied person in idleness or to compensate any person in disproportion to services rendered.[21] In addition, annuities could be suspended or forfeited for a willful refusal to pay "just obligations."

The new amount of the annuity, the time of payment, and the type of taxes represented major compromises in the original Townsend Plan. H. R. 7154 specified that annuities correspond to the pro rata amount arrived at by dividing the tax revenue by the number of qualified applicants. The $200 figure was retained, but only as the maximum amount. Since administrative expenses had to be met and a reserve fund maintained for the payment of delayed applications, this system provided no guarantee that an annuity would equal $200 or $25.

In the committee hearings on the original Townsend bill, congressmen had severely criticized the provision for the immediate payment of pensions from general revenues before Townsend taxes were collected. As in the case of the $200 pension, this promise of immediate payments to the aged was also diluted in H. R. 7154. All taxes were payable upon transactions occurring thirty days after the act went into effect, while annuity payments were to commence in the fifth month. The second month's revenue would be paid in the sixth month, and so on.

The 2 per cent transaction tax remained the principal financing device. However, three supplementary taxes were included in the new bill: a 10 per cent increase in the federal income tax, a 2 per cent inheritance tax and a 2 per cent tax on gifts exceeding $500. These additions represented, in part, a maneuver to placate those congressmen who had condemned the sales tax nature of the transaction tax.

Although Dr. Townsend had previously rejected any means test, asserting that what was desired was an army of spenders, H. R. 7154 did incorporate a crude means test. No annuity was to be paid anyone whose net income exceeded $2,400 a year. If an outside income was received which was less than this amount, the annuity was to be reduced to insure a total monthly income equalling the pro rata sum the annuitant would otherwise have obtained. All income had to be spent under the same conditions as that of the annuity.

Its financial and administrative features strengthened, this version of the plan seemed more expedient for congressional maneuvering than H. R. 3977. Yet, within seventeen days after its introduction, H. R. 7154 was revised and decisively defeated. Opponents quickly pounced upon a number of obvious flaws, and even those mollified by its compromises denounced the bill as favoring big business and chain stores.

A revised version of H. R. 7154 was presented for debate after Congressman James W. Mott (Ore., R), the floor leader of the Townsend bloc, had acknowledged the validity of these objections.[22] All reference to $2,400-a-year or $200-a-month annuities was completely eliminated; these sums had become political liabilities. Governmental bonds and transactions were exempted from the transaction tax, and the inheritance tax was limited to items taxable under the laws of the United States. The most significant new features sought to counter the charge that a transaction tax discriminated against small and independent businesses. Where several transactions occurred in the course of the production, manufacture, distribution or sale of property or services, all such transactions were declared taxable whether they were carried on in whole or in part, by, within or under a single person or firm. The Secretary of the Treasury was granted sweeping powers to prescribe what constituted a transaction in such cases. Each person engaged in the retail sale of goods, however, was deemed an independent operator and not an agent.

The brief debate on this bill was precipitated by a maneuver on the part of Townsend congressmen to amend the revised H. R. 7154 onto the social security bill which was before the House.[23] However, many of the drafters of the Townsend bill made no attempt to defend it, while those few who did participate in the debate indulged in highly emotional speeches. Congressman Mott, who was the only proponent to present a reasonable case for H. R. 7154, sought desperately to exclude the issue of $200 pensions from debate, realizing that it would discredit the bill. Agreeing that a transaction tax constituted a multiple sales tax, he contended that such a tax would be unfair if used solely to raise money for ordinary governmental purposes; it was justifiable when used for the direct and special benefit of those who paid it.

The opposition did not marshall its full strength, for passage of the social security bill was inevitable. Despite the fact that the $200 pension and Townsend testimony at the hearings were not germane to this version of H. R. 7154, they provided the principal ammunition for discrediting it. Opponents emphasized the multiple sales tax nature of the transaction tax and the increased cost of living that would ensue if the Townsend financing system were adopted. The new amendments were criticized for favoring big business and for removing any maximum from annuity payments. Since virtually all of the Townsend letters from constituents had demanded passage of the original plan or bill, congressmen were assured that they could vote safely against the revised bill as it did not represent the wishes of the aged.

Blunders and lack of coordination within their congressional bloc plagued Townsend efforts to the very end. In reading the bill for amendment, the Clerk of the House had employed the $2,400 figure which had been specifically extracted by the Townsendites in their last revision. Congressman Mott's request for unanimous consent to strike out what he termed a "typographical error" failed, and the Townsend bloc was left with a bill containing the $2,400 figure which they had previously repudiated. After an amendment to substitute a capital tax levy for the transaction tax was rebuffed, the Townsend bill was rejected on a division vote: 206 to 56.[24]

If the OARP, Ltd., and the plan had descended upon Congress

as a threatening political force, they departed meekly, having been assessed and found wanting. And yet the defeat of H. R. 7154 and the passage of the Social Security Act did not signify the demise of the Townsend Plan or of old-age politics. The demand for old-age pensions arose out of a basic insecurity which remained partially unresolved. A resurgence of the pension issue was inevitable, granted three factors: an inadequate social security system, the depression, and an active pressure organization.

CHAPTER V

THE TOWNSEND PLAN
IN CONGRESS (continued)

Period II: 1937–1939

A Townsend bill did not reemerge as a major issue in Congress until 1939. In the interval the Townsend National Recovery Plan, Inc. (TNRP, Inc.), as the pension organization was now titled, was preoccupied chiefly with organizational problems and with efforts to realize its goals through the avenue of political parties. A discharge petition for H. R. 4199, the Townsend bill for 1937–38, had gained 136 signatures which indicated that a substantial number of congressmen were being kept aware of the plan. And Dr. Townsend as well as his legislative representative appeared before a special Senate committee studying unemployment in 1938 to urge the adoption of their bill.

In 1938–39 the plan acquired new significance in both congressional and party politics as a result of deficiencies in the Social Security Act, the recession of 1937–38, and the ability of Townsendites to capitalize upon these circumstances in the elections of 1938. With the presidential race of 1940 looming on the political horizon, the Townsend Plan and the revision of the Social Security Act became important issues of maneuver between the major parties.

I THE SOCIAL SECURITY ACT AND OLD-AGE PENSION POLITICS

Ironically, provisions of the Social Security Act were conducive to a renewal of pension politics. Old-age insurance ben-

efits were not scheduled to begin until 1942, seven years following the adoption of the act. The Act omitted millions of workers from old-age insurance coverage and failed to provide voluntary insurance either for them or for the self-employed.
Eligible workers were not assured adequate insurance payments
since employment was necessary in "covered" industries for a
specified period of time; to leave such employment meant the
loss of an opportunity to secure benefits or to augment the
amount one might receive. Consequently, millions of workers
as well as adults in middle-class families possessed either no protection whatsoever for their period of old age or prospects for
very inadequate retirement income. In case of need, their sole
alternative, under the Act, was to request old-age assistance from
their states. All persons already over sixty-five years of age were
excluded from the old-age insurance system.

The President's Committee on Economic Security had recommended that old-age assistance be granted on the basis of "reasonable subsistence compatible with decency and need." This formula, however, was not incorporated in the "needs test" provision
of the Social Security Act of 1935. Since determination of need was
left to the state governments, many of them imposed rigid standards or limited eligibility through the adoption of relative-re-
sponsibility clauses.

An additional feature of the Social Security Act contributed
to its reconsideration in 1939. Congress had imposed a sharply
rising tax rate in order to accumulate a reserve fund large enough
to preclude contributions by the national government to the insurance system. Business dissatisfaction with prospects of a huge
reserve fund was expressed in the hearings on this issue held
by the Senate Committee on Finance in 1938. Since old-age insurance taxes were scheduled to rise to 3 per cent in 1939, imple-
menting the large reserve plan, a clash over increasing taxes was
inevitable. A Republican leader in the United States Senate,
Arthur H. Vandenberg (Mich.), had already seized upon it as a
viable political issue.

The major stimuli for congressional evaluation of the Social
Security Act in 1939 were political in nature. An inadequate old-
age assistance program generated one set of pressures. States were
financially unable to meet the maximum federal grant of $15
per person for old-age assistance. By September, 1938, over 22 per
cent of the population past the age of sixty-five, or about 1,737,-

000 persons, were receiving old-age assistance. Although nearly three years had elapsed since the enactment of the Social Security Act, only the state of California, which paid an average pension of $32.39 a month, matched the maximum federal grant. Only Arizona and Colorado paid pensions to recipients under sixty-five years of age, Colorado having dropped its eligibility age to sixty. However, the national government did not match grants for the aged group below sixty-five. Old-age assistance in the nation averaged $19.21 a month; the lowest state aid was $6.37.

As a result of a sharp recession extending from 1937 to 1938, the financial situation of many states deteriorated still further. At the same time, since the Social Security Act empowered the states to determine their own contributions as well as to define "need," and also permitted the states to set their own retirement age limits up to seventy years until 1940 and below sixty-five at any time that the states desired, they were placed squarely in the center of old-age pension politics.

Old-age pension propositions were placed upon the ballot in seven states in 1938. The California electorate voted upon a scrip money scheme paying "$30 Every Thursday" to all who would retire at age fifty. Oregon voters confronted two choices, a "baby"-Townsend Plan promising the aged $100 a month upon retirement, and a proposal that the state legislature petition Congress for a constitutional convention to draft a Townsend amendment. A graduated income tax was proposed in Washington to increase old-age assistance, and an amendment legalizing slot machines was sponsored by the aged in Nebraska. In North Dakota a proposal for pensions of $40 at sixty-five years of age was considered, while even more liberal provisions were envisaged in Arkansas—$50 at age sixty. In Colorado, on the other hand, a fight developed to repeal assistance benefits adopted previously under pressure from local pension organizations. Politicians and the aged were also reported flirting with proposals for higher benefits in Arizona, Florida, Georgia, North Carolina, Oklahoma, and Texas.[1] The Administration in Washington become sufficiently alarmed for the President to find it necessary to warn the nation against allowing itself "to be misled by those who advocate short cuts to utopia or fantastic financial schemes."[2] Although the more exotic proposals were defeated, the "Ham and Eggs"—Townsend candidate, Sheridan Downey, was elected United States senator in California.

The success of a Townsend-Republican coalition in the 1938

congressional elections and national old-age pension agitation combined to guarantee consideration of the entire issue of social security as well as the Townsend Plan. Skillfully exploiting this ferment over pensions, the TNRP, Inc., was able to undertake a very successful membership drive in 1938 which also extended into 1939. The greatest expansion of new clubs and members occurred in the Central and Eastern states and in parts of the South, areas wherein the Townsendites had previously lacked sufficient strength. As a result of its identification with the groundswell of protest and votes, and its successful organizing campaign, the TNRP, Inc., became an important factor to be considered in congressional and state elections.

Out of power since 1930, sizeable elements within the Republican Party desperately sought Townsend support in an attempt to win election to Congress. The widespread agitation for adequate pensions assured Republican politicians that attacks upon inadequacies in the Social Security Act would be politically advantageous. Over ninety Republicans who were committed in some degree or other to the plan's support were elected in 1938,[3] more than one-half the entire Republican membership in the House of Representatives.

Democrats were shaken by their losses, having dropped from 328 in the House to 226. That the significance of the pension issue in the Republican upsurge was not lost upon Democratic leaders is revealed in Harry L. Hopkins' appraisal that ". . . Democratic Congressmen were pitched out and . . . Republican Congressmen went in because they promised bigger and better old-age pensions. I think, politically, they were very smart and intelligent."[4] To conciliate the national demand for increased old-age security, to head off the demands by radical pension lobbyists, and to cut the ground from under the Republicans, the Democratic leadership undertook to liberalize its Social Security Act.

President Roosevelt and his congressional leaders presented the new Congress in 1939 with a constructive revision of the Social Security Act built upon a two-fold approach: beginning old-age insurance benefits by 1940 and liberalizing the benefits to be paid; making proportionally larger federal grants-in-aid to those states with limited financial resources.[5] The proposed reforms would have extended the coverage of old-age insurance to many of the self-employed and to all of the workers who had been excluded previously, expanded the insurance system to include survivors' insurance for widows and orphans, and paid part of the eventual cost of the insurance plan out of taxes other than those levied against payrolls. Improvements in the federal-state assistance program were also recommended.

Only two major changes in the Social Security Act were actually adopted by Congress, however—an increase in old-age assistance grants and the earlier commencement date for insurance benefits. Both reforms were politically motivated, reflecting the influence of Townsend-Republican politics. The "variable" federal grants principle for old-age assistance was rejected. However political expediency demanded some action and a straight $5.00 a month raise in federal contributions was granted despite the inability of many states to match existing federal grants. Since the Social Security Board had strongly opposed a flat increase, it can be attributed, in part, to a reaction to the pension politics which preceded the 1938 elections.[6]

There is little doubt that Townsend-pension pressure also helped provide the political motivation for congressional acceptance of President Roosevelt's recommendation that the initial date for old-age insurance benefits be advanced from 1942 to 1940.[7] Nor was it a coincidence that the new date insured an outflow of insurance payments during a presidential election year. Both liberalizations adopted by Congress were aimed not only at strengthening the Social Security Act, but at stemming the tide of the Republicans and the Townsendites.

II THE DEMOCRATIC LEADERSHIP PROMOTES A
VOTE ON THE TOWNSEND PLAN

In 1939, the House Ways and Means Committee again afforded the Townsend Plan a hearing. This time, however, it also reported an amended version to the floor of the House which subjected the bill to the test of a record vote. The hearing, report and vote were directly attributable to the political pressure generated by the Townsend forces. Essentially, however, both the report and the vote constituted maneuvers by the majority party to embarrass Republican congressmen and to dispose of the Townsend Plan.

(A) *The Revised Townsend Bill, H. R. 2.*—H. R. 2, the Townsend bill which was considered by the Ways and Means Committee, in 1939, had been pigeonholed in that committee for the previous two years as H. R. 4199.[8] Some of the complexities had been eliminated from the last Townsend bill of 1935—barter transactions were excluded from taxation, the income tax abandoned, administration removed from the Administrator of Veterans' Affairs, and the means test dropped. Nevertheless, new provisions in H. R. 2 raised additional problems, and sections included solely to attract greater political support actually weakened the bill.

Revenue for the annuities was now to be raised through an "excise" tax of 2 per cent upon the gross dollar value of all transactions and upon the gross market value of transfers of money or property by devise or gift. The term "transaction" was carefully redefined to exclude loans, deposits, and withdrawals from deposits, wages, salaries and commissions, and transactions involving governmental agencies or securities. A transaction was defined as the sale, transfer, or assignment for a consideration of real or personal property, including stocks, bonds, and equity in property. An attempt was made to insure the full application of the tax to chain stores and vertical concerns as well as small businesses.

Taxes were to go into effect three calendar months after the enactment of the bill, with no tax return necessary if the total amount due any month was less than one dollar. The detailed formula for the pro rata payment of annuities remained intact, but the $200 maximum, excluded from the Townsend bill which was voted upon in 1935, now reappeared. In the fifth month after the act went into operation, those applicants registered in the first month were to receive their pro rata sums of the revenues collected during the first month of tax payments, and so on.

The bill, itself, authorized and appropriated annuity payments from the special tax fund and such sums from the government's general fund as were necessary to establish and maintain the act. To make the proposed legislation more palatable to Congress, any surplus in the special fund after maximum $200 annuities were paid was to be utilized to repay the national debt. Once that had been achieved the surplus was to become part of the general fund.

Applications as well as the monthly reports required of annuitants were to be processed through the Post Office Department. Local postmasters were to be responsible for checking such applications and returns and for forwarding them to the Secretary of Treasury or, if necessary, to the United States District Attorney for prosecution.

As in previous bills, the retirement age was set at sixty, annuitants could not engage in gainful pursuits, and annuities had to be spent within a month (and five days). A new provision authorized annuitants to support a dependent spouse, a former spouse, or dependent child. The 10 per cent limit upon gifts and the payment of debts was retained, however, and money or property received through the annuity had to be spent in a similar manner as the annuity.

The support of labor, business, Southerners, and church elements was deliberately cultivated by the inclusion of new provisions which limited the use of the annuities by the aged.[9] Annuitants were forbidden to spend money for gambling or, upon penalty of permanent loss of a portion of the annuity, to "unreasonably and unnecessarily maintain any able-bodied person in idleness, or any person in drunkenness or gambling." Services purchased by an annuitant had to be "rendered, to his best knowledge and belief, by citizens of the United States," and the commodities purchased had to be manufactured, to his best knowledge and belief, in the United States.

Penalties were increased for both misdeeds and the fraudulent filing of reports by annuitants and taxpayers. Annuitants also forfeited, to the extent of the amount received, the right to any other benefits to which they were entitled under federal law. Finally, all federal acts in conflict with any term of the bill were repealed to the extent of such conflict.

(B) *A Hearing before the Ways and Means Committee.*—Although the Ways and Means Committee was primarily concerned with the President's recommendations, a major portion of its hearing was devoted to the Townsend bill. Aside from whatever political considerations may have entered into the granting of such a hearing, it represented a personal decision by Chairman Robert L. Doughton. According to Doughton, his decision to hold hearings on social security had been directly influenced by the campaigning of Dr. Townsend's son, Robert, who had canvassed the congressman's district in 1938 with a sound truck and "tons of literature" in an effort to defeat him on the issue of the Townsend Plan.

. . . in the campaign conducted against me by a man favoring the Townsend plan, it was stated boldly that had it not been for me the old people would have gotten $200 a month; that I alone was responsible for the failure of the Townsend bill, and the only way in the world to get any relief was to bring about . . . my defeat. That was the issue all the way through.[10]

The congressman informed the committee that during that campaign he had promised that while he did not think it an opportune time to hold hearings, if he were reelected he would push for hearings at the first session of the new Congress. While such action ran contrary to his better judgment, he had deemed it politically expedient.

Determined to subject the Townsend bill to an exhaustive study, the committee called upon a number of prominent economists for their evaluation. Among those whose opinions were solicited were Dr. J. F. Dewhurst (Twentieth Century Fund), Dr. H. G. Moulton (Brookings Institution), Professors F. D. Graham (Princeton University), S. H. Slichter (Harvard University), and E. E. Witte (University of Wisconsin). Appearing after the major Townsend witnesses had testified, these economists effectively demolished the claims that had been advanced for the plan. The economists attacked both the economic assumptions and administrative provisions of the Townsend bill, and they were unanimous in their conclusion that it would adversely affect business.

Maximum pensions of $200 a month were ridiculed as imposing a fantastic and impossible burden upon the economy. It was the unanimous opinion of the economists that H. R. 2 would not accelerate money velocity through the payment of annuities; increased velocity was caused by improved business and not vice versa. If hoarded monies were placed into circulation, business and money velocity might be stimulated, but the Townsend Plan taxed spending rather than hoarding, they pointed out.

Their assessment of the transaction tax was that it would transfer to the aged money that would otherwise be spent by the general populace. Consequently, the Townsend Plan would neither increase the amount or velocity of money in circulation nor increase purchasing power or business activity. Graham and Slichter asserted that a reduction might even occur in velocity due to deflationary provisions of the bill. If businesses withdrew money from operation to pay their taxes and the federal government reserved this revenue for the payment of annuities in the fifth month after the act went into effect, extraction of this money from circulation for the first three months or more would create a dangerous deflationary situation.

The effect of the tax would be harmful to the general welfare, the economists contended. To the extent that the seller would absorb the tax, it would tend to reduce or eliminate his profit.

Levied on all gross incomes, the tax would cause bankruptcies and unemployment since many businesses operated on a net loss or a small profit. If passed on to the consumer, the tax would raise prices and cut into purchasing power.[11] The regressive nature of the transaction tax was also severely condemned. With the exception of Slichter, all the economists felt that the Townsend bill would stimulate monopoly and the concentration of wealth, and that it would adversely affect independent concerns in relation to chain stores and vertical businesses. Those portions of H. R. 2 designed to prevent such consequences were declared impossible to understand or enforce. Furthermore, an army of clerks, investigators, economists, and tax experts would be necessary to administer the bill, to check the monthly reports of millions of annuitants, enterprises, and self-employed persons as well as to determine at what stage in the process of each industry a transaction had occurred.

There was no general agreement, among those economists who advanced estimates, on the monthly annuity which the Townsend bill would provide. According to Slichter, $5.5 billions could be raised at the business level prevailing in 1937. Divided among eight million annuitants, this would yield $700 a year or less than $60 per month. Dr. Moulton doubted the possibility of obtaining more than $30 per month for ten million aged, although Dewhurst's analysis demonstrated that sufficient revenue might be raised to pay annuities of $50 a month to this number of applicants.

Representatives of business, labor, the unemployed and humanitarian organizations also opposed the Townsend bill as did private individuals. Both the executive secretary of the American Association for Social Security and the president of the Workers' Alliance of America testified against it. A National Association of Manufacturers' representative asserted that the plan would harm business while a vice-president of the American Federation of Labor assured the committee, "There is no question about it; we are opposed to the Townsend bill, and the principle underlying it."[12] The chairman of the Social Security Board and the Secretary of the Treasury both expressed the Administration's opposition to H. R. 2. The American Retail Federation conducted a special poll of its members and reported to the committee unanimous disapproval of both transaction and gross income taxes. Such popular writers on economics as David G. Coyle and John T. Flynn condemned the bill. And in response to special

TABLE VIII

ESTIMATED TAX YIELDS AND PENSIONS PAYABLE UNDER H. R. 2*

(Prepared by Dr. J. F. Dewhurst)

Gross Transactions and Transfers	*(Billions)*
Total gross transactions (or gross income) 1936	$449
Estimated transfer of money by devise, bequest, etc., 1935	2.5
Estimated transfer of money by gift, 1935	1.1
Total transactions and transfers	$452.6

Estimated Exemptions and Deductions	
Payment for personal service of employees	$37.368
Gross income to government (1937)	12.5
Estimated sale of government securities	3.0
Estimated shrinkage from security transactions— 2 per cent tax	76.288
Estimated shrinkage from sale of tangible goods— 2 per cent tax	14.483
Total exemptions and deductions	$143.639

Total transactions and transfers	$452.6
Total exemptions and deductions	143.639
Theoretical taxable balance	$308.961

Yield of 2 per cent transaction tax	$6,179,220,000
Average annual pension under H. R. 2	612
Average monthly pension under H. R. 2	51

* *Hearings before the Committee on Ways and Means relative to the Social Security Act Amendments of 1939,* U. S. House of Representatives, 76th Cong., 1st Sess. (Washington, 1939), vol. 1, p. 789. Dr. Dewhurst's table has been condensed from his original presentation and his totals have been rounded off for purposes of clarity.

queries by committee members, a number of prominent businessmen were also placed on record as opposing the plan.

H. R. 2 was sharply attacked by another pension group with
a competing bill. Representing the General Welfare Federation
of America, Inc., a splinter group of former Townsendites, Congressman Harry R. Sheppard (Calif., D) and Arthur L. Johnson,
its legislative secretary, appeared in support of H. R. 11, their
own bill for the aged. In addition, they denounced Dr. Townsend for perpetrating a fraud upon the old people. Since the
congressman had been chairman of the Townsend Steering Committee in 1937 and Johnson the Townsend legislative representative at that time, their testimony was all the more damaging.
Both opposed the Townsend bill which they had previously
sponsored and which Johnson had personally drafted as H. R.
4199, of which H. R. 2 was an exact duplicate.

The proponents of the Townsend bill conducted a much more
professional lobbying operation in 1939 than that undertaken in
1935. More modest and more carefully drafted, their new bill
contained provisions whose patriotic, moral, and economic overtones were especially adapted to the congressional frame of reference. Townsendites marshalled, moreover, an impressive array
of congressional witnesses whose testimony was buttressed by
non-organizational proponents as well as the chief officers of the
Townsend National Recovery Plan, Inc.

Thirty-seven congressmen appeared or wrote letters in favor
of H. R. 2, three of them senators. Such a sizeable bloc indicated
considerable support within Congress itself. The Far West contributed its usual contingent: Arizona—1, California—6, (including a senator), Colorado—1, Idaho—1, Montana—1, Oregon—3,
Washington—2. But as distinct from 1935, the Townsendites had
now developed appreciable strength in the agricultural and industrial sections of the Midwest and Northeast: Indiana—3, Iowa
—1, Maine—1, New Jersey—1, North Dakota—1, Ohio—4, Pennsylvania—1, Wisconsin—4. Six from Florida, including both senators, constituted the sole representation from the Southern bloc
in Congress.

Furthermore, the Townsend pressure organization had finally
registered some success in securing the endorsement of other
groups. Its legislative representative introduced a list of eighty
union locals, seventeen city labor councils and one state union
conference which had endorsed the plan as of September 1, 1938.
Yet the committee did not receive a single communication from

a union in support of H. R. 2. While the president of the Florida
A. F. of L. personally urged its passage before the committee, he
spoke solely for himself, his organization having never taken official action. He was joined, however, by two other Florida citizens,
one a businessman who also testified favorably.

With minor exceptions the witnesses were moderate in their
discussion of the bill and its possible revenues, and all appeared
to be familiar with its features. To anticipate objections against
the transaction tax, some cited sponsorship of a federal turnover
tax by the tax committees of the National Association of Manufacturers and the United States Chamber of Commerce in 1921.
Specific questions, however, concerning the transaction tax and
the economic effects of the bill were referred to a Townsend tax
expert who was to testify. The experience of Hawaii and Indiana
with the gross income tax was cited as exemplifying the operation of a successful financing device similar to that of the transaction tax.

H. R. 2, it was claimed, would provide an American market
for American goods, insure recovery and provide employment
for millions through additional purchasing power and increased
money velocity. A few congressmen indulged in fanciful flights,
predicting that insanity would be reduced by one-half and
divorces by 75 per cent if the bill were passed, that religious
organizations would be strengthened, and that a large proportion
of crime would be eliminated! More specifically, representatives
from Florida, Indiana, Iowa, Ohio, and Oregon stressed the
strength of the Townsendites in their constituencies.

Under cross-examination from committee members, major
flaws developed in the defense of the bill by Townsend congressmen. Senator Claude Pepper (Fla., D) conceded that he was
uncertain as to whether the plan would accelerate or diminish
transactions. Congressman James W. Mott (Ore., R) suggested
extracting the provision for a separate fund in view of his doubts
as to its constitutionality. He was also willing to sacrifice the $200
monthly maximum and to forgo the compulsory spending provision, although Townsend Floor Leader Joe Hendricks (Fla.,
D) had informed the committee that he would oppose the bill if
the latter provision were removed. Damaging admissions were
elicited from the more moderate proponents—the tax was a multiple sales tax; prices would pyramid; the bill would foster considerable litigation; provisions requiring the spending of annuities for goods "manufactured" in the United States could

be interpreted to exclude American agricultural products. A number of congressmen also weakened the case for the Townsend bill by endorsing as satisfactory either H. R. 2 or H. R. 11, the General Welfare Federation's bill. Others indicated that they would abide by whatever the committee decided in liberalizing the Social Security Act.

When the leaders of the TNRP, Inc., appeared, they proved incompetent to defend their own bill. Responding to committee member Roy O. Woodruff's (Mich., R) observations that the Townsend tax would overprice American commodities and thereby permit foreign goods to undersell them, the vice president of TNRP, Inc., L. W. Jeffery, proposed a higher tariff as a remedy! Jeffery's admission that no penalty existed if annuitants failed to purchase American goods and services nullified, in effect, the advantages of that particular provision. He conceded, moreover, to the bill's weakness "in definition and mechanism." All questions regarding its tax features he referred to the tax expert whom the pension group had scheduled to testify.

To the committee's astonishment, the Townsend legislative agent, Otis J. Bouma, refused to testify regarding the major provisions of his bill. He, too, deferred to the Townsend tax expert. In addition, he questioned the enforceability of the "buy-American" provision, and he conceded that both transaction and pay-roll taxes would have to be paid simultaneously since the bill neglected to repeal social security taxes. Bouma further undermined his own bill when he implied that a basic difference existed between the Townsend Plan and H. R. 2.

Mr. Bouma.	. . . I do not say the passage of this bill would bring about recovery. But I believe that the passage of a bill containing the fundamental principles of the Townsend plan would bring about recovery. . . .
Mr. McCormack.	Is not this bill carrying out the principles of the Townsend plan, or the plan advocated by Dr. Townsend? . . .
Mr. Bouma.	I do not know.[13]

The Townsend tax expert was Louis C. Silva, Deputy Tax Commissioner for the Territory of Hawaii, on a one-year leave of absence with the TNRP, Inc. Silva's initial statement revealed that he would be a poor witness for H. R. 2 as he was not thoroughly familiar with the bill. He was certain, however, that the "transaction tax, was not a definite, usable instrument." If it were a tax upon business measured by gross income, he deemed it usable. But the sale of real property, stocks, and bonds, should be exempt, he explained, for such sales represented transfers of capital assets and not taxable gross income. Nevertheless, the bill specifically taxed these items.

So embarrassed was this witness by his bill's tax, that in answer to a direct question whether he could recommend that the committee report the bill with or without recommendation, he replied: "No; honestly I could not, not in the present form the bill is phrased in."[14] Moreover, Silva implied that a compulsory spending system could not operate except through the issuance of scrip money.

The committee's attitude after two score favorable witnesses had appeared is best summarized by Congressman Frank H. Buck's (Calif., D) exasperated remark:

. . . so far nobody has appeared . . . who has had any knowledge whatsoever of what the legislation as offered means, and I feel that somebody ought to interpret it. Otherwise it is a gross imposition on the committee to have its members listen to people who do not know what their legislation proposes. . . . [15]

The principal concluding advocate was Dr. Townsend. Whereas other proponents had avoided reference to the $200 maximum on annuities and had agreed that starting sums would approximate $50 a month, Dr. Townsend insisted that $200 was not a high maximum and that it would eventually rise to $300 a month. He contradicted his fellow witnesses by asserting that the tax would produce almost immediately more than $100 a month annuities. Testimony by Townsend Congressman Martin F. Smith (Wash., D) and Ralph O. Brewster (Me., R) that an increase in the cost of living would result from the bill was waived aside by the pension leader as an opinion only; *he knew* that the tax would be absorbed in a reduction of profit.

Seemingly unaware of political realities, Dr. Townsend admitted that the transaction tax would eliminate smaller businesses. He dismissed the middleman and the small businessman as not worth preserving. This statement was seized upon by committee members to elicit hostile responses from business witnesses who had otherwise been unconcerned with the bill. It stimulated one business group to poll its members and send a special witness to report their unanimous rejection of the tax.

The validity of the bill was also impugned by Dr. Townsend's proposal at this time for a special amendment to the Constitution. If the bill were passed and held constitutional, he informed the committee, he would probably not favor an amendment. But this implied that Townsendites questioned the constitutionality of their bill and that the amendment was being offered to insure its legality.

(C) *A Vote on the Townsend Plan.*—The debate and vote on the Townsend bill in 1939 constituted a maneuver by the Democratic leadership to embarrass the large number of Republicans elected with Townsend support.[16] The elimination of the plan from any further consideration in the field of social security was a secondary goal. With the House leadership expediting passage of the Townsend bill through two crucial committees, Ways and Means as well as Rules, some constructive action by either the TNRP, Inc., or Townsend congressmen might have enhanced their bill's prospects. Instead, blunders during debate, in drafting a new bill and its presentation to Congress nullified this opportunity.

At the time he testified, Dr. Townsend had promised the Committee on Ways and Means that on the following day he would offer amendments which would strengthen his bill. Three months elapsed, however, before they were introduced in the form of another bill. It was his understanding, Dr. Townsend wrote to Congressman Hendricks on May 15, that if a new bill were submitted with these amendments, the committee would report it, although without recommendation.[17] On May 17, 1939, H. R. 6378 was introduced by Hendricks. Omission of the compulsory spending provision necessitated a further delay and the introduction of yet another bill, H. R. 6466, on May 23.

The Committee on Ways and Means and the Democratic leadership had ample reason not to report H. R. 6466. In an effort to rush the bill to a vote, however, they took unprecedented action. Although no hearings were held on the bill, the committee voted to report it to the House, but without recommendation.[18] The committee's chairman pointed out that in all the years he had been a member, this was the first bill reported in such a manner by his committee.[19] He explained to his colleagues in the House that twenty-five thousand letters recommending action had been received by his committee and that hundreds of House members had called for a vote on the Townsend Plan.

In the Rules Committee, a body hostile to unorthodox legislation, the bill was quickly cleared for debate and vote.[20] Except for the fact that the measure had for years claimed public attention throughout the country, Chairman Edward E. Cox explained to the House, the ". . . Committee on Rules would probably have not, even upon request of the Committee on Ways and Means . . . reported a resolution for the consideration of a measure that was reported out without any recommendation whatever."[21] Whatever the reason, within the very brief period of eight days after H. R. 6466 was introduced, it had been acted upon by two committees and reported to the House for debate and vote.

Through Hendricks, Townsend congressmen were directed neither to oppose a rule forbidding amendments nor to recommit the bill in final debate; either step would be construed by Dr. Townsend to be a vote against his bill. A "gag" rule, Hendricks explained, was favored in order to obtain a vote upon the issue and not simply a "scrap of paper." House Resolution 205, limiting general debate to four hours, controlled by the chairman and by the minority leader of the Ways and Means Committee, and permitting no amendment except one motion to recommit, was passed on May 31, 221 to 53.[22]

H. R. 6466 represented a drastic revision of the Townsend Plan. The transaction tax was abandoned and the magical 2 per cent rate altered in favor of a gross income tax which varied from one-half of one per cent to 2 per cent. Ostensibly patterned after the Hawaiian gross income tax, the new tax included bonds, stocks and real property as taxable items, although Silva, the Townsend tax expert, had raised serious doubts as to the validity of including such items. Tax exemptions for personal services by employees were omitted from H. R. 6466, and the exchange of property was also now taxable. Annuities could be spent for agricultural products, the taxes upon such products being limited to one-half of one per cent. To forestall the problems implicit in the "Buy and Hire American" provision, a clause "with preference given, as far as possible," was appended. The customary prohibition against spending more than 10 per cent of an annuity for gifts or contributions was deleted as was the requirement that additional income be spent in a similar manner to that of the annuities.

The significant changes involved the new tax, the exemptions, and the reduced tax rates. Wholesalers or jobbers, producers, and manufacturers were to be taxed one-half of one per cent on monthly gross receipts. If they sold directly to consumers, their tax rose to the full 2 per cent which all other businesses, retailers, professions, etc., had to pay. A large number of organizations, chiefly of a charitable, educational and non-profit nature, were exempt from the tax.

In the debate, forty-three congressmen from nineteen states spoke in favor of the Townsend bill.[23] Almost all attacked the Social Security Act for paying inadequate benefits, covering insufficient numbers of Americans and for building a huge trust fund. Old-age assistance was condemned as constituting charity. In contrast, the Townsend Plan was praised for its universal coverage, generous annuities as a matter of right, and its excellent financing device.

Republicans George H. Bender (Ohio), Brewster (Me.), and Francis H. Case (S. D.) sought to impress upon their party colleagues that the Townsend bill was consistent with the Republican national platform of 1936; a vote for H. R. 6466 would redeem the party's pledge of a pay-as-you-go program financed by a widely distributed direct tax. H. R. 6466 was guaranteed to bring about recovery, reduce unemployment, and relieve the states of the burden of caring for the needy aged.

Representative Mott (Ore., R) conceded that the amounts of revenue to be raised and the annuities to be paid were uncertain. No new tax, however, could be accurately estimated in advance, he contended. Mott agreed that a gross income tax constituted a multiple sales tax, but, he asserted, objections to this tax were invalid if its revenues were to be used for the special benefit of its payers. Seeking to discredit the economists who had testified against the Townsend bill, Hendricks (Fla., D) pointed out that they had failed to agree upon a single point except to condemn the Townsend bill.

The floor fight by the Townsend supporters was very poorly coordinated. Hendricks maintained that wages and salaries were not taxable under H. R. 6466; they had deliberately been exempted. Opponents pointed out, and proponents John A. Martin (Colo., D) and Martin F. Smith (Wash., D) concurred, that under the language of the bill, wages and salaries were taxed! Hendricks referred to initial annuity payments of from $50 to $75, but Clyde H. Smith (Me., R), stated that the payments would be lower. Both Homer D. Angell (Ore., R) and Hendricks characterized the new tax feature as similar to that of H. R. 2, whereas Martin and Smith (Me., R), insisted that it constituted a significant change, a drastic narrowing of the tax base. A number of Townsend congressmen, Francis H. Case (S. D., R), Charles Hawks (Wisc., D), Carl Hinshaw (Calif., R), Martin (Colo., D), and John R. Murdock (Ariz., D), protested that the bill was imperfect and that they were precluded from amending it by the "gag" rule.

An impressive bipartisan attack was marshalled by the opponents of the Townsend bill.[24] The chairman of the Committee on Ways and Means read to the House letters urging the defeat of the bill which had been written by the president of the A. F. of L., the Washington representative of the National Grange, and the presidents of the American Farm Bureau Federation, the Railway Labor Executives Association and the American Association for Social Security. Other congressmen cited the adverse criticism by businessmen and economists before the Ways and Means Committee. It was stressed repeatedly by those who called for the defeat of H. R. 6466 that despite ample opportunity to vote for a favorable report, no member of either the Ways and Means or the Rules committees had expressed approval for the bill.

The concluding speeches in the debate were monopolized by the opposition although traditionally such time is allotted to an opponent and a proponent. Addressing himself specifically to those Republicans who had not yet concluded how they would vote, Everett M. Dirksen, (Ill., R) charged that the Townsend leaders themselves did not want their bill adopted, that L. W. Jeffery had specifically informed him, " 'We do not want this bill to pass.' "[25] The vice-president of the Townsend organization had personally told him, Dirksen pointed out, that a constitutional amendment was necessary, and that at least a year was required in which to rewrite the bill. Democrats were assured by John W. McCormack (Mass., D) that they would have an opportunity to vote for a sound measure to liberalize social security. A vote for the Townsend bill, he warned, was a vote against the best interests of the farmer and the businessman. After a motion to recommit had been rejected, H. R. 6466 was defeated on a roll call vote, 302 to 97, fifty-five Republicans, forty Democrats, one Progressive and one Farm-Laborite voting favorably.[26] The Townsend bloc had splintered badly; the Democratic maneuver had succeeded.[27] Since one-third the Republican contingent in the House of Representatives had voted for the Townsend bill, Democratic National Chairman James A. Farley took to the national radio networks to mock the Republican Party: "In view of the voting . . . I insist that ours is the conservative party and the Republicans are the radicals."[28]

(D) *Townsend Activities in the Senate.*—In 1939, for the first time, Townsend senators sought to advance their bill in the Senate. However, by the time the Committee on Finance met to consider amendments to the Social Security Act,[29] H. R. 6466 had been defeated in the House. Perhaps this helps explain why Senators Sheridan Downey (Calif., D) and Claude Pepper (Fla., D), who testified in favor of the Townsend Plan, each advocated a different version.

Downey favored a 2 per cent transaction tax and asserted that under the plan the sale of stocks and bonds was exempt from taxation. But this tax had already been abandoned and the second provision had never been part of the Townsend Plan. Pepper recommended a strange amalgam, superimposing the Townsend Plan upon the existing social security program of old-age assistance. He proposed minimum federal assistance of $40 a month for single persons and $60 for married couples sixty years of age or older. It would be foolish, he informed the committee, to substitute immediately an untried plan such as the Townsend Plan. Therefore, he suggested adopting on an experimental basis a one per cent gross income tax, the division of revenue from this tax for pensions on a pro rata basis, and a means test.

Committee members were now completely confused as to what the plan embodied. Senator Josiah W. Bailey's (N. C., D) query whether Pepper was simply proposing a program of his own elicited the following response:

> The Townsend plan is . . . exactly what I am describing, Senator, and if you had Dr. Townsend here you would see I am right, because I conferred with him . . . only a few days ago; I went over in more or less detail with him in substance what I am saying now.[30]

Whatever modifications in the plan its leaders may have contemplated, none was introduced in the Senate. So certain was the defeat of the plan that Dr. Townsend personally urged Pepper not to offer it as an amendment to the social security bill.[31] He feared that such a defeat would militate against a proposed campaign to enact a constitutional amendment permitting a general federal tax for old-age assistance. A Townsend maneuver to recommit the social security bill failed.[32]

As early as 1936 Townsend leaders must have begun to question the constitutionality of their plan. At the Second National Convention of Townsend Clubs the doctor proposed a constitutional amendment which incorporated the most extreme version of the plan.[33] No efforts were initiated to secure the adoption of such an amendment at that time.

A Townsend-sponsored constitutional amendment was originally proposed in the House in 1939,[34] but it was eclipsed by the conflict on the Townsend bill. Resolutions providing for a constitutional amendment to grant Congress the power to levy taxes for old-age assistance were introduced that year in the Senate by Charles O. Andrews (Fla., D) and Ernest Lundeen (Minn., F-L). The Judiciary Committee subsequently approved and reported out, 10 to 6, a similar resolution, S. Jt. Res. 145, introduced by Andrews for himself and Senator Henry Cabot Lodge (Mass., R).[35] These two senators spoke in behalf of their amendment, but never made a determined effort to bring it up for consideration; the Townsend issue was no longer politically important in the 76th Congress.

Period III: 1940–54

After 1939 the Townsend Plan never regained the degree of political eminence characteristic of the first two periods. No Townsend bill was ever again granted the consideration by Congress which it received in 1935 and in 1939; the Townsend Plan had ceased to be a meaningful alternative in the field of social security reform.

A major change in the Townsend Plan appeared in H. R. 8264, introduced by Hendricks (Fla., D) on February 1, 1940, which established the gross income tax as the new financing device. This bill reintroduced the straight 2 per cent tax instead of the sliding tax rate incorporated in H. R. 6466. For the first time a Townsend bill excluded from its tax gross income up to the amount of $3,000 a year.[36] The complicated formula for determining when taxes were to be paid was abandoned in favor of a more simplified administrative procedure. And the concept of a special fund was also discarded; tax revenues were to flow into the general funds of the Treasury. The bill authorized an annual appropriation equal to estimated revenues; a "General Welfare

Account" was to be credited each month with an amount equal to the revenue to be collected.

TABLE IX

TOWNSEND BILLS INTRODUCED IN CONGRESS, 1935 THROUGH 1954*

Date	Congress	Bill No.	H.	S.	Sponsor
1935					
Jan. 16	74:1	H. R. 3977	x		McGroarty (Calif. D)
April 1	74:1	H. R. 7154 (2 versions)	x		"
1937					
Feb. 2	75:1	H. R. 4199	x		Crosby (Pa. D)
1939					
Jan. 2	76:1	H. R. 2	x		Hendricks (Fla. D)
May 17	76:1	H. R. 6378	x		"
May 23	76:1	H. R. 6466	x		"
1940					
Feb. 1	76:3	H. R. 8261	x		Hendricks (Fla. D)
Feb. 1	76:3	S. 3255		x	Downey (Calif. D)
1941					
Jan. 3	77:1	H. R. 1036	x		O'Connor (Mont. D)
1943					
Feb. 2	78:1	H. R. 1649	x		Cannon (Fla. D)
Feb. 11	78:1	S. 706		x	Langer (N.D. R)
1945					
Feb. 16	79:1	H. R. 2229	x		Cannon (Fla. D)
Feb. 16	79:1	H. R. 2230	x		Angell (Ore. R)
Mar. 6	79:1	S. 690		x	Pepper (Fla. D)
Apr. 2	79:1	S. 809		x	Langer (N.D. R)
1947					
Jan. 2	80:1	H. R. 16	x		Angell (Ore. R)
Jan. 6	80:1	S. 57		x	Langer (N.D. R)

* Identical bills were introduced by Democrats and Republicans in the House and Senate, commencing with the 79th Congress, to permit greater bipartisan support and to deny a Congressman the excuse of refusing to support the Townsend bill because it was not introduced by a member of his party. In 1953, one bill, H. R. 1436, introduced by Van Zandt (Pa., R), differed from the officially sponsored Townsend bills in its provision for a gross income tax of 3 rather than 2 per cent.

TABLE IX (cont.)

TOWNSEND BILLS INTRODUCED IN CONGRESS, 1935 THROUGH 1954

Date	Congress	Bill No.	H.	S.	Sponsor
1947					
Mar. 10	80:1	H. R. 2476	x		Peterson (Fla. D)
Mar. 24	80:1	H. R. 2752	x		Poulson (Calif. D)
June 26	80:1	S. 1510		x	Pepper (Fla. D)
1949					
Feb. 2	81:1	H. R. 2135	x		Blatnik (Minn. D)
Feb. 2	81:1	H. R. 2136	x		Angell (Ore. R)
Feb. 14	81:1	H. R. 2677	x		Withrow (Wis. R)
Feb. 15	81:1	H. R. 2743	x		Van Zandt (Pa. R)
Feb.16	81:1	H. R. 2792	x		Peterson (Fla. D)
June 30	81:1	S. 2181		x	Pepper (Fla. D)
					Downey (Calif. D)
					Thomas (Okla. D)
					Taylor (Idaho D)
					Langer (N.D. R)
1951					
Feb. 15	82:1	H. R. 2678	x		Angell (Ore. R)
Feb. 15	82:1	H. R. 2679	x		Blatnik (Minn. D)
1953					
Feb. 2	83:1	H. R. 2446	x		Angell (Ore. R)
Feb. 2	83:1	H. R. 2447	x		Secrest (Ohio, D)

In the 78th Congress, the Townsend bill, H. R. 1649, incorporated fundamental alterations and additions which were retained in succeeding Townsend bills. The gross income tax was increased to 3 per cent (reduced to 2 per cent in 1953). Benefit coverage was widened to include citizens between the ages of eighteen and sixty who were disabled for periods longer than six months and mothers (later replaced by widows) caring for one or more children under the age of eighteen. With the United States at war and inflation an imposing threat, the compulsory spending provision was declared inoperative until six months after hostilities had ceased. In 1947, the compulsory spending of annuities within thirty days was once again reinstated in the Townsend bills.

The $200 annuity figure, a maximum since April, 1935, was finally eliminated in H. R. 1649. Thereafter, no Townsend bill contained a maximum amount for annuities. The prohibition against spending annuities for gambling as well as the requirement to spend annuities for American goods and services were both deleted, and the administration of the Act was entrusted primarily to the Secretary of the Treasury rather than to the Post Office Department.

H. R. 1649 reduced the exemption from the gross income tax to the first $100 income per month and confined the exemption to personal incomes only. In the 81st Congress the personal exemption was raised again to $250 a month. With the changes in the amount of personal exemption, its limitation to personal income, and the reinstatement of the compulsory spending provision, the Townsend bills from the 78th through the 83rd Congress were identical except on minor points.

In each Congress Townsendites endeavored to obtain a hearing for their bills. In April, 1940, Senator Downey (Calif., D), a leader of the Townsend forces in the Senate, became chairman of a special committee to investigate the old-age pension system.[37] Townsend witnesses were treated courteously, but committee members evidenced little interest in the plan. Neither the chairman nor committee member Pepper, another Townsend supporter, undertook to employ the committee as a sounding board for the plan. Downey subsequently introduced a bill to establish a state-administered federal pension system, but only one feature, retirement at sixty, bore any resemblance to the Townsend bill. The Committee on Finance also held hearings, but its members displayed a similar disinterest in testimony by Dr. Townsend and Representative Martin F. Smith (Wash., D) on behalf of their bill, H. R. 1036.

In the 1946 hearings on social security conducted by the House Committee on Ways and Means, an economist for the first time reported enthusiastically on a Townsend bill.[38] Dr. John Donaldson of George Washington University had been employed by Townsend leaders to undertake an analysis of the plan. He characterized as cursory and biased all previous studies. It was his conclusion that net gross revenues for annuities under the Townsend Plan would have provided more than $16.5 billions in 1942 and $23.4 billions in 1943. Payments to an estimated 16 million applicants would have amounted to $91.60 a month in 1942 and $122.00 a month in 1943. However, in spite of his favorable testimony, the committee did not interrogate Dr. Donaldson or seriously concern itself with other Townsend witnesses.

In the 81st Congress, the Townsend bill was provided a hearing both before Senate and House committees.[39] Dr. Townsend, Robert C. Townsend and a Townsend statistician testified as did a number of Townsend congressmen. Among their witnesses this time were four senators: Downey, Pepper, Margaret Chase Smith (Me., R) and Glen H. Taylor (Idaho, D). Again neither committee was concerned with the Townsend bill. The plan was no longer a serious issue and its adherents were merely provided the same opportunity to testify as was granted other groups. Subsequent hearings in later Congresses confirmed this pattern.

Townsend efforts on the floor of the House and Senate also proved futile. All the discharge petitions on Townsend bills failed. More material favoring the plan was inserted in the *Congressional Record* through the extension of remarks than in actual speeches on the floor, a revealing index of the disinclination of congressmen to press for the bills. Petitions from state legislatures urging Congress to enact or consider Townsend bills soon ceased altogether. In 1942, Representative Robert A. Green (Fla., D) attempted unsuccessfully to offer the Townsend bill as a rider to legislation repealing the granting of congressional pensions. And in 1946, Senator Downey offered H. R. 2229, one of the Townsend bills, as a substitute for Senate amendments to the Social Security Act; it was rejected without a record vote.[40]

The plan was regularly introduced in legislative form in each Congress, but there was no real expectation among its congressional supporters for its enactment. As expressed publicly by one of the "101 Immortals," so titled because they had championed the bill in the 1939 vote, ". . . there is now little hope of getting any of the so-called Townsend bills enacted into law under the changed conditions of today."[41] Congressmen who had been endorsed by the Townsendites for election continued to sign discharge petitions, request hearings, speak for the bills and insert material in the *Congressional Record*. Many of them, no doubt, would have voted for the bills if such an opportunity arose. But an appreciable number turned to bills which proposed reform within the existing framework of the Social Security Act as the only realistic opportunity for effective action.

CHAPTER VI

THE POLITICAL MACHINE: ELECTION AND CONTROL OF CONGRESSMEN

To venture into election-party politics, an undertaking in which few pressure organizations presume to engage and in which still fewer succeed, demands intelligent leadership, a shrewdly designed policy, strong group cohesion and optimum exploitation of political tactics. As in the case of congressional efforts to enact the plan, Townsend political behavior was characterized by an absence of these essentials. Whatever advantages did accrue through an accidental coalescence of these factors were never adequately exploited. Failure of the Townsend lobby in Congress is attributable in large measure to this inability of the pressure organization to operate effectively as a political machine.

Congressional Endorsements: Primaries and Final Elections

Supporting one's friends and opposing one's enemies is considered the most rewarding technique whereby pressure groups may intervene directly in the election process. Professor V. O. Key, Jr., has observed, however, that the influence exerted by pressure groups upon nominations and elections is a matter about which there is little precise knowledge: "The chances are that the bark of most of the organized groups is more terrifying than their bite on election day, but there is little convincing evidence bearing on the question one way or the other."[1] Excluding for the moment the broader factors conditioning the Townsend "bite," emphasis in this section is placed on the efforts and achievements of the Townsend organization in terms of its own actions and internal structure.

I THE COORDINATION AND CONTROL OF ENDORSEMENTS

A skillful endorsement policy is indispensable if a pressure organization is to benefit from its intervention in the election process. Not only should the recommended candidate be sufficiently committed to the support of its policies, but his personality and party affiliation must offer reasonable assurance of his election. At the same time, the endorsement must be acceptable to that segment of the pressure group located in the candidate's district.

One major political weakness of the Townsend Movement was its inability to develop a coherent endorsement policy due to inept leadership and a poor organizational apparatus. Initially, Robert E. Clements and Dr. Townsend had proposed a centralized procedure. Under the guidance of the two leaders, the First National Convention of Townsend Clubs in October, 1935, voted them sole and unqualified right to fix national policy, endorse candidates and commit Townsend clubs to the support of these candidates.[2] It was contemplated that club representatives in each congressional district would evaluate candidates and forward their names to National Headquarters where the founder and co-founder would review the selections and grant those approved the endorsement of the Old Age Revolving Pensions, Ltd.

Early in 1936 the leaders dissolved their partnership and Clements, who had been responsible for organizational affairs, left the Movement entirely. Dr. Townsend devoted some attention to congressional races in the fall of 1936, but his primary objective throughout the campaign was the defeat of President Franklin D. Roosevelt. The pension leader had neither the time nor the inclination to devote himself to the selection of candidates. Ironically, part of his plan to unseat Roosevelt was premised upon the election of a Townsend bloc holding the balance of power in the event the House of Representatives chose the president.

Consequently there was little if any central leadership, no over-all coordination, and only minor attempts to insure the endorsement of congressional supporters seeking reelection in 1936. Townsend clubs, congressional district boards and conventions, state boards and state managers operated independently in endorsing whomever they desired. The confusion was further compounded by Dr. Townsend's insistence upon his personal right to endorse in his own name and in that of the OARP, Ltd.

What ensued was a complete fiasco. Townsendites forfeited any meaningful choice in twenty-two districts since they had endorsed candidates who did not even run for election! Of those who did compete, twenty-two received 2,600 votes or less, obviously nonentities. A penchant for independent party candidates proved costly since of these eighty-one endorsees who ran, a mere eight were elected to office. Out of a total of 249 individuals who were endorsed for Congress, only seventy-two or 28.8 per cent were elected.[3]

TABLE X

TOWNSEND CONGRESSIONAL ENDORSEMENTS-ELECTIONS, 1936–1952*

Year	Endorsed	Did Not Run	Duplicate Endorsements†	Elected	Per Cent Elected of Total Endorsed Candidates
1936	249	22	5	72	28.8
1938	264	1	22	147	55.7
1940	227	0	8	132	58.1
1942	285	4	9	172	60.3
1944	229	0	5	172	75.1
1946	275	2	26	182	66.2
1948	206	18	11	135	65.5
1950	230	3	9	174	75.7
1952	226	3	8	173	76.5

* Endorsement-Election figures compiled from lists of Townsend-endorsed candidates found in the *Weekly,* October–November issues, 1936–1952 and from U. S. Congress, Clerk of the House of Representatives, *Statistics of Congressional Elections,* 1936–1952. Townsend-endorsed candidates for the U. S. Senate are included in the figures used in this table. Abstracted from the figures used in this table, they reveal the following endorsement-election data: 1936, 17–6; 1938, 19–14; 1940, 20–15; 1942, 24–12; 1944, 0–0; 1946, 14–7; 1948, 1–1; 1950, 9–4; 1952, 10–6.

† Number of election contests where two or more candidates were endorsed in the same congressional district.

A determined effort was made in the 1938 and 1940 elections to avoid similar errors by centralizing endorsements entirely within Townsend National Headquarters. Responsibility for endorsements was delegated by Dr. Townsend to Vice-President L. W. Jeffery of the Townsend National Recovery Plan, Inc. This method was sanctioned by the Third National Convention of Townsend Clubs which voted in 1938 that clubs should govern their political activities in accordance with instructions from National Headquarters and endorse candidates only with the permission of Dr. Townsend or National Headquarters.[4]

Armed with this authority and granted almost complete autonomy by the doctor, Jeffery became the official contact man between candidates and the TNRP, Inc. According to Robert C. Townsend, the entire endorsement policy was conceived and implemented by the vice-president of the organization.[5] Although 90 per cent of the confusion which had characterized the 1936 campaign was eliminated, an endorsement policy directed by National Headquarters still did not guarantee club cooperation.

Dissatisfaction with Jeffery's endorsements must have alarmed National Headquarters, for special bulletins to the clubs and instructions in the *Weekly* sought to justify all recommendations even to the point of conceding that certain endorsements might be misunderstood and questioned by clubs. That some clubs resisted the national policy was exemplified in Representative W. Sterling Cole's (N. Y., R) complaint that, despite his election pledge to national Townsend officers, clubs in his district had actively opposed him.[6] Clubs were also assured that endorsements were made irrespective of party, reflecting perhaps a protest against excessive Republican endorsements: Republicans—169; Democrats—77; Independents—17. Jeffery was an ardent Republican and his partisanship undoubtedly influenced his selections.[7]

A refinement in the centralized endorsement policy was initiated in 1940 through the establishment of a Townsend National Voters League. Its genesis stemmed from the critical questioning of Townsend leaders in 1939 by Democrats on the House Ways and Means Committee.[8] Jeffery was queried as to how candidates were endorsed, what part the TNRP, Inc., had played in the 1938 election, and why no financial statement had been filed under the Corrupt Practices Act. In spite of his having campaigned actively for certain candidates, Jeffery attempted to disassociate the Townsend corporation from the political

San Diego—Dr. Francis E. Townsend addressing a huge gathering at the California Scientific International Exposition in the Ford Bowl.

DISCUSS PENSION BILLS

Francis E. Townsend (center), Old-Age Pension advocate, is shown discussing with Sen. Claude Pepper (right) (D–Fla.) and Rep. Joseph Hendricks (left) (D–Fla.) the pension bills they introduced in the two houses of Congress opening day.

TABLE XI

TOWNSEND CONGRESSIONAL ENDORSEMENTS-ELECTIONS, BY PARTY, 1936–52

		Republicans			Democrats			Independents		
Year	Total En-dorsed*	End.	Elect.	Per Cent Elected	End.	Elect.	Per Cent Elected	End.*	Elect.	Per Cent Elected
1936	249	73	16	21.9	73	48	65.7	81	8	9.9
1938	264	169	101	59.7	77	43	55.8	17	3	17.6
1940	227	139	75	53.9	81	54	66.7	7	3	42.8
1942	285	122	105	86.0	141	63	44.7	18	4	22.2
1944	229	142	109	76.8	84	61	72.6	3	2	66.6
1946	275	133	124	93.2	135	57	42.2	5	1	20.0
1948	206	108	68	62.9	76	66	86.8	7	1	14.0
1950	230	93	88	94.6	133	86	64.7	1	0	0
1952	226	105	100	95.2	118	73	61.9	0	0	0

* Minus the candidates who did not run. Hence the figures under Total Endorsed do not equal the sums of the endorsed Republican, Democratic and Independent candidates.

activities of the Townsend Movement. The national Townsend organization had never campaigned, he contended, for the *Townsend National Weekly* and the clubs, which did engage in politics, were separate and distinct from the TNRP, Inc. Since both were, in fact, completely controlled by the latter corporation, this was a totally specious argument.

Dr. Townsend, who disclaimed responsibility for most of the endorsement policy, attributing it to his political advisers, did admit that the TNRP, Inc., had engaged in politics. Such was its purpose, he asserted. There was no need to file under the Corrupt Practices Act, Dr. Townsend explained, for the TNRP, Inc., did not engage in corrupt practices and had not contributed large sums of money for congressional campaigns!

In the 1940 election Townsend leaders sought to retain absolute national control over the endorsement policy and its implementation and at the same time to circumvent the Corrupt Practices Act. The Fourth National Convention of Townsend Clubs in 1939 authorized Dr. Townsend to appoint a group to supervise political activity. From this committee originated the Townsend National Voters League.[9] The Townsend National Recovery Plan, Inc., was proclaimed to be an educational organization and could not participate in political activities. On the other hand, the Voters League could support candidates favoring the Townsend Plan and receive contributions for political activities.[10] Clubs were to be notified of the Voters League's recommendations through the *Weekly*.

In reality the Voters League remained a paper organization, its officers being identical with those of the TNRP, Inc. Dr. Townsend served as chairman, Robert C. Townsend as vice-chairman, and L. W. Jeffery as executive-secretary. Neither individual nor group memberships in the Voters League was solicited, and control of endorsements remained centralized in the National Headquarters of the TNRP, Inc.

A complete shift in responsibility for endorsements occurred after the 1940 elections, official recommendations being made thereafter by district and state councils of Townsend clubs. Officially the TNRP, Inc., did not, therefore, engage in the endorsement of candidates or in election politics. The need to establish an integrated policy, however, compelled the reintervention of National Headquarters. What evolved was an awkward arrangement which attempted to reconcile the local autonomy of Townsend clubs and the ostensible non-intervention of the national organization in politics with the necessary control and direction from headquarters.

In 1942, all clubs were notified of the non-partisanship of the TNRP, Inc., in the ensuing election. Neither Dr. Townsend, the *Weekly*, headquarters nor the Washington staff would recommend candidates; as an "educational" organization, the TNRP, Inc., would not endorse candidates for public office.[11] Clubs represented in congressional district and state councils were to be responsible for official endorsements. The *Townsend National Weekly* would publicize those endorsees recommended through the councils. This policy was ostensibly followed thereafter in each congressional election.

In practice, however, the national Townsend organization participated actively in endorsements. Through the medium of the *Weekly* it attempted to insure the inclusion of pro-Townsend candidates on the endorsement list irrespective of action by the councils. No data is available for the years 1942 or 1944 to indicate the nature of endorsements. That National Headquarters incorporated its own choices among those recommended in 1942 is obvious, however, from an explanation accompanying the list of candidates in the *Weekly*;[12] in 1944, no such explanation of endorsements was provided. On the other hand, detailed figures for the period 1946 through 1952 illustrate the operation of an endorsement policy in which the national leadership of the Townsend Movement exercised a predominant influence.

TABLE XII

ENDORSEMENTS OF CONGRESSIONAL CANDIDATES BY DISTRICT COUNCILS AND
NATIONAL HEADQUARTERS, 1946–52*

Year	Total End. Elect.	Council End. Elect.	Headquarters End. Elect.	Joint Council & Headquarters End. Elect.
1946	275–182	51–13	160–121	64–48
1948	206–135	33–12	134– 92	39–31
1950	230–174	41–11	99– 88	90–75
1952	226–173	57–14	99– 92	70–67

Of those endorsed during this period, twenty-six were not candidates for election: eight recommended by the Councils, eighteen by Headquarters. In the following number of contests Headquarters inserted on the recommended lists names of incumbents who had supported the Plan, but whose opponents were endorsed by Councils: 1946, 18; 1948, 9; 1950, 8; 1952, 3.

* Data abstracted from the recommended lists of candidates for Congress contained in the *Townsend National Weekly,* November 2, 1946; October 30, 1948; October 21, 1950; November 1, 1952. Prior to 1952 it was officially denied that anyone except the District Councils endorsed candidates.

While National Headquarters assumed a major role in the endorsement policy, its participation did not guarantee an accurate or intelligent guide to Townsend voters. This was especially evident in 1948 when fifteen candidates inserted by headquarters did not compete in the election! Without the intervention of national leaders, however, many pro-Townsend congressmen would never have received endorsement and support. The Twelfth National Convention of Townsend Clubs, which met in 1952, belatedly authorized the *Weekly* to endorse candidates in certain cases.

II   THE BASIS OF ENDORSEMENTS

In the process of selecting their candidates, local Townsend units originally relied primarily upon an oral interview. As not all the major party candidates appeared at Townsend meetings, numerous nonentities were endorsed. Moreover, the less sophisticated club members were incapable of distinguishing between ambiguous promises and concrete commitments. A New York

Times's editorial in 1936, when the nature of endorsements first became apparent, touched upon this fundamental weakness: Townsendites were easy to please; one either said nothing against them or employed vague generalities.[13] The national organization, on the other hand, always sought a written commitment whenever possible. While many candidates complied with this demand, the discarding of all such records by the headquarter's staff prior to 1948 and the unavailability of subsequent records has made impossible any evaluation of this technique.

More important than the method of ascertaining the candidates' views is the nature of the commitment demanded of the candidates, the most desirable being a "hard and fast" pledge to fight and vote for the organization's goals. Obviously such is not always obtainable, but if an organization is willing to forgo such commitments in search of greater legislative representation, it runs the risk of relying upon a group of legislators whose responsiveness may not be proportionate to the demands imposed by the pressure organization. Willingness to accept a diluted commitment indicates that the pressure organization is being duped or that it is too weak to command more or that it feels sufficiently powerful to force a greater compliance than the commitment would indicate.

Townsend endorsement records reveal a contradictory, self-negating policy, for while the most definite commitments were sought and obtained at times, these were often ignored. Responding to a Townsend questionnaire in 1935, forty-nine congressmen pledged themselves to vote for the Townsend bill while twenty-eight indicated they were undecided.[14] Of the forty members in the first group who ran for reelection in 1936, thirteen failed to receive a Townsend endorsement while seven of those undecided did receive this endorsement.

Logically a disposition to vote for the plan should have invested incumbents with a preferred status; self-interest should have dictated maximum cooperation on the part of the Townsend leaders to assure their reelection. In many cases, however, the Townsend endorsement record suggested a reversal of the familiar dictum so as to read—ignore or oppose your friends and comfort some of your enemies. Fifty-six members of the House of Representatives responded favorably to a division vote on the Townsend bill in 1935.[15] Of the fifty-nine included in a Townsend Honor Roll of these congressmen, nine did not seek reelection in 1936, and two of the twenty-six who were endorsed gained little therefrom since their opponents were also endorsed. Townsendites either failed to endorse twenty-four or else granted their opponents this support. Over 50 per cent of those on the Honor Roll who offered themselves for reelection did not benefit from their loyalty to the Townsend bill. Included among those whose opponents were endorsed were some of the plan's leading proponents as well as legislators who had signed discharge petitions or answered favorably all Townsend questions relating to the plan.

A roll-call vote on the Townsend bill in 1939 elicited ninety-seven "ayes" and four favorable pairs, a total of 101 representatives committing themselves to the plan. Although the pressure organization recognized the validity of the vote as an excellent basis for endorsement, two of the "101 Immortals," as they were gratefully entitled, campaigned without endorsement in 1940. Yet Townsend Vice-President Jeffery had announced that all seeking reelection would be recommended. Apparently the leadership had also neglected to scrutinize the names of those voting negatively, since nine were endorsed, four of whom had been elected with Townsend support in 1938 and had subsequently voted to defeat the bill!

Despite the pension leaders' continued pledge of support to the "Immortals," four failed to receive endorsement in 1942, three of whom were defeated by Townsend-endorsed opponents, and one who won reelection despite his being deprived of his Townsend label. In addition, two endorsed "Immortals," competed against endorsed opponents. At the same time, thirty-two congressmen who had voted against the plan in 1939 were endorsed, apparently because they had signed the current discharge petition.

A major criterion for endorsing incumbents became their willingness to sign the Townsend discharge petition although such action did not signify a favorable attitude toward the bill. Before 1942, the signing of a Townsend discharge petition did not insure endorsement. In 1938, at least eighteen signers were not endorsed for reelection; nine of them competed against Townsend-approved opponents. Five others gained little from their support as their opponents were also endorsed. In 1940, of those incumbents voting against the Townsend bill in 1939 who subsequently signed a discharge petition, four were endorsed and sixty-five received no support. Commencing in 1942, however, endorsements were given all who signed petitions, who participated in Townsend steering committees, co-sponsored Townsend bills or testified in their behalf.

Many incumbents who had not committed themselves in any way or who furnished only partial assistance were termed "supporters" by the Townsend organization. Of the 160 candidates whom National Headquarters inserted within the list of club-approved candidates in 1946, eleven had merely voted against a "gag" rule prohibiting alterations in proposed amendments to the Social Security Act. They had never signed a discharge petition, appealed for a hearing on the Townsend bill, voted for such a bill or testified in its behalf. Nevertheless, support had been promised those who would oppose the "gag" rule regardless of their attitude toward the plan. Fifty-six were endorsed for reelection because they had signed a discharge petition although they, in turn, had not furnished supplementary support. Seven incumbents were endorsed whose records were barren of any affirmative action whatsoever.

The Townsend organization might have claimed after each election that many endorsed candidates were elected who were pledged to, favored or were friends of the plan, but it could never be certain that they were *committed* to the plan or would furnish even minimal support. On those rare occasions when the organization imposed maximum demands, the consequences were disastrous for the plan.

III SUPPORTING ENDORSED CANDIDATES

Pressure-group endorsements are generally of little value in elections unless an effort is made to activate the cooperation and voting support of the group. The *Weekly,* subscribed to individually and sold at club meetings, provided the Townsend organization with a vehicle for influencing its members. Techniques of name familiarity and identification with leadership approval and with the plan were employed in the Townsend press and by club speakers to assure a favorable response toward endorsed candidates. Recommended lists of candidates appeared in three or four consecutive issues of the *Weekly* before each election.

"Get-out-the-vote" committees in the clubs encouraged members to register and vote. Clubs engaged in letter-writing drives as well as door-to-door campaigning for their candidates, and held public rallies at which their endorsed candidates appeared with national Townsend leaders.

In 1936 and 1938, National Headquarters ordered that those candidates who had not been endorsed be forbidden to appear before a club and that no one be allowed to speak in their behalf. At one time, the Townsend leadership, in demanding the maximum support for its candidates, insisted that those members objecting to them abstain from club activities.[16] On occasion, National Headquarters intervened in the campaigns of its friends, sending its representatives into their districts to speak in their behalf.

Participation in election campaigns was limited in comparison to the number of candidates endorsed and the total number of elections. Two auxiliary agencies, the Townsend National Voters League and the Trailblazers, which might have furnished organization, leadership and direction, were not permitted to develop beyond their initial stages. A strong independent political arm of the Movement was never encouraged since many revolts and attempts to capture control from Dr. Townsend had occurred. Such an organization with its inevitable special leaders and the power and prestige adhering to their positions might have undermined Dr. Townsend's supremacy. In 1952, Townsend leaders for the first time sought to establish local Townsend National Voters League units to unite the aged, labor, church groups and others. These endeavors proved largely futile.

IV PRIMARIES

While an effort was made to influence the choice of candidates, Townsend leaders never systematically devoted themselves to the primary process. Endorsements in primaries were reported sporadically or not at all in the Townsend press. Although Townsend leaders participated in some primary campaigns, in general the primary appears to have been considered incidental to the election process, not crucial.

The Townsendites might have played a more effective role on this level, for the plan was an important issue in a number of primary campaigns, particularly in Idaho, Florida and Michigan during 1935–36. After flirting with the Townsendites in 1935, Senator William E. Borah (Idaho, R) branded the plan as impracticable, and advocated, instead, pensions of $50 to $60 a month at sixty years of age. The Senator knew that the plan had a strong following in Idaho; Townsendites there boasted that they controlled 90,000 votes. "I am also aware," he wrote to a constituent, "that it will likely defeat me, should I be a

candidate for reelection."[17] Both the state Townsend organization and National Headquarters endorsed Borah's opponent in
the Republican primary, Byron Defenbach. Dr. Townsend, who
was personally fond of Borah, vacillated in his attitude toward
the Idaho senator, praising as well as criticizing him. A massive
Townsend vote never materialized, and Borah overwhelmed his
opponent. Ironically, in the November election, Borah campaigned with Dr. Townsend's full endorsement.

In the Democratic primary campaign for United States senator from Florida the reverse occurred, the Townsend issue being
considered the deciding factor in Judge C. O. Andrews' victory.[18]
In the same primary Claude Pepper, a Townsend Club member,
ran unopposed for the other senatorial nomination. Andrews, a
particularly inconspicuous political figure, opposed former Governor D. E. Carlton. Both appealed to the state Townsend convention for endorsement, but whereas Andrews promised to support the plan, Carlton merely indicated a favorable attitude
toward pensions.

Until the plan appeared as an issue, a sweeping victory had
been predicted for Carlton, and several large newspapers had
advised Andrews to avoid embarrassment by withdrawing from
the race.[19] But Andrews persisted and captured the nomination,
unofficial returns from almost all precincts giving him a slender
margin of 4,492 votes, 64,374 to 59,882.[20] In view of the 42,147
paid members and 208 clubs claimed by the Townsendites in
Florida at the time, it is probable that Andrews obtained his
winning margin from the ranks of the organized aged.

The most comprehensive Townsend victory, albeit a Pyrrhic
one, occurred in a 1935 Republican primary in Michigan's third
congressional district. The OARP, Ltd., and local clubs coordinated a successful drive to nominate and elect their candidate, Verner W. Main, who swept the Republican primary on
the basis of the Townsend issue and defeated his Democratic
opponent in the final election. Since this victory led directly
to the establishment of a special congressional investigating committee designed to destroy the political strength of the Townsendites, it will be discussed in conjunction with the investigation in Chapter VII.

V THE TOWNSEND MACHINE AND ITS OPPONENTS

Was the Townsend machine capable of defeating those whom
it singled out for special opposition? Defeat of five members of

the House committee investigating the Townsend Movement was pledged in 1936: C. Jasper Bell (Mo., D), Joseph A. Gavagan (N. Y., D), Clare E. Hoffman (Mich., R), John B. Hollister (Ohio, D), Scott W. Lucas (Ill., D). Although the opponents of four were endorsed, the incumbents were easily reelected that year. Hollister, alone, was defeated, but by an opponent who had not been endorsed. Lucas was elected United States senator over his Republican-Townsend-endorsed opponent and encountered no further Townsend opposition during his political career.

From 1938 through 1946, Bell thwarted Townsend attempts to defeat him, retiring unbeaten in 1948. Gavagan encountered no endorsed opponents in 1938 or 1940; he was endorsed in 1942, presumably because he had signed the discharge petition. Hoffman, on the other hand, faced persistent Townsend opposition from 1938 through 1942. Despite his vote against the Townsend bill in 1939, he was endorsed in 1944 and 1946 for signing the discharge petitions. In the Republican-controlled 80th Congress he again refused to cooperate with the Townsendites; obviously his signature represented political expediency only. He was not endorsed in 1948, but his willingness to sign the petition in the 81st Democratic Congress restored him to the good graces of the Movement.

Representatives who led the debate in Congress against both Townsend bills which were voted upon were never defeated by the Townsendites in spite of attempts to eliminate them in both primary and final elections. Those who broke with the Townsend leadership, although not necessarily with the plan, were also bitterly opposed. John S. McGroarty (Calif., D), who had introduced the first two Townsend bills, was opposed in the 1936 primary and final elections. He was reelected, but did not seek the seat in 1938. Dr. Townsend personally campaigned in Oklahoma, in 1938, to defeat Gomar Smith, a former vice-president of the OARP, Ltd., who sought the Democratic nomination for United States senator.

In 1937–38 Representatives Charles N. Crosby (Pa., D), Harry R. Sheppard (Calif., D), Charles H. Leavy (Wash., D), Jerry J. O'Connell (Mont., D), James C. Oliver (Me., R) and John M. Coffee (Wash., D) established a rival steering committee in competition with Dr. Townsend's committee. Except for the latter two who repledged their faith in the Townsend leadership, all were opposed in 1938. Crosby was eliminated in the primaries by an opponent who was assisted in his district by a special Townsend agent. Sheppard was reelected over his Republican-Townsend-endorsed opponent by a majority virtually identical with the one he achieved in 1936, despite a national Republican upsurge in 1938. Leavy won both primary and final elections over Townsend opposition. Leavy's and Sheppard's votes for the Townsend bill in 1939 earned them endorsements in 1940 and thereafter. O'Connell, on the other hand, who had rejoined the ranks of the loyal committee, failed to secure an endorsement in 1938.

Because of his attack upon Dr. Townsend on the floor of the House in 1947, John C. Butler (N. Y., R) forfeited Townsend support in 1948. Although defeated without Townsend opposition, he was reelected in 1940 despite such opposition. On the other hand, Harold Knutson (Minn., R), who was declared a traitor by the Townsendites, was defeated in 1948 by a sufficiently small majority to suggest that their votes may have played a vital role in eliminating him.

A special "political arm" of the Townsend National Recovery Plan, Inc., the Townsend Trailblazers League, was created to defeat those incumbent congressmen who had voted against the Townsend bill in 1939 despite Townsend endorsement in the 1938 election.[21] The Trailblazers League consisted of squads of special organizers, later local volunteers, who canvassed crucial congressional districts in order to stimulate club growth and influence subsequent voting behavior. Typical of many Townsend undertakings, it was haphazardly executed, insufficiently financed, and abandoned in 1939 *before* the 1940 primaries and final elections.

Of the fifty-three congressmen whose votes in 1939 repudiated their Townsend endorsements of 1938 and who sought reelection, seventeen were opposed by Townsend-endorsed candidates in 1940 and only four were defeated. Thirty-two were unopposed by the Townsend Movement; all but one were reelected. The remaining four were reendorsed and reelected. In 1942, forty-three campaigned for reelection. Nineteen of the twenty actively opposed by Townsend-endorsed candidates were elected and thirteen won election without Townsend intervention in their campaigns. Nine of the group which in 1940 ran unopposed and unendorsed were endorsed in 1942.

The Townsend Lobby and Its Congressmen

To establish close, cooperative relations with those congressmen whom it helps elect, to provide them maximum assistance and guidance, to weld them into a solid bloc of maneuverable supporters—these are primary tasks for a pressure organization. They are fundamental to the effective use of the lobbying technique which premises an implicit reciprocal relationship between the pressure organization and its legislative supporters—responsible leadership on the one hand and the redemption of pledges on the other. Where either of these are nonexistent or are inadequately grounded in political reality, the relationship is distorted so as to sap the effectiveness of the election-lobbying technique.

I THE WASHINGTON LEGISLATIVE BUREAU

A Washington office to lobby for the plan was established early in 1935, and the Townsend national headquarters was subsequently transferred from Los Angeles to the capital. Pressure was applied through a congressional campaign committee and the personal lobbying of Dr. Townsend, Mr. Clements, their national publicity director and Charles H. Randall, a former congressman from California.[22] Within the original Washington lobby all did not progress well, a reflection in part of its composition—national leaders, local club representatives and hired lobbyists. Most club representatives withdrew charging the founders with manifesting a greater interest in financial remuneration than in the passage of the Townsend bill.

After 1935, National Headquarters alone controlled the Washington lobby. A special legislative representative was appointed in 1937 and a permanent legislative bureau was established in 1938. The bureau maintained close liaison with individual congressmen, attempting to persuade them to favor the Townsend bills. It arranged for testimony at committee hearings and solicited signatures for discharge petitions. It served as the immediate contact between the Townsend organization and its congressional steering committee and as the source of information from the nation's capital through the *Weekly* and its own publication, *The Townsend Flash*.

Except for one brief period in 1937, Townsendites were never able to secure a qualified legislative representative who combined legislative experience, legal training and a dynamic personality. Very few were ever retained for a sufficient period to provide the wide acquaintanceship and political maturity necessary for the position. In the late 1940's a more permanent staff was finally appointed, including among its ranks a Townsend statistician.[23]

II LEADERSHIP AND CONGRESSIONAL UNITY

Cooperative relations between a pressure group and its congressional supporters demands responsible leadership on the part of the former. More is required than the marshalling of data for debate and the effective presentation of a bill before legislative committees. For the leadership to place its legislative supporters in an untenable political position or to introduce extraneous issues is to destroy the basis of unity and seriously impair its own cause. It was in the critical years, 1935–39, when the Townsend Movement was at its height and the plan still a significant issue, that the Townsend leadership forfeited unity within its congressional ranks by its irresponsible behavior.

In 1936, the Townsend Congressional Steering Committee sharply reprimanded OARP, Ltd., leaders on two counts. Despite repeated admonishments by his co-founder and by his principal legislative adviser, Dr. Townsend had publicized in 1935 his intention to organize a third party. Embarrassed committee members, 90 per cent of whom were Democrats and Republicans, issued a warning that any move toward a Townsend Party would be "unwise and against the best interests of the Townsend Movement in Congress."[24] Although no Townsend Party was established, Dr. Townsend subsequently cooperated with the Reverend Gerald L. K. Smith and Father Charles E. Coughlin in supporting William Lemke's Union Party (see Chapter VIII).

The second protest by the steering committee involved a more sensitive issue, that the *Weekly* was misrepresenting the Townsend bill and ignoring their advice that the aged be informed regarding the amount of the annuity which the bill would pay. The economist presented by Townsend leaders before the congressional committees in 1935 had testified that $200 a month pensions as proposed in the initial bill would be impossible to provide. In the second bill, $200 was converted to a maximum and in a subsequent version the sum was eliminated entirely.

Old Age Recovery Plan, Inc., leaders, however, assured their followers that their bill had undergone no basic revision. The fact that Townsend congressmen had felt compelled to remove all reference to the $200 figure was never publicized. Through the *Weekly* and over the radio, Dr. Townsend and his aides continued to reassure the clubs that there had been no compromise on their demands nor would there ever be. In an official interview Co-Founder Clements declared unequivocally:

There has been no compromise. The sum of two hundred dollars per month as the pension demanded under the Townsend Plan is not open to compromise. . . . Any compromise or acceptance of a lesser figure would not be the Townsend Plan nor would the payment of a lesser sum be as certain a recovery measure.[25]

Although never specifying that the new Townsend bill incorporated the $200 pensions, propaganda releases from National Headquarters rarely, if ever, stated that it did not. Only after a special congressional investigating committee had publicly exposed this deception in 1936 did Townsend literature affirm that the $200 figure constituted a maximum sum only.

In the debate and vote for the second bill in April, 1935, and thereafter, the congressional supporters were continually embarrassed by the Townsend leaders, lecturers and press who identified the $200 pension with their new bill. Some of the Townsend congressmen were placed in an untenable position *vis-à-vis* the clubs in their home districts. As late as 1938, Representative James W. Mott (Ore., R), one of the most aggressive proponents in the House, charged that he had been savagely criticized by Townsend club members in his own district for stating in debate that the bill made no provision for $200 pensions. Rather than a thankful membership ready to cast its votes for him, he encountered hostility in the clubs. "In fact, in one or two places I was told that I would be mobbed if I tried to enlighten the members of the Townsend Clubs on this point [the $200 issue]."[26]

In 1936, Dr. Townsend quarreled also with the sponsor of his first two bills, John S. McGroarty (Calif., D).[27] Due in part to the doctor's drift toward a third party and to his sharpening conflict with Co-Founder Clements, the schism with McGroarty had wider ramifications. In his foreword to a book by Sheridan Downey that year, which severely criticized the transaction tax, Dr. Townsend repudiated any absolute commitment to this tax and endorsed, as deserving consideration, Downey's suggestion of a ten billion dollar bond issue.[28] Congressional supporters discovered their ground cut out from under them or so McGroarty felt. Dr. Townsend had now declared dispensable that which had been extolled as the sole instrument with which to finance pensions and insure recovery. A ten billion dollar bond issue violated a principal Townsend tenet that the plan would be self-financing and would not increase the national debt. To McGroarty, this constituted a repudiation of both the Townsend bill and its steering committee.

McGroarty had planned, moreover, to run a Townsend slate of delegates in the California Democratic presidential primary in 1936 with himself designated as the "favorite-son" candidate. It was his intention, he claimed, to use this delegation as a bargaining tool for the insertion of a Townsend plank in the party's platform. Co-Founder Clements had approved this plan which was to be publicized as a state Townsend venture only: "I told John [McGroarty] we would have nothing to do officially with such an election, but . . . so long as the delegates chosen . . . were hundred-per cent Townsendites and had no connection whatever with E. P. I. C. and Sinclair, I thought such a ticket would win."[29] Dr. Townsend, however, disassociated the OARP, Ltd., completely from McGroarty's proposal and condemned it publicly. At the time the doctor envisaged backing Senator Borah (Idaho, R) as the Townsend presidential candidate. Dr. Townsend later protested that McGroarty had attempted to hand Townsend delegates over to the Democratic Party.

It was immaterial to the doctor that the plan might have secured excellent publicity, and that the parties might have been compelled to consider Townsend demands more seriously if the delegation had been elected or had secured a significant vote. So fanatical was Dr. Townsend at this time in his determination to prevent votes from accruing to the national leader of the Democratic Party that he was prepared to forgo all the advantages of McGroarty's maneuver and to break totally with the congressman whom he had praised as having done more than any one in the national legislature to promote the plan.

In 1937–38 the Townsend steering committee was rent asunder as a result of a personal political venture by Dr. Townsend.[30] Against the advice of his legislative agent, his vice-president and other subordinate leaders, Dr. Townsend insisted upon opposing President Roosevelt's court reform plan. In a fighting editorial in the *Weekly,* entitled "My Attitude on the Supreme Court Issue," he conceded that his friends had warned him to leave the issue alone because it was "too hot" and of no consequence to the Townsend Movement.[31] If the Townsend bill were passed, he warned, and some future Congress and venal President "packed" the Supreme Court, the plan could be declared unconstitutional!

This led to a special meeting of the steering committee, called by the Townsend congressmen on June 3, 1937, at which time Representatives Crosby (Pa., D), its chairman, and Sheppard (Calif., D) accused the doctor of impairing the work of his supporters and the chances for his bill. It was difficult, they contended, to solicit congressmen to support the plan when they were simultaneously threatened with regard to another measure. For their bill to pass, they required Democratic cooperation and the President's signature.

In the general unburdening of complaints, an old controversy was rekindled. Representative Leavy (Wash., D) protested the identification by official Townsend speakers of the $200 pension with their bill. In answer, Dr. Townsend is reported to have compared the $200 sum to the old saw about the wisp of straw held in front of an ox to lead him on. To a number of the congressmen $200 as a wisp of straw held forever in front of the aged constituted opportunism, evidence that the Townsend leaders were misrepresenting the plan and misleading the aged.

Asked by Sheppard if the Supreme Court fight was of greater importance and interest to the aged than the Townsend bill, Dr. Townsend replied in the affirmative and threatened to campaign personally for the defeat of those voting to enlarge the Court.[32] In response, the chairman of the steering committee, Crosby, the floor leader, Sheppard, and Leavy as well as a number of others—Coffee (Wash., D) O'Connell (Mont., D) and Oliver (Me., R)—openly repudiated Dr. Townsend's leadership. They were joined by the Townsend legislative representative, Arthur L. Johnson, who castigated Dr. Townsend bitterly for his attitude with regard to the $200 pension and for promoting "pet theories" on public issues having no relation to the Townsend bill. The Townsend name, he pointed out, had become a definite handicap for those attempting to secure passage of the bill since there was a ". . . marked hesitancy to espouse the cause because no one can tell what outside issues you would take up the next day, whose toes you would step on, or which man of shady reputation you would tie up to next."[33]

A General Welfare Steering Committee was organized by these congressmen who united with the Townsend legislative representative and other rebellious leaders of the TNRP., Inc., to establish the General Welfare Federation of America, Inc. This new pension organization captured a number of Townsend clubs and organized its own clubs. Although the General Welfare Federation steering committee campaigned in 1938 for H. R. 4199, the Townsend bill, it subsequently abandoned the Townsend Plan and introduced its own pension legislation.

III   THE CONGRESSIONAL RESPONSE AT THREE CRITICAL JUNCTURES

In the final analysis, the response of its legislative bloc is the crucial test of a pressure group which seeks to affect the election of legislators as well as their decisions. The nature of this response reflects the organization's endorsement policy as well as its leadership and the features of its proposals. If the political underpinnings of support are basically weak, the action of its legislators will not correspond to the demands imposed upon them.

At three crucial points in the relationship between the Townsendites and their congressmen, the pressure organization could not control a solid, wieldable bloc of congressional supporters commensurate with its claims: the vote in 1939 on H. R. 6466; the discharge petition of 1943–44; the occupancy of strategic congressional positions by Townsend congressmen. The 1935 vote on H. R. 7154 is excluded from consideration since, with minor exceptions, the OARP, Ltd., was not very active in the 1934 congressional elections.

(A) *The Vote on H. R. 6466.*—By expediting consideration of the Townsend bill in 1939, the Democratic leadership forced those elected with Townsend support to the crucial test of casting a public vote. In November, 1938, 148 candidates had been elected to Congress with Townsend endorsement, 134 of them to the House of Representatives: Republicans—93, Democrats—38, Progressives—2, Farmer Laborite—1. Under the compulsion of a public vote the so-called Townsend bloc revealed its true character—only seventy-three, or approximately 54 per cent, voted for the measure; one Progressive was paired favorably and one Democrat did not vote. From outside its endorsed group, the Townsend forces secured only twenty-four votes and three favorable pairs.

TABLE XIII

VOTE BY TOWNSEND-ENDORSED CONGRESSMEN (AND ALLIES)
ON H. R. 6466, JUNE 1, 1939*

Endorsed Congressmen in Favor of H. R. 6466

Democrats 23	Republicans 48		Farmer-Labor 1	Progressive 1
Murdock (Ariz.)	Anderson (Cal.)	Jenks (N.H.)	Buckler (Minn.)	Hull (Wisc.)
Ellis (Ark.)	Carter (Cal.)	Jeffries (N.J.)		
Elliott (Cal.)	Eaton (Cal.)	Powers (N.J.)		
Tolan (Cal.)	Englebright(Cal.)	Wolverton (N.J.)		
Martin (Colo.)	Gearhart (Cal.)	Crowther (N.Y.)		
Cannon (Fla.)	Welch (Cal.)	Harter (N.Y.)		
Green (Fla.)	Chiperfield (Ill.)	O'Brien (N.Y.)		
Hendricks (Fla.)	Wheat (Ill.)	Burdick N.D.)		
Peterson (Fla.)	Grant (Ind.)	Lemke (N.D.)		
White (Idaho)	Harness (Ind.)	Bender (Ohio)		
O'Connor (Mont.)	Johnson (Ind.)	Lewis (Ohio)		
Schwert (N.Y.)	Landis (Ind.)	Seccombe (Ohio)		
Hunter (Ohio)	Springer (Ind.)	Angell (Ore.)		
Kirwan (Ohio	Dowell (Iowa)	Mott (Ore.)		
Secrest (Ohio)	LeCompte (Iowa)	Gartner (Pa.)		
Sweeney (Ohio)	Guyer (Kan.)	Gross (Pa.)		
Pierce (Ore.)	Brewster (Me.)	McDowell (Pa.)		
Myers (Pa.)	Oliver (Me.)	Van Zandt (Pa.)		
Garrett (Texas)	Smith (Me.)	Case (S.D.)		
Murdock (Utah)	Clason (Mass.)	Mundt (S.D.)		
Coffee (Wash.)	Holmes (Mass.)	Hawks (Wisc.)		
Hill (Wash.)	Andresen (Minn.)	Johns (Wisc.)		
Smith (Wash.)	Knutson (Minn.)	Keefe (Wisc.)		
	Thorkelson (Mont.)	Murray (Wisc.)		

* See *Townsend National Weekly,* October 31, 1938; November 7, 1938; June 30, 1939; *Congressional Record,* 76th Cong., 1st Sess., (June 1, 1939), 6524–25. One Townsend-endorsed congressman did note vote, Maciejewski (D. Ill.).

TABLE XIII (cont.)

Non-Endorsed Congressmen in Favor of H. R. 6466

Democrats 17		Republicans 7
Ford (Calif.)	Collins (Miss.)	Ford (Calif.)
Geyer (Calif.)	Scrugham (Nev.)	Hinshaw (Calif.)
Havenner (Calif.)	Sutphin (N.J.)	Winter (Kan.)
Izac (Calif.)	Cartwright (Okla.)	Pittenger (Minn.)
Sheppard (Calif.)	Massingale (Okla.)	Risk (R.I.)
Voorhis (Calif.)	Leavy (Wash.)	Shiffler (W.Va.)
Fries (Ill.)	Magnuson (Wash.)	Bolles (Wisc.)
Jacobsen (Iowa)	Wallgren (Wash.)	
Houston (Kan.)		

Endorsed Congressmen Against H. R. 6466

Democrats 14	Republicans 45	
Patrick (Ala.)	Church (Ill.)	Stearns (N.H.)
Cummings (Colo.)	Dirksen (Ill.)	Cole (N.Y.)
Caldwell (Fla.)	Johnson (Ill.)	Culkin (N.Y.)
Schaefer (Ill.)	Sumner (Ill.)	Reed (N.Y.)
Mills (La.)	Gillie (Ind.)	Brown (Ohio)
Connery (Mass.)	Halleck (Ind.)	Elston (Ohio)
Lesinski (Mich.)	Jensen (Iowa)	Jenkins (Ohio)
Tenerowicz (Mich.)	Martin (Iowa)	Jones (Ohio)
Anderson (Mo.)	Talle (Iowa)	Routzohn (Ohio)
Crosser (Ohio)	Carlson (Kan.)	Vorys (Ohio)
Allen (Penn.)	Lambertson Kan.)	White (Ohio)
Walter (Penn.)	Rees (Kan.)	Corbett (Penn.)
Gossett (Texas)	Martin (Mass.)	Darrow (Penn.)
Mahon (Texas)	Rogers (Mass.)	Fenton (Penn.)
	Treadway (Mass.)	Gerlach (Penn.)
	Blackney (Mich.)	Jarrett (Penn.)
	Dondero (Mich.)	Kunkel (Penn.)
	McLeod (Mich.)	Rutherford (Penn.)
	Shafer (Mich.)	Rich (Penn.)
	Maas (Minn.)	Simpson (Penn.)
	Short (Mo.)	Tibbott (Penn.)
	Stefan (Neb.)	Thill (Wisc.)
		Horton (Wyo.)

Paired Votes in Favor of H. R. 6466	
Paired Votes Endorsed	Paired Votes Non-Endorsed
Gehrmann (Prog.-Wisc.)	Wood (D.-Mo.)
	Alexander (R.-Minn.)
	Schulte (D.-Ind.)

As a result of this large-scale defection among Townsend-endorsed congressmen, one of the Townsend congressional leaders,
Joe Hendricks (Fla., D), conceded:

> I must be frank in admitting that many . . . endorsed by the Town-
> send organizations never actually promised to vote for the plan. Neither
> did they—only in one or two exceptional cases—say they would not.
> They only led the old people to believe that they would when they
> knew in their own minds that they would not, which is simply cruel
> and indefensible.[34]

TNRP, Inc., leaders had led their followers to assume that those
whom they endorsed would favor the plan. Yet some of the most
bitter attacks against the bill were directed by Republicans who
had received Townsend endorsement and support.[35] Ostensibly
Townsend-endorsed Republicans should have held firm in view
of the political victories in 1938 achieved in cooperation with
the Townsend Movement and in the absence of a party leadership committed to the Social Security Act. Yet forty-five of the
ninety-three Republicans elected with Townsend endorsement,
or over 48 per cent, deserted the plan. Only seven non-endorsed
Republicans joined the Townsendites to vote favorably. Conversely, Townsend-endorsed Democrats who were under the
greatest pressure from their party leaders proved more reliable,
twenty-three or 60 per cent of this group voting in the affirmative. An additional seventeen Democrats from outside the Townsend bloc also voted for the bill.

(B) *The discharge petition of 1943–44.*—In the discharge petition, the pressure organization possesses an instrument with
which to circumvent the House leadership if the latter is reluctant to permit legislation to be considered. A legislator may
file a petition to withdraw for consideration by the House any
bill pigeonholed in committee. On the other hand the requirement of 218 signatures is a formidable obstacle. A summary of
discharge petition action from 1935 to 1948, for example, re-

vealed that 204 discharge petitions were introduced, but only seventeen received the necessary signatures.[36] Of this number, ten bills passed the House and one was eventually enacted into law.

Efforts by Townsendites to withdraw their bill from committee through the discharge petition proved unsuccessful. Up to the 83rd Congress, nine Townsend discharge petitions were filed. None attained the requisite 218 signatures, although most surpassed the former discharge rule of one-third of the House. Since the required number of signatures was raised from 145 to 218 in 1935, the very year in which the Townsend bill first appeared in Congress, Townsend leaders developed an obsession that the increased severity of the rule was aimed primarily at their legislation.

TABLE XIV

TOWNSEND DISCHARGE PETITIONS, 1935–52*

Congress	Year	Petition No.	Bill	Author	Signatures
74:1	1935	?	H.R. 3977	Kramer (Calif. D)	57–?
74:1	1935	?	H.R. 7154	Monaghan (Mont. D)	63–?
75:1–3	1937–38	12	H.R. 4199	Sheppard (Calif. D)	136
76:3	1940	28	H.R. 8264	Hendricks (Fla. D)	175–180
77:1–2	1941–42	7	H.R. 1036	O'Conner (Mont. D)	193
78:1–2	1943–44	17	H.R. 1649	Cannon (Fla. D)	213–217
79	1945–46	None filed			
80:1–2	1947–48	7	H.R. 16	Angell (Ore. R)	179–182
81:1–2	1949–50	15	H.R. 2135	Blatnik (Minn. D)	201
82:1–2	1951–52	4	H.R. 2678	Angell (Ore. R)	188

* None of the signature totals is official for the Clerk of the House refuses to make them public unless the full 218 signatures have been affixed. With three exceptions, noted below, the totals used here have been abstracted from the *Weekly*, 1935–1952, which raises the possibility of error. The totals are probably accurate, for those congressmen whose names were mistakenly included have protested, and the *Weekly*, with disdain and no little threat,

In the 78th Congress, after intensive efforts on the part of TNRP, Inc., and its steering committee, 217 representatives were persuaded to sign Discharge Petition No. 17.[37] So confident were the pension leaders of obtaining the required number that a meeting was called by their steering committee to plan strategy for handling the bill on the floor of the House. The signatures decreased to 213, however, when Representatives Grant Furlong (Pa., D), Francis E. Walter (Pa., D), Joe L. Smith (W. Va., D) and Foster Stearns (N. H., D) withdrew their names, at which point the 78th Congress was terminated.

Discharge Petition No. 17 could have been completed despite this withdrawal if the Townsend congressional bloc of 172 had remained unified. The critical signatures were available within the group of thirteen endorsed congressmen who failed to sign.[38] When it was imperative that congressmen reciprocate for election-endorsements and support, and when it was within the power of the legislative bloc to affix the required signatures, the response again proved inadequate.

On at least two other occasions endorsed legislators did not add their signatures to discharge petitions. Seven endorsed congressmen refused to sign the Townsend petition in the 77th Congress and twelve in the 81st Congress, ten of the latter being Democrats who had been willing to sign in the previous Republican Congress.

It must be stressed that the discharge petition imposed only minimal demands upon a legislator. Congressmen were not being requested to commit themselves in favor of the bill or even to vote for the motion to withdraw it from committee. Signing simply facilitated House consideration of the question of whether or not the bill should be discharged. If an endorsed congressman would not sign under these circumstances, it is reasonable

---

removed their names from its lists. Figures for the 74th Congress are especially vague. In the *Congressional Record*, 74th Cong., 1st Sess., April 2, 1935, 4883, after H. R. 3977 had been officially abandoned by the Townsendites, John H. Hoeppel (Calif., D.) announced that only fifty-seven had signed its discharge petition. In outlining the composition of the Townsend Steering Committee in 1936, Joseph P. Monaghan (Mont., D.), its chairman, mentioned that its members were chosen from the sixty-three who had signed the discharge petition for H. R. 7154. See *Congressional Record*, 74th Cong., 2nd Sess., January 15, 1936, 424. Figures for the 1937-38 petition were obtained from *Congressional Record, Appendix*, 75th Cong., 3rd Sess., June 16, 1938, 3225. At least three representatives, perhaps five, withdrew their names in 1940; four did so in 1944 and three in 1948.

to surmise that he had never favored the plan and that he was reluctant to have it even considered.

(C) *Strategic congressional positions.*—Another test for assessing the Townsend bloc when its response was crucial to the success of the plan lies in analyzing the role played by individual Townsendites who occupied key congressional positions. To what extent did they advance the Townsend Plan as necessary legislation by virtue of their strategic positions? If they did not, it may be concluded that for them the plan was merely a convenient device for securing their reelection or a means of liberalizing the Social Security Act.

Only once, in 1939, was the Townsend bill reported out by a legislative committee, the House Committee on Ways and Means.[39] Its hearing should have provided an excellent opportunity for those eight members who had been endorsed in 1938 to welcome the Townsend bill and attempt to secure for it a favorable recommendation. The eight, all Republicans, were Frank Carlson (Kan.), Frank Crowther (N. Y.), Bertrand W. Gearhart (Calif.), Benjamin Jarrett (Pa.), Thomas A, Jenkins (Ohio), Harold Knutson (Minn.), Daniel A. Reed (N. Y.) and Allen T. Treadway (Mass.). Throughout the hearings, however, only two members of this group assumed a friendly posture. Although for the most part Knutson remained silent throughout the discussion of the plan, he did offer some assistance. Only Gearhart of California encouraged Townsend witnesses and attempted to undermine the adverse testimony presented by the economists. Even he, a club member before his election to Congress, a drafter of the second Townsend bill, and a member of all the steering committees, refused to commit himself to the plan. At one point a fellow committee member, Frank H. Buck (Calif., D), became so incensed with Gearhart's leading questions that he demanded to know whether he favored the bill. He was for any bill, answered Gearhart, that was based on a pay-as-you-go principle. This was not the degree of support commensurate with Gearhart's Townsend activities. By avoiding a positive identification with the plan, he implied that he, too, could not recommend it to the committee. Not one of the eight members attempted to secure a favorable recommendation by the committee when a Townsend bill was reported out. On the final roll call vote in the House of Representatives, five opposed it and only three voted favorably: Crowther, Knutson and Gearhart.

Senator Sheridan Downey (Calif., D), a leading Townsendite, became chairman of a special committee in 1941 to investigate old-age pensions. Downey had sought the Democratic nomination for Congress on a Townsend platform in 1936; he had once served as Dr. Townsend's personal attorney, and he had been active in the pension movement since 1934. He was the author of a number of pro-Townsend books, including *Why I Believe in the Townsend Plan*.[40] His election to the Senate in 1938 represented a victory for the Townsendites as well as for the "Ham and Eggs" pension group in California. Two of the other members of Downey's committee were J. W. Elmer Thomas (Okla., D), who had campaigned in 1938 with strong Townsend support, and Claude Pepper (Fla., D), who had been elected in 1936 and reelected in 1938 with the plan as one of his principle issues. Although proponents of the plan obtained an opportunity to testify before the committee, none of these senators took advantage of their special position to advance the cause of the Townsend bill.

A brief case history of Congressmen Harold Knutson (Minn., R) and Ralph O. Brewster (Me., R) completes this analysis of Townsend-endorsed congressmen in key posts. Knutson had voted for the Townsend bills in 1935 and 1939; he had participated in the rewriting of the second Townsend bill of 1935. The Townsend forces repeatedly endorsed Congressman Knutson for reelection. In the Republican 80th Congress he became chairman of the important Committee on Ways and Means. "The 80th Congress is a Townsend Congress," rejoiced the Townsendites. At the termination of that Congress, however, the Townsendites were no closer to their goal; Knutson had failed to utilize his chairmanship in behalf of the plan.

Knutson's inactivity was sharply attacked by a fellow Republican, Representative Merlin Hull (Wisc.), who accused the chairman of blocking consideration of the Townsend bill.[41] Hull's accusations were printed in the *Weekly* which demanded that Knutson commit himself on the plan. In his rebuttal, Knutson reminded the Townsendites of his past loyalty to the plan, but all that he was willing to suggest as chairman was that the Townsend bill could be considered any time a committee majority of thirteen desired to do so.[42] A bitter *Weekly* editorial condemned Knutson for his failure to support the Townsend Plan and for his failure as chairman to initiate a committee vote. This controversy was climaxed by an intensive campaign against

Knutson in 1948, and his defeat by a Townsend-endorsed Democrat in a district that had returned Republicans to office for over forty years.

Ralph O. Brewster was elected to the House of Representatives in 1936 with strong Townsend support. He, too, signed all the discharge petitions, participated in the steering committees and voted for the bill in 1939. Before the Third National Convention of Townsend Clubs in 1938 and upon the floor of the House, he had contended that a vote by Republican congressmen for the Townsend bill would redeem their party's platform pledge.

In 1950, as a member of the Senate Committee on Finance which considered the plan, he addressed the following remarks with regard to the plan: "I would not have either provision, that they [the pensioners] must spend it, or that they must not earn. That has always been my philosophy."[43] Yet the compulsory spending and retirement features lay at the heart of the Townsend Plan. And the bill for which he had voted in 1939 and which he had urged upon his party contained identical compulsory spending and retirement provisions.

To leave the impression that the great number of endorsed congressmen refused to cooperate with Townsend legislative efforts would be misleading. It may be hypothesized, however, that had they in turn occupied similar positions of responsibility, their response would have corresponded to that of their fellows.

IV   THE GEOGRAPHICAL LIMITS OF TOWNSEND STRENGTH

Townsendites were unable to overcome an additional obstacle in their efforts to secure the adoption of the plan in the U. S. House of Representatives. Their legislative strength was restricted to a fixed and limited regional pattern which militated against efforts to win support from outside their endorsed group of legislators.

In the vote on the Townsend bill of 1939, approximately 75 per cent of the congressmen from the Far West supported the plan. The region providing the next highest level of support was the Midwest—28.5 per cent. Of the eight state delegations voting unanimously for the bill, five came from the Far West—Arizona, Montana, Nevada, Oregon, and Washington—and two from the Midwest—North Dakota and South Dakota; the Maine delegation was the sole exception. Over 70 per cent of the congressmen who voted for the plan came from states of the Far

TABLE XV

TOWNSEND CONGRESSIONAL ENDORSEMENTS-ELECTIONS, BY REGIONS, 1936–52*

Region	1936 End.	Elect.	1938 End.	Elect.	1940 End.	Elect.	1942 End.	Elect.	1944 End.	Elect.	1946 End.	Elect.	1948 End.	Elect.	1950 End.	Elect.	1952 End.	Elect.
Far West	48	22	48	26	46	39	59	44	40	36	59	35	44	28	46	36	44	30
Midwest	88	23	132	69	103	55	120	69	110	79	124	84	79	51	103	71	105	77
Northeast	63	10	65	37	58	28	82	43	61	41	65	39	47	37	60	51	58	50
South	28	17	18	15	20	10	20	16	18	16	25	24	21	19	18	16	16	16

* The endorsement figures in this table do not include those candidates who did not compete in the congressional elections: 1936–22; 1938–1; 1942–4; 1946–2; 1948–15; 1950–3; 1952–3.

West and Midwest. And the greatest gains from outside the group of Townsend endorsees occurred in the delegations from the Far West, twelve votes as against twelve from the three other regions combined.

Eleven of the fifteen state delegations furnishing 100 per cent of their available signatures in support of the 1944 discharge petition were Far Western and Midwestern. Several states in these regions had a signature record of from 75 to 99 per cent.

With four exceptions, Delaware, New Hampshire, Maine and Vermont, those state delegations which responded 75 to 100 per cent in support of the various discharge petitions, in the period 1935–52, were also from the Far West and Midwest. In addition, five of the nine representatives who served as Townsend steering committee chairmen during this period came from these areas: McGroarty (Calif., D) Monaghan (Mont., D), O'Connor (Mont., D), Homer D. Angell (Ore., R), and John A. Blatnik (Minn., D). Two, Crosby (Pa., D) and James E. Van Zandt (Pa., R) represented the East; two, Pat Cannon (Fla., D) and Hendricks (Fla., D), the South.

From the above figures, confirmed in other modes of Townsend support, it is evident that the Far West, especially, and the Midwest occupied predominant positions in the sum total of Townsend congressional support. Since, however, the Far West sent the smallest delegation to the House of Representatives, only forty-three to fifty-seven members from 1935 through 1952, the region with the highest degree of Townsend strength had the weakest representation in the House.

From within the delegations of the northeastern states, the Townsendites failed to capture sufficient support with which to transform their Western votes into a majority. The Northeast sent the largest delegation to the House, 129 to 133, in the period under consideration. In the 1939 vote, eighteen of the endorsed representatives from this region stood firm for the bill; twenty or approximately 53 per cent voted against it. Only three votes were obtained for the bill from outside the Townsend group in these Eastern delegations. The twenty-one Eastern representatives who voted for the Townsend bill comprised only 15.6 per cent of the membership in the twelve Eastern delegations.

On the 1944 discharge petition, congressmen from only one state from this region cooperated 100 per cent, and only two state delegations granted a support ratio of 75 to 99 per cent.

All of the four signers who withdrew their names were from the Northeast.

The Southern bloc in the House, comprising between 120 and 122 members in the period 1935 through 1952, was largely impervious to Townsend appeals; its congressmen furnished the bulk of the opposition to the plan. An inability to penetrate this bloc was clearly revealed in the 1939 vote, the Townsend bill failing to receive a single favorable vote from eight of the thirteen Southern delegations: Alabama, Georgia, Kentucky, Louisiana, North Carolina, South Carolina, Tennessee and Virginia. Six Townsend-endorsed Southerners voted for the bill while five voted against. Only nine Southern votes were cast for the Townsend bill, a mere 7.5 per cent of the Southern Congressional bloc.

In 1944, the four state delegations which failed to provide a single signature for the discharge petition were all from the South—Mississippi, North Carolina, Tennessee, and Virginia. Of the thirteen endorsed representatives who failed to sign the petition that year, four were from this region.

Townsend overtures toward the Southern representatives proved useless although almost continuously, from 1937 to 1948, a Florida legislator chaired or co-chaired the Townsend steering committees and, at one time or another, a small number of Southern congressmen participated in its meetings. In 1941 Dr. Townsend addressed a special letter to seventy Southern congressmen in which he stressed the South's self-interest in the plan; that pensions would recompense their states for the financial drain imposed by federal taxes and discriminatory freight rates.[44] He returned to his campaign of wooing Southerners in 1943, his letter this time emphasizing that the plan would provide the South additional purchasing power and free it from Northern bankers and industrialists.[45] Whatever the explanation—the racial question, an absence of Townsend clubs at the political grass roots, hostility on the part of the Democratic Party leaders, or a general conservatism—the Townsendites were largely isolated from the sizeable and powerful bloc of Southerners in the House of Representatives.

CHAPTER VII

CONGRESS INVESTIGATES
THE TOWNSEND MOVEMENT

Congress is no mere passive agent responding positively or negatively to pressure. Its machinery screens the demands of competing groups and its composition forces them to confront the political-geographic imperatives involved in obtaining a majority vote. At the same time Congress is capable of assuming a positive role in initiating counter pressure. A congressional exposé of the Townsend Movement in 1936 affected decisively the latter's political behavior and organizational structure.

The congressional investigation originated primarily in the threat posed by Townsend strength to the future of large numbers of congressmen. After having secured only fifty-six votes in the House of Representatives in April, 1935, and with the new Social Security Act on the statute books, the Townsend Plan had apparently shot its political bolt. A startling Townsend electoral victory in November, 1935, however, marked a tremendous resurgence in the plan's popularity and strength. More ominous for politicians was the realization that the Townsend Movement had broken out of the confines of the Far West.

To attain the political strength commensurate with its ambitions, the Old Age Recovery Plan, Ltd., undertook an extensive organizational drive after its April legislative defeat. The response was so encouraging that four regional headquarters were established to direct Townsend activities throughout the nation, and pension leaders spoke before overflowing audiences in Indiana, Michigan, Minnesota, and Ohio, relatively virgin territory for them up to this time. The increase in clubs was phenomenal, 982 new charters being issued from November 11, 1935, through January 7, 1936,[1] the greatest gains occurring in the Midwestern and Eastern states.

Financially the OARP, Ltd., reaped an ever-increasing bounty. From March through December, 1934, $84,959.78 had been collected. In only the first quarter of 1935, over $99,400 poured into the Townsend treasury, while by September 30, 1935, the sum total of revenue collected up to that time was reported to be $636,803.21.[2]

An opportunity for exerting the power of this new strength presented itself in a special election held in Michigan's Third Congressional District in November, 1935.[3] One of the four candidates for the Republican nomination, Verner W. Main, a leading "dry" and a prominent church leader, campaigned principally on a Townsend platform. He was supported by the local Townsend clubs and the national pension leaders, including Dr. Townsend and Robert E. Clements, who campaigned in his district in behalf of his nomination and election. Main captured the primary by a tremendous majority despite the hostility of the regular party organization. He credited his success to Dr. Townsend's speeches and to a large bloc of Townsend votes. In the final election he defeated a Democrat who centered his campaign upon an attack on the plan.

Capture of the Republican primary by a Townsend candidate forced many politicians to reappraise the Movement's political significance; it now appeared to represent a political force with a dangerous cutting edge. The new organizational growth and financial position acquired added significance in view of the Michigan election. The unexpectancy of the Townsend victory and the tendency of the press to emphasize the sensational over-exaggerated, moreover, the importance of the election. The venerable New York *Times* furnished it front-page coverage and publicized an alarming dispatch from Washington that leaders of the major parties were seriously impressed by the plan's ability to attract votes.[4] Capitalizing upon this new strategic position and free publicity, Townsend leaders warned that they would campaign against all candidates in 1936 who opposed their plan.

Congressional offices were again deluged with Townsend letters; the chairman of the House Appropriations Committee reported receiving over 5,000. Conservative news analysts, whose columns were studied for an indication of political trends, pre-

dicted that all candidates would be under pressure to endorse
the Townsend Movement or suffer the consequences. It was the
responsibility of the nation's political leaders to unite in meeting this challenge, Arthur Krock warned, in order "to avert this
threat of the destruction of our economic system."[5] Michigan
Senator Arthur Vandenberg's (R) disclosure that the plan
possessed a tremendous following "here and elsewhere" confirmed the gravity of the situation.[6] Vandenberg suggested, moreover, that Townsend Democrats would vote for the Townsend-
endorsed Republican. This implied that party lines might not
withstand the attraction of the plan. The shock and fear generated by the Townsend election victory in Michigan was reflected in almost all of the popular journals dealing with public
affairs and political events. It was impossible for congressmen
to avoid the contagion of their leaders and of the press, especially since 1936 was an election year.

Congressmen whose political futures are threatened become
formidable opponents. Within two months after the second
session of the 74th Congress had convened, a special investigating committee was probing into the OARP, Ltd. H. Res. 443
authorized an investigation of old-age pension plans submitted
as legislation to the House and specifically cited the Townsend
bill.[7] Inquiry was to be directed "with special reference" to promoters of such legislation, their records, their methods of collecting and spending money.

The emphasis placed upon internal organization and finances
rather than upon an economic analysis of the plan testifies to
the political nature of the investigation. Its purpose was to discredit the Townsend Movement, thereby destroying its effectiveness as a political machine in the 1936 elections. Although the
plan was susceptible to serious economic questioning, a discussion
of the transaction tax and its other features was not the most
favorable grounds on which to launch the attack, nor could it
provide the lurid reading material which would attract public
interest.[8]

In exposing and crippling the practices of another old-age
pension organization in 1934, Congress had before it a useful
precedent for its attack on the Townsend Movement. The investigation of Dr. E. J. Pope and his National Old Age Pension
Association had revealed highly derogatory information to the
effect that his pension movement was actually a lucrative racket.[9]

Chiropodist Pope had enticed through the mails more than $60,000 in contributions from aged people.

Sufficient evidence existed to indicate that this type of legislative investigation might also prove profitable with the Townsend Movement. Bitter revolts within the Townsend Movement in 1935 had led to serious charges against the doctor and the co-founder. Prominent club leaders had joined with the former national publicity director in denouncing Dr. Townsend and Clements for transforming the Movement into a racket.[10] It was asserted that whereas Clements had been penniless when the Movement was initiated, he was now living a luxurious life. The co-founders were accused of reaping handsome dividends from the *Weekly* and of delaying passage of their bill in order to collect more money from the aged.

The immediate goal of the investigation was to smear, to insinuate, if possible to prove the Movement a racket operated for personal gain at the expense of the faith and pennies of the aged. Here were weak links in the Movement, the areas already exposed and sensitive to attack. It was a crucial maneuver, moreover, since the first club convention had granted the two leaders absolute control over the endorsement of candidates, complete direction over the "millions" of Townsend ballots. By undermining confidence in the Townsend leadership and destroying the identification and self-interest of club members and the aged in general with the leaders, the political efficacy of the Movement might be destroyed.

Almost immediately after the Michigan primary an investigation of this nature appears to have been contemplated. In a letter written on December 13, 1935, to a Washington administrator, the former executive secretary to the President's Committee on Economic Security, Edwin E. Witte, referred to a proposed investigation of Townsend financial transactions in the coming congressional session.[11] Although he expressed the doubt that a demonstration of venality would disrupt the Movement, it is clear that political leaders had already appraised a weakness in the Townsend position.[12]

From the first day of the second session of the 74th Congress, in 1936, the Townsend Movement became a major issue of debate, the focus of a bitter and mounting attack led chiefly by Representatives C. Jasper Bell (Mo., D), Thomas L. Blanton (Tex., D), Charles L. Gifford (Mass., R) and Clare E. Hoffman (Mich., R). The allegations raised by the Townsend rebels in

1935 were reprinted in the *Congressional Record,* and an invidious parallel was drawn between Dr. Pope and Dr. Townsend. Pro-Townsend congressmen confined themselves to defending the plan and to assertions of Townsend voting strength; little was said to refute the serious charges of corruption and fraud. Recognizing, however, the inevitability of the investigation, Townsend supporters in the House subsequently announced that it would be welcomed by the Movement.

The House leadership exercised considerable care to insure the proper planning and reliable direction of the investigation. Representative Marion A. Zioncheck (Wash., D), who had introduced the initial resolution for an inquiry into pension bills or rackets, was sidetracked as being too erratic to be entrusted with the task the leaders had in mind. Washington was a strong Townsend state and Zioncheck had vacillated from voting for the plan in 1935 to condemning it and subsequently promising to vote for it. Bell, who had also introduced a resolution for an investigation, appeared to be a more reliable choice. Not only had he consistently opposed the bill, but he represented a safe Missouri district.

It was undoubtedly true, as the press reported, that Bell's resolution was drafted with the help and approval of the House leadership.[13] A careful effort seems also to have been made to induce the Republicans to co-sponsor the investigation. The New York *Times* reported that the Rules Committee had abstained from acting on Bell's resolution until Democratic leaders had conferred with Republican House chieftains.[14] Apparently a bipartisan investigation was agreed upon, for an amended resolution, H. Res. 418, was reported favorably which deleted all reference to the Townsend Plan, but increased the number of committee members from seven to eight.[15]

It was no usual practice to divide assignments on an important committee equally between the two major parties, especially when one commanded an imposing majority in the House. This constituted a maneuver by Democratic leaders to prevent their party from falling sole heir to the onus of the investigation in the event it backfired. The Republicans participated, it was pointed out at the time, because ". . . the [Townsend] threat . . . has cut across party lines and many members on both sides of the House are fearful of their seats if the Movement gains or even continues at its present force."[16]

On February 22, the Speaker appointed to the investigating

Wide World Photos

DR. TOWNSEND QUITS HEARING

Cleveland—Accompanied by his attorney, Sheridan Downey (right), Dr. Francis E. Townsend walked out of a deposition hearing on the Townsend Organization today. Attorney Benjamin F. Sacharow, conducting the hearing, obtained a citation for contempt of court and had Dr. Townsend stopped in East Cleveland.

TOWNSEND AND SMITH AT MEETING

Cleveland—The Rev. Gerald L. K. Smith (right) of Louisiana, head of the "Share-the-Wealth" movement and a director in the Townsend Organization, shown conferring with Dr. Francis E. Townsend on the platform during a session of the Townsend National Convention.

committee Democrats Bell as chairman, Scott W. Lucas (Ill.), Joseph A. Gavagan (N. Y.) and John H. Tolan (Calif.) and Republicans Samuel L. Collins (Calif.), J. William Ditter (Pa.), Clare E. Hoffman (Mich.) and John B. Hollister (Ohio). H. Res. 418 was subsequently replaced by H. Res. 443 which specifically designated the Townsend Plan as the subject of inquiry, and an appropriation for $50,000 was voted to finance the committee.

Two events occurred, meanwhile, which seemed to justify congressional hopes of uncovering scandals in the Townsend Movement. Robert E. Clements resigned from the OARP, Ltd., because of "irreconcilable differences" with Dr. Townsend. Although his resignation in no way concerned the investigation, it left the impression that something was amiss and provided excellent advance publicity for the committee. The Townsendites suffered a further blow as a result of the cancellation of all surety bonds on Townsend employees by the company issuing them.

Public hearings by the Select Committee to Investigate Old Age Pension Organizations were held intermittently from the end of March to June, 1936, and two subcommittees were active in California and Michigan. Except for Tolan, who alone fought its excesses and sought to aid the Townsendites, and Collins, who remained neutral, the committee adopted a hostile attitude toward the Townsend Movement. Chairman Bell, Hoffman, Lucas, Gavagan, and the counsel were particularly vitriolic and insulting.

Together, counsel and the hostile majority of the committee indulged in the most unscrupulous browbeating and questioning of witnesses. Dr. Townsend and Clements were compelled to comment upon quotations and testimony deliberately abstracted from context to trick them into damaging admissions. Witnesses hostile to the leaders were encouraged to indulge in exaggerated and sensational conclusions.

Although the committee had anticipated capitalizing upon differences between the leaders, Clements' testimony indicates that he refused to permit himself to become such an instrument.[17] He denied that either he or Dr. Townsend knew that the OARP, Ltd., could be dissolved at any time and its assets divided among the doctor, himself, and Walter Townsend, the third "member" of the corporation. Moreover, Clements assumed full responsibility for administering the Movement, asserting that Dr. Townsend's role was to advance the plan. The co-founder was scrupulously fair to Dr. Townsend throughout his entire testimony and refused to accede to suggestions that the doctor had swindled or defrauded club members. Clements adamantly repudiated counsel's charges that Dr. Townsend had encouraged patent medicine advertisements in the *Weekly,* thereby violating ethical standards.

Clements made important admissions, however, regarding finances and organizational control which the committee was able to exploit, principally because they originated from the co-founder and not from minor malcontents, many of whom also testified. He substantiated charges raised by Townsend rebels that both he and his partner had benefited financially from the Movement. Close questioning revealed that the Prosperity Publishing Company and the OARP, Ltd., had provided Clements with approximately $79,000 in two and one-half years. Whereas the counsel implied fraud and deception on the part of both leaders, Clements asserted that this income represented both salary and dividends, of which $25,000 constituted Dr. Townsend's dividend which he had employed to purchase Clements' share of the Prosperity Publishing Company.

In contrast with Dr. Townsend, Clements had never contributed any significant sum to the Movement; he had not felt a moral responsibility to do so, he explained. Yet the OARP, Ltd., had paid him over $9,000 in salary for two and one-half years in addition to a very generous expense account. The committee members emphasized repeatedly that these sums were all derived from the nickels and dimes of the impoverished aged who were continuously solicited by the Townsend leaders for greater contributions to keep the Movement alive.

The First National Convention of Townsend Clubs in 1935 had been informed that the two leaders received only $50 a week plus expenses. Soon afterwards they increased their own salaries to $100 a week plus expenses and, in January, 1936, to $250 a week. The clubs were never informed of the latter increase. There was nothing fraudulent or illegal involved in these increases, but the committee was again able to point out the contrast between the income of the leaders and the poverty of the aged people supporting them.

The suspicion which the committee sought to foster, that the leaders misled the Movement and mulcted it for their personal gain, appeared to find some confirmation in the secrecy surrounding the partners' ownership and control of the key Townsend corporations. The Bell committee publicized what had never been officially disclosed to the rank and file, but which had been reported before the Senate Committee on Finance in 1935, that Dr. Townsend, his brother, Walter Townsend, and Robert E. Clements owned and controlled the corporation which chartered the clubs, OARP, Ltd. It is true that with regard to the *Weekly,* Dr. Townsend and Clements had publicized their personal ownership of the newspaper late in 1935 and again early in 1936. However, the *Weekly* had at no time revealed, as the committee was able to demonstrate, that substantial profits were being earned from the newspaper or that over $65,000 in dividends had been paid out. Just the reverse, the Townsend leadership had deliberately fostered the impression among the clubs that the paper barely covered its expenses! Sold as the Movement's official organ, its revenues had actually accrued to Dr. Townsend and Clements alone.

Two independent witnesses who testified helped contribute to the committee's case against Dr. Townsend and Clements. The conclusions of an accounting firm, which had inspected the financial records of the OARP, Ltd., at the request of the committee, cast suspicion upon the financial honesty and integrity of the pension leaders. Whereas club members had been assured that all financial records were in order, the committee was informed by the accountant that these records were extremely confused and that they did not reflect accurately receipts and disbursements.

Dr. Robert R. Doane, the economist who had testified on the plan at Dr. Townsend's request in the 1935 congressional hearings, was the other hostile witness. He accused the pension leaders of deliberately distorting his testimony. They had ascribed to him statements which he had never made—that he had verified the feasibility of the transaction tax and the plan. Dr. Doane charged that he had personally informed Dr. Townsend and Clements before and after the 1935 hearings that the $200 pensions were unobtainable, and that they had acknowledged this fact to him. Nevertheless, prominent Townsend speakers had led old people to believe that $200-a-month pensions would be forthcoming upon enactment of the bill.

With the encouragement of various committee members, Dr. Doane undertook to furnish an economic analysis of the plan, although he balked at their insistence that he predict that the plan would inevitably lead to "commissars and bayonets." Obviously embarrassed at times by his testimony at the 1935 hearings, Dr. Doane adhered to his charges against the pension leaders and his present economic analysis that enactment of the plan would have a disastrous effect upon the economy. The committee subsequently called one other economist, Dr. A. G. Hart of the University of Chicago, who also condemned the Townsend Plan.

A number of spectacular and damaging charges were levied against Dr. Townsend, Clements and the entire Townsend leadership by witnesses who had in one way or another been in personal contact with the organization and the two partners. These former Townsendites were eager to label the leaders as opportunists, racketeers, swindlers and atheists. Much of this type of defamation was actively solicited by counsel and by the committee which encouraged the most extreme statements. It was alleged that Dr. Townsend and Clements held their aged followers in profound contempt, referring to them with such terms as "old fossils" or "We don't give a damn about the old people."[18] The partners were accused of having agreed to a financial deal to throw Townsend support to the Republican candidate for governor of California in 1934 in return for the sum of $12,000. O. Otto Moore, a prominent Colorado lawyer, who as a club leader had participated in the Townsend national lobby in 1935, charged that a member of the Townsend Board of Directors had attempted to bribe him to prevent his exposing the irresponsibility and misappropriations of Clements and Dr. Townsend.

Moore also accused the two of transmitting false information through the mails to raise funds. The case of the "Townsendgram" was perhaps one of the most serious charges made against the two leaders since it raised the question of the fraudulent use of the mails, a federal offense. Of the $22,500 collected for the congressional action fund to finance the Townsend lobby in 1935, only $2,404.96 had been spent during the four months that it was active in Washington. In spite of a large surplus, the two leaders had issued a "Townsendgram," stressing that further contributions were necessary if the Townsend lobby were to remain in Washington. Moore's charges were substantiated by a former California congressman, Charles R. Randall (R), who had been employed as chairman of the Townsend National Strategy Committee in 1935. He complained that his name had been forged to communications sent through the mails in order to stimulate the flow of financial contributions from the clubs.

Evidence from a number of Townsendites revealed that considerable racketeering by local leaders and organizers had occurred and that the Movement contained leaders with unsavory reputations. Dr. Frank Dyer, a national lecturer for the OARP, Ltd., was charged with having represented himself as a "Father Sylvester," who traveled throughout the United States in a monk's robe, lecturing and collecting money. The area state manager for Lower Michigan admitted having been a Ku Klux Klan organizer in that state for two years. The letters of the Eastern regional director, the Reverend Clinton Wunder, were deliberately included in the record to reveal him as inordinately preoccupied with sex. The committee was forced to delete large sections of his letters for their obscenity.

The committee's chief prize was Northern California Area Manager Edward J. Margett who had been indicted in the past for grand larceny, obtaining earnings from a prostitute, and bootlegging. Clements testified that Dr. Townsend had refused to replace Margett, and the committee stressed repeatedly that Dr. Townsend had knowingly supported a man whose character and reputation proved him unfit for responsible leadership. Although the indictments against Margett had been dismissed, they provided lurid reading in the nation's press.

By the time Dr. Townsend was permitted to testify, a damaging case had been established and extensively publicized. Having previously ignored his demands that he be called, the committee could now attack the doctor frontally. Nevertheless, he was able to blunt their attack by disclaiming all responsibility for past organizational and financial activities of the Movement. He contended that the organization of the Movement had been Clements' domain whereas he was primarily in charge of advancing the plan before the nation. When confronted with the charges made by previous witnesses, Dr. Townsend categorically repudiated them all.

Dr. Townsend was forced to concede, however, that he had employed OARP, Ltd., money for his own political use in an attempt to establish a third party in California. Clements had testified that he had advised his partner that such expenditures were not permissible under the OARP, Ltd., charter as an eleemosynary corporation.

Dr. Townsend denied amassing a fortune from the Movement. His $25,000 dividend from the Prosperity Publishing Company he had paid to Clements, and he had utilized the major part of another $7,500 dividend in building a visual education program for the Movement. Since he had become sole owner, he stated, 90 per cent of the revenues which the *Weekly* earned had been assigned by him to the OARP, Ltd. He affirmed a moral responsibility, as Clements had not, to help advance the Movement.

Unable to uncover illegal or fraudulent practices, the committee belabored the doctor with the accusations that had been raised against him. His letters were cited to prove his intent to reap millions from the Movement, although it was apparent that their meaning differed from the one fashioned by the committee. His words were so misconstrued by his inquisitors that at times he despaired of answering, and he agreed with their wildest assertions. So confused did Dr. Townsend become under this sledge-hammer questioning that he contradicted himself on the most simple items.

After three days of such pressure, Dr. Townsend refused to participate further in the hearings. In a short speech before the committee, the chairman having denied him permission to read a statement, he announced that he would not remain a party to such an "inquisition"; only under arrest would he return.[19] Upon that note, Dr. Townsend abandoned the committee chambers.

Without Dr. Townsend or his chief assistants, who obeyed his orders to ignore the committee's subpoenas, the hearings were shorn of their dramatic appeal. The investigation was protracted for a short period to introduce the absurd notion that the *Weekly* constituted an organ for Communist propaganda, and to allow additional Townsendites to testify. Subsequently the committee voted six to two in favor of citing for contempt Dr. Townsend and two of his regional directors, the Reverend Clinton Wunder and John P. Kieffer. In spite of efforts by Townsend congressmen to delay action, the House on a division vote, 271 to 41, accepted the committee's recommendation.[20]

To prevent Dr. Townsend from exploiting any element of martyrdom for political purposes, the charges were not pressed until after the 1936 election. In 1937, Dr. Townsend was adjudged guilty, his co-defendants having broken with him in the meantime and having testified against him. An appeal from a sentence of $100 fine and one year's imprisonment was unsuccessfully carried to the United States Supreme Court, and only a last-minute unconditional pardon by President Roosevelt in 1938 saved the pension messiah from prison.

As a result of the congressional investigation the organizational structure of the Townsend Movement was undermined and the Townsend leadership placed on the defensive from which it never completely recovered. Initially the investigation had been openly welcomed, the attitude presented to the clubs and the public being one of utmost confidence. Clements had boasted that the Townsendites were the ones who forced the House leadership to adopt Bell's resolution, and that "these monkeys have played right into our hands," by providing publicity through which the Movement would be exonerated.[21] By the middle of March, however, the committee was labeled a "gestapo," and accused of conducting a campaign of espionage and inquisition. "Is this investigation to be another Hitler blood purge?" trumpeted the *Weekly*.[22] A determined effort was made to prevent Townsendites from reading or believing the daily press; the truth, it was asserted, was to be found only in the *Weekly*. The *Weekly*, on the other hand, did not report testimony in full so that unfavorable evidence concerning high salaries and Margett's indictments never appeared therein except indirectly.

To counteract the accusations of the committee and its witnesses, Dr. Townsend renounced all further salary from the OARP, Ltd. In addition, he enlarged his Board of Directors from three to seven, and granted it a greater voice in the corporation. And he called for the election of a council of "Citizens Maximi" to provide the clubs with a share in directing the Movement.

The reiteration of such charges as personal enrichment, dictatorial control, irresponsible conduct, and racketeering aroused widespread mistrust among Townsend Club members. In April, 1936, Townsend National Headquarters called for a pledge of faith in its leadership, asking the 7,000 clubs to forward affidavits that no pressure had been exerted for funds, that members had voluntarily contributed money to be used as their leaders deemed necessary. By the end of May, Congressman John H. Tolan (Calif., D) announced receipt of affidavits from 4,450 clubs representing 1,456,000 members.[23] Over a third of the clubs had failed to furnish a vote of confidence.

Financially the Townsend Movement suffered severely from the investigation. Clements had testified that the quarterly rate

of income had leaped to $350,000 by the end of 1935. In the first
quarter of 1936, it shrank to $180,000. In many districts, clubs
ceased entirely to collect for the state or national organizations.[24]
When Clements had resigned he had informed the investigating
committee that the Townsend treasury contained approximately
$130,000. At the end of the investigation, Reverend Wright, a
member of the Board of Directors, estimated that only about
$30,000 remained.

Serious divisions developed within the leadership of the
Townsend Movement. Resignations and expulsions occurred on
all levels from the Board of Directors, OARP, Ltd., down
through state and area managers. The political consequences
were equally disastrous. Lack of finances and the disruption of
the organization affected the political potential of the Movement as did the forfeiture of public confidence and the weak-
ening of faith on the part of many Townsendites. The plan did
become a major issue in the Maine Republican primaries, the
Florida Democratic primaries and in the primaries of both major
parties in California, but on the whole Townsend candidates
fared badly.

CHAPTER VIII

PARTY POLITICS
AND STATE INITIATIVES

The Townsend Movement did not confine itself to any single aspect of politics or level of government. Its leaders committed it to the selection and election of presidential as well as congressional candidates and to the shaping of party platforms; in one state the Townsend Movement undertook to operate as a political party. And through the use of the "initiative," it circumvented the parties altogether by appealing directly to the electorate to enact the plan into state law.

Although such versatility maximizes opportunities for shaping public policy, it involves considerable risks. Identifying its cause with that of one major party or attempting to defeat both parties may impose severe strain upon the internal cohesion of the pressure group. The political system in the United States militates, moreover, against successful third-party undertakings. And by subjecting itself to a popular test, the pressure group is exposed to an objective measurement of its political strength, a potentially dangerous undertaking.

Participation in Political Parties

In two of the five presidential elections during the period 1936–52, the Townsend leadership was committed to the defeat of the Democratic national candidate and the election of his Republican opponent. At the same time, Townsendites supported, officially and unofficially, a national third party in 1936 and a state third party from 1938 to 1942. Their involvement in one of the national third parties of 1948 was actively solicited, and initially, at least, sympathetically considered by Dr. Townsend.

This erratic pattern is explained in part by Dr. Townsend's personal hatred for President Franklin D. Roosevelt, an obsession which dominated his political behavior up to and including the 1940 election. The doctor's ambivalent attitude toward the major parties—the simultaneous rejection and acceptance of the two—and the refusal of either major party to endorse the Townsend Plan also helps explain the relationship between the Townsend Movement and the party system. As a result of the pension leader's dominance within the Movement, his views and its behavior were inextricably interrelated.

I   THE ANTI-ROOSEVELT PHOBIA: MATRIX OF TOWNSEND-
NATIONAL PARTY BEHAVIOR, 1936–40

Dr. Townsend's attitude toward President Roosevelt originated in the latter's refusal to grant him an interview in December, 1934.[1] Proud of his Movement and confident that his new idea would rescue the country, the pension leader resented bitterly this indifference. "President Roosevelt even refused to meet Dr. Townsend—that is an insult that the masses of the people should resent," proclaimed a *Weekly* editorial in February, 1935.[2] "We have aristocracy in the White House—not democracy."

As late as August, 1935, a political informant reported to the White House that the pension leader's antagonism to the President originated in this rebuff.[3] Democratic leaders from outside as well as within the Townsend Movement, concerned over the possible consequences this ill-feeling might have for their party, sought a meeting between the two.[4] Dr. Townsend failed, however, to receive any invitation to meet with the President. Roosevelt never commented publicly upon the Townsend Plan, but he was held personally responsible by its proponents for sabotaging their bill in Congress since his representatives had attacked it before the Committee on Ways and Means in 1935.

The congressional investigation in 1936 transformed the doctor's resentment into active hatred. This attempt to besmirch his personal reputation and that of his plan and Movement, he attributed to the hostility of the Administration. Dr. Townsend was convinced that the President was the evil genius behind his persecution; the contempt citation by the House of Representatives was construed as an act of malevolence on the part of Roosevelt. The major obstacle to his plan, progenitor of the despised Social Security Act, President Roosevelt become Dr. Townsend's personal "devil" whom he was determined to exorcise.

In 1935 and again in 1936, Dr. Townsend had considered creating a third party in the presidential campaign. The Bell investigating committee provided the final impetus for this move since it caused him to focus upon one goal, the defeat of Roosevelt. In addition, it led him directly into the political arms of a confirmed Roosevelt-hater, the Reverend Gerald L. K. Smith, and subsequently into a coalition with Father Charles E. Coughlin.

Reverend Smith was a demagogue in search of a cause and a following, having been driven from Huey Long's machine after the assassination of the Kingfish. He encountered the pension leader at a propitious moment, when the latter, humiliated and defiant, stalked out from the committee's session. Smith escorted him from its chambers, his arm around the old man. As the doctor recounted this story, Smith emitted a Southern yell, took him by the hand and brushed aside all those who would have held him back: ". . . an inward force caused him to leap to my side and risk possible jail sentence for contempt."[5]

From this fateful meeting, his first encounter with the pension leader, Smith became Townsend's most intimate adviser. Smith was an individual of unbounded ego and ambition. In ministering to the doctor's wounded self-esteem, Smith counseled him to undertake a retaliatory campaign against the President. "We are going to drive that cripple out of the White House—and we are going to do it in 1936," he had bellowed at a Talmadge-sponsored convention in Georgia earlier in the year.[6] Dr. Townsend was so immersed in his own desire for revenge that he ignored Smith's reputation as an anti-Semite and a prominent member of the Ku Klux Klan.

Within a short time, Dr. Townsend and Smith announced a union of forces to present "a common front against the dictatorship in Washington."[7] They would strive for Roosevelt's defeat, and their groups would meet in a convention with representatives of Father Coughlin. "Anybody but Roosevelt" would be their slogan. At Dr. Townsend's insistence, Smith was made a member of the Townsend Board of Directors, and the Reverend proclaimed himself in charge of the Movement's political activities.[8] Smith became the pension leader's alter ego, traveling with him throughout the country on a joint speaking tour, negotiating with Coughlin and Lemke, and issuing statements in the name of the Townsend leadership.

It was inevitable that the new allies would join a third malcontent who shared their hatred for President Roosevelt. Father Charles E. Coughlin, at one time a strong supporter of the President, had become his bitter opponent. His emotional radio "sermons" combining an advocacy of inflation and economic security with attacks upon bankers, Jews and Communists had catapulted him to national prominence and provided him with an organized following, the National Union for Social Justice.

On May 27, 1936, Father Coughlin declared that he would not support a third party even though he was opposed to Roosevelt and was unable to support Landon. But the "hate-Roosevelt" forces must have discovered common ground, for by the middle of June, Dr. Townsend had proclaimed an alliance with Smith, Coughlin, and Lemke to create a new party to defeat the President and eliminate the "gang-ridden" old parties:

> I have no wish that the Townsend Movement shall become the sole factor in creating this new political alignment, and I have no desire to gain political leadership of any new party. But I do want the Townsend Movement to do its full part in creating such a fundamental change in our political life."[9]

Within a week, William Lemke, a North Dakota congressman and a former Non-Partisan League leader, had initiated his candidacy under the Union Party banner and a platform which incorporated most of Father Coughlin's principles.[10]

Although Father Coughlin adopted Lemke as his candidate, Dr. Townsend and the Reverend Smith announced that they would withhold their endorsement until after they had consulted their followers. The mutual suspicion which was to flourish in this coalition may have already developed or perhaps Lemke had not committed himself sufficiently to the plan. It is more likely, however, that Dr. Townsend and his adviser were saving their endorsement for the Second National Convention of Townsend Clubs.

From the outset the new political alignment was a precarious one. In 1935 Father Coughlin had denounced the Townsend Plan as impracticable, while Dr. Townsend, in turn, had publicly indicated his contempt for Father Coughlin's program.[11]

The Reverend Smith, a proponent of the late Huey Long's Share-Our-Wealth philosophy, catered to the doctor whose movement he desired to control. Neither Coughlin nor Townsend wished to lose the identity of his own group within the coalition. Their desire to defeat President Roosevelt was the sole cement which bound them together.

Consequently the third party was premised upon an inherently unstable coalition. Any success would depend upon the cooperation of the three as well as Lemke's ability to hold them together until the election. Of equal uncertainty was their ability to deliver the votes of their supporters. The coalition was principally a creation by three individuals for personal and political reasons, detached from any spontaneous popular demand. No massive ground-swell of popular protest against the major political parties was involved. Just the reverse, President Roosevelt had effectively mobilized the support and allegiance of the great masses of discontented Americans.

Father Coughlin, who claimed to control at least nine million votes, encountered no difficulty in persuading his National Union for Social Justice to accept Lemke. The Reverend Smith represented himself as the leader of the Share-Our-Wealth clubs encompassing six million members. Actually he exercised no control over the remnants of Huey Long's movement, a fact obvious to Father Coughlin and most observers although not to Dr. Townsend. Smith's position depended solely upon his influence over the pension leader.

On the eve of the Townsend convention in July, the doctor engaged in a series of seemingly confusing maneuvers.[12] He announced his hesitancy regarding Lemke's candidacy since the latter had never fully committed himself to the plan. Moreover, club mail indicated that many local units opposed a third-party coalition. The matter would be decided by the convention, he stated, but he was prepared to suggest a candidate if the delegates so desired. The following day the pension leader proclaimed his opposition to any endorsement of Lemke by the OARP, Ltd.; he doubted seriously if any independent candidate could win a place on the ballot in November! Either the doctor was reacting to protests from Townsend leaders and clubs opposing a third party or he was endeavoring to drive Lemke into a more positive endorsement of the plan.

Whatever Dr. Townsend's intentions, the convention became completely embroiled in an "elect Lemke–hate Roosevelt" controversy. Since stenographic records are not available, it is impossible to verify charges by former Congressman Gomer Smith (Okla., D), then vice-president of the OARP, Ltd., that Dr. Townsend and Reverend Smith sought by resolution to join the pension movement to the third party.[13] However, bitter opposition developed against an attempt to stampede the convention into the Lemke camp, and the convention adopted a nonpartisan position as a compromise.

Dr. Townsend's welcoming speech to the delegates constituted an attack upon President Roosevelt for seeking to undermine the American form of government. He was followed by the Reverend Smith who whipped the delegates into an emotional frenzy with his denunciation of Roosevelt as a "communistic atheist." On the second day, Father Coughlin was unexpectedly introduced to influence the delegates. As he explained later, Dr. Townsend had telegraphed him the night before requesting him to speak in order to prevent "Farley's man, Gomer Smith," from capturing the convention.[14] In a dramatically staged appearance, Coughlin denounced Roosevelt as a liar, a betrayer, an ally of the "money changers" and a proponent of communism. The Union Party, he assured the thousands of cheering delegates, incorporated Dr. Townsend's principles and constituted the only means for saving the country from the gold standard, the Communists, the "double-crossing" Democrats. Virtually everyone rose when he demanded to know how many would follow Dr. Townsend into the third party.

Dr. Townsend announced that Father Coughlin, Reverend Smith, William Lemke and he would tour the country in support of Lemke's candidacy. They would attack President Roosevelt, the New Deal and its "alien and communistic trend." Prior to its termination, the convention was addressed by Lemke who endorsed old-age revolving pensions, praised Dr. Townsend and promised to sign a Townsend bill.

The attack upon the President and the Democratic Party as well as the attempt to wed Townsendites to Lemke did not pass unchallenged in the convention. Delegates were warned by their temporary chairman, Democratic Congressman Martin F. Smith (Wash.), to refrain from any formal alliance with political parties. Endorsed Democratic and Republican congressional candidates who were introduced before the assembled delegates recommended continued loyalty to the established parties. After Coughlin's speech a bitter battle was waged from the floor by

Gomer Smith, vice-president of the OARP, Ltd., and a member of its Board of Directors, who contended that the Townsend Movement should concentrate upon the plan and not follow the chimera of a third party. The Reverends Coughlin and Smith, he attacked as religious bigots; Roosevelt, he assured the delegates, was a God-fearing, church-going citizen. In response, Dr. Townsend reprimanded Gomer Smith for personal disloyalty and for introducing personalities and controversy into the convention!

The rebellion was more widespread than Dr. Townsend had realized. Sheridan Downey, his personal counsel and former adviser, supported Gomer Smith's position. To Dr. Townsend's consternation, these speakers received as much applause as had he and his allies. Opposition to the third party threatened to divide the convention and the Movement into two irreconcilable camps.

The dissenters were strong enough to compel the adoption of a resolution declaring the Movement to be non-partisan and inviting all presidential candidates, with the exception of the Communist, to address the convention. Only Norman Thomas, the Socialist candidate, accepted, and he was roundly booed for his frank and critical examination of the Townsend Plan. Resolutions proposing the endorsement of presidential candidates were barred by the convention's chairman, but the records are too incomplete to determine whether his action forestalled a move to endorse Roosevelt or whether Dr. Townsend had introduced a resolution to endorse Lemke but had reconsidered.

Two resolutions precluding third-party activity were adopted with Dr. Townsend's approval. The first forbade the OARP, Ltd., through its Board of Directors or "Citizens Maximi" to endorse any presidential candidate. Since it neglected to specify the president of the OARP, Ltd., he was technically exempt from its restrictions and, therefore, promptly endorsed Lemke at the convention. The second proclaimed that the Movement should strive to elect the greatest number of congressmen pledged to the plan in view of the possibility that no candidate would receive an electoral majority.

The coalition between Coughlin, Smith and Dr. Townsend was characterized more by bickering and indecision than cooperation. Joint speaking engagements which the three had originally contemplated were summarily abandoned. Father Coughlin permitted the other two to address the convention of his National Union for Social Justice, but made little effort to disguise his distaste for them or for their programs. The Reverend Smith he dismissed contemptuously as one who pretended to a following which did not exist; the Townsend Plan, he claimed, was mathematically unsound.[15] Dr. Townsend's rejoinder was that Father Coughlin's famous sixteen-point program contained "fourteen points too many."[16] Dr. Townsend and the Reverend Smith campaigned together until the latter announced his intention to form a "nationalist" movement, at which time Dr. Townsend immediately disavowed him and the two parted company.

Lemke, who had assured his reelection to Congress as a matter of precaution, could not maintain the coalition. Nevertheless, he continued his efforts to secure Townsend votes, promising to recommend the plan in his first message to Congress, to invite Dr. Townsend to confer with him in the White House on strategy for his bill, and to sign the Townsend bill into law. During the campaign Dr. Townsend gave Lemke his fullest cooperation, editorially as well as through personal campaigning in his behalf throughout the country. But their first objective, Townsendites were informed, was Roosevelt's defeat, their second, Lemke's election.[17]

The strategy of Dr. Townsend and the Reverend Smith, from the outset, had revolved around the hope of diverting from Roosevelt sufficient votes to throw the election into the House of Representatives.[18] To accomplish this end, Dr. Townsend endorsed the Republican as well as the Union candidate for President! Alfred M. Landon, both as governor of Kansas, in 1935, and as Republican presidential candidate, in 1936, had personally informed the doctor of his opposition to the plan. Yet Landon had been willing to meet with the pension leader and had treated him courteously. Prior to the organization of the third party, Dr. Townsend had suggested that Governor Landon was not inclined to imprison those who differed with him. He subsequently designated Landon his second choice should Lemke fail to capture a popular following.

As the campaign progressed, hints appeared in the Townsend press that the doctor would prove receptive to Republican overtures. Once it became apparent that Lemke would not be placed upon the ballot in all states, Dr. Townsend assumed the initiative and endorsed Landon. On October 7, 1936, he wired Edward J. Margett, his California state manager, to support

Landon as "the lesser of the two evils," and he warned against wasting ballots on a write-in campaign for Lemke.[19] According to Margett a special poll of California Townsendites, to which 40,000 to 50,000 had responded, indicated 6 per cent favored a write-in campaign for Lemke, 28 per cent favored Roosevelt, and 62 per cent favored Landon; the rest were undecided.[20]

Subsequently, Dr. Townsend issued a formal appeal to his followers to vote for Landon in all states where Lemke was not on the ballot. It was imperative that Roosevelt be defeated if the Townsend Plan were to be enacted into law, he explained. For his part, Landon was prepared to offer concrete evidence of his disposition to cooperate. In a letter written to the California state Townsend manager on October 21, 1936, and authorized for public release the day before the election, the Republican presidential candidate promised that if elected President he would do everything within his power to see that the Townsend group received a fair and impartial hearing; he was also prepared to discuss the plan with Dr. Townsend in the White House.[21]

In a series of special dispatches to the New York *Times,* James A. Haggerty, traveling with the Landon campaign train, revealed that Republican strategists contemplated winning California through Townsend votes.[22] The Republican nominee's sudden decision to campaign in California was due principally, he disclosed, to the shift of Townsend support to Landon. The Republican move was a reasonable one in view of the above cited Townsend poll and the fact that the *Literary Digest* polls indicated a close race in California where Townsend Club members were estimated to number between 500,000 and 700,000. In his single speech in California, Landon included a condemnation of the congressional investigating committee which was anathema in Townsend circles.

In campaigning for his two candidates, Dr. Townsend concentrated primarily upon attacking the President. The Roosevelt administration, he charged, was wasting the country's money, subverting the democratic form of government, establishing a dictatorship in Washington. A "Roosevelt-Farley machine" was pictured as determined to destroy the Townsend Movement, and President Roosevelt was characterized as a "political savage" who indulged in cheap, dishonest politics.

The election of 1936 represented Franklin Delano Roosevelt's greatest electoral victory; both the Union and the Republican parties were overwhelmingly defeated. The 882,479 ballots cast for Lemke demonstrated the futility of the coalition and the inability of its leaders to deliver their "20 million" followers to the third party. Landon captured only two states, Maine and Vermont. In California, where Republicans had relied heavily upon Townsend support, Roosevelt won by more than 900,000 votes.

Within the Movement, internal unity and cohesion were undermined by Dr. Townsend's political leadership. His crusade against Roosevelt shattered completely the core of experienced leaders who had remained loyal despite the Bell investigation. Vice-president Gomer Smith was eliminated from the Movement through the doctor's efforts, and Sheridan Downey was excluded from national Townsend leadership. The dismissal by Dr. Townsend of three senior officials who had been regional directors was undoubtedly motivated by their opposition to his political policies. The Southern regional director resigned voluntarily in protest against the doctor's partisanship. At least two members of the Townsend Board of Directors repudiated the doctor's political leadership and urged their followers in Kansas and Oregon to vote for their own party's choice for President. The Townsend National Secretary conceded publicly that many club members had protested Dr. Townsend's political leadership, and that they had written indignant pleas for their National Headquarters to abstain from the politics it was pursuing.[23]

In 1940 as in 1936, Dr. Townsend sought to array the old-age pension movement against President Roosevelt's reelection. Again Republican leaders, desperate for votes, obtained Dr. Townsend's endorsement. In contrast with 1936, the doctor's efforts to lead the movement in the direction which he favored were more successful. By this time, virtually all independent intermediary leadership had been driven from the Movement. Those remaining were either partisan Republicans such as L. W. Jeffery, vice-president of TNRP, Inc., or individuals personally loyal to or dependent upon the doctor such as his son, Robert C. Townsend. Sheridan Downey, now the Townsend leader in the United States Senate, was himself opposed to a third term for the President. The 1940 Townsend convention approved with comparatively little opposition Dr. Townsend's resolution:

> Resolved, that this Organization go on record as being irrevocably opposed to a third consecutive term for any President of the United States.[24]

Having achieved considerable success in the 1938 congressional elections with the pension-Townsend issue, Republican leaders undoubtedly concluded that their party could once again profit from such an alliance. Evidence warranted the assumption that positive Republican action might attract a significant number of Townsend votes; the doctor boasted of five to six million.

On the basis of a letter written on August 6, 1940 by Oregon's Senator Charles L. McNary, the *Weekly* proclaimed that the Republican vice-presidential candidate had endorsed the Townsend Plan.

My dear Dr. Townsend:

A few days ago I had the pleasure of discussing with you various pension proposals that have been introduced into the Congress, and in my opinion Senate Bill 3255, introduced . . . by Senator Downey of California, is a sincere attempt to have the national government insure all citizens a comfortable retirement annuity when the age of sixty is reached. I believe the nation would prosper and human happiness be vastly increased if this were done. This measure should receive thoughtful and sympathetic consideration.

Very truly and cordially yours,

(signed)   CHARLES L. MC NARY[25]

It is obvious that McNary's letter did not endorse the plan as embodied in S. 3255. Nevertheless, it became the center of a campaign by Dr. Townsend and Jeffery to defeat President Roosevelt. Disappointed with the Republican presidential candidate's position on old-age pensions. Dr. Townsend insisted, nevertheless, that McNary had accorded the Townsend bill a strong commitment and that Wendell Willkie would eventually do so. Despite the pension leader's announcement in October that both Willkie and McNary had informed him that they would not oppose his plan, an endorsement from Willkie did not materialize. And with the Democratic victory of 1940, President Roosevelt ceased to be a center around which Townsend national politics revolved.

II AN AMBIVALENT APPROACH TO POLITICAL PARTIES

The ambivalence with which Dr. Townsend viewed the political parties also affected the Movement's approach to politics. On the one hand he recognized that the plan's prospects would be enhanced if it were identified with the self-interest of the major parties. And yet, at the same time, he rejected the two-party system in an idolation of the third-party technique.

Cognizant of the power and prestige of the major parties, the Townsend leadership regularly proposed to the two national conventions that they incorporate the plan within their platforms. Neither party ever adopted this proposal. Nevertheless, the Townsend representatives who appeared at the major party conventions in 1936 reported that the Republican platform committee had devoted one-half hour to a discussion of the plan.[26] Dr. Townsend, who attended both major party conventions in 1936, scored a minor success at the Democratic conclave when the Washington state delegation voted in caucus to demand a Townsend Plank.[27] Ironically the pension leader had already publicized his intention to align himself with a new third party.

In 1940, Dr. Townsend announced that the Movement was prepared to cooperate with either party's presidential candidate in return for inclusion of the plan within the party's program. The *Weekly* claimed that, at the Republican Convention, Senator Henry Cabot Lodge, Jr., of Massachusetts had sought the adoption of a plank embodying the plan's principles, but that he was defeated in committee.[28] Sending a special delegation to the 1943 Republican policy conference at Mackinac Island, the doctor announced that one-half million dollars of national newspaper and radio advertising was available to the political party which endorsed the plan in 1944.[29] Three to five million Townsend votes were also assured the party which accepted. In spite of this tempting (sic) offer, coupled with a warning that the vote of the aged would prove decisive with the younger men away at war, neither party was receptive. After 1940 not even the Republican presidential candidates endeavored to solicit Townsend support, the Townsend Movement having suffered a precipitous decline in membership and strength.

At the same time that Dr. Townsend sought to persuade the major parties to embrace the plan, he attacked them as being undemocratic, un-American, gang-ridden and as being controlled by sinister (financial) forces. This hostility stemmed possibly from a heritage of Midwestern populism and his early membership in the Socialist Party which equated the Democratic and Republican parties with plutocracy and Wall Street. The refusal of either major party to endorse his plan was, of course, the primary factor.

The political history of the Townsend Movement is replete with attempts by its leader to involve it in a third party despite the protests of his co-workers. A May, 1935, *Weekly* editorial entitled, "No Third Party," obviously inspired by Co-Founder Clements, stressed the problems involved in organizing one and disclosed that the clubs were opposed to such a venture.[30] Nevertheless, Dr. Townsend wrote in September to Clements that the time had arrived to organize their own Townsend Party, not to expect the major parties to adopt the plan:

> I tell you, old fellow, the way for us to lick the stuffing out of the old parties is to become militant and go after them hammer and tongs for being totally incompetent, as we know they are. If either of the old parties adopted our program it would be for strategic purposes only and their promises would be forgotten the next day after the election. The cry everywhere I go is, "Why don't we have our own party?" Now, that is just the thing I believe we should begin to do, talk about the Townsend Party, not wait in the foolish hope that one of the old groups will adopt us. If they ever do they will treat us like poor adopted trash. To hell with them. If we begin to announce ourselves soon and work like the dickens for the next year we shall be able to lick the stuffing out of both of them.[31]

Apparently the anti-third party logic prevailed for the First National Convention of Townsend Clubs voted in 1935 against involvement with any party.

At least three times in 1935, *after* the convention's decision, Dr. Townsend announced on his own initiative plans to place a Townsend Party in the 1936 presidential campaign. Retractions followed immediately upon the demands of his partner, Clements, his legislative leader, Congressman John S. McGroarty, and the vice-president of the OARP, Ltd., Gomer Smith.[32] So determined was the doctor to activate a Townsend Party that before the year was out he had spent thousands of dollars of his own money and that of the OARP, Ltd., in a futile attempt to establish such a party in California. A joint statement by Gomer Smith, Robert E. Clements and Dr. Townsend in December, 1935, indicated that it had been necessary to placate the doctor by taking some action to initiate a national third party.[33] Townsend clubs were informed that third-party petitions would be filed in numerous states, but the leaders promised not to exercise the third-party privilege should either major party change its attitude.

A principal factor in the break between Dr. Townsend and

his associates in 1936 was his insistence upon complete freedom
to invoke at will the third-party tactic. And in the end, although
he rejected an invitation from the liberal American Commonwealth Federation to cooperate in creating a "progressive" third
party, he campaigned for the Union Party's candidate in 1936.
While in the midst of his campaign for Lemke, the pension
leader informed his followers that it was a ". . . lamentable
thing that we did not organize *our own party* for the November
elections."[34]

So deeply ingrained was the third-party concept in the doctor's political thinking, that after the 1940 presidential election
a formal call for a new party was issued through the *Weekly*.[35]
His followers were urged to suggest a name, his own tentative
choice being the "Power Age Pension Party." Although headquarters reported receipt of thousands of letters, three to one
in favor of the new party, no further action was taken. In 1943
he was prepared to create a "Freedom From Poverty Party."[36]

The Progressive Party of 1948 appeared for a time to be the
instrument through which the Townsend Movement might fulfill this third-party role so desired by the doctor. Its leaders were
prepared to adopt a very generous social security position and
they desperately needed mass organizational support. Here was
Dr. Townsend's long-sought-after opportunity, a national third
party to combat the major parties and one soliciting his aid.

From the outset, Dr. Townsend's activities in behalf of Henry
A. Wallace and the Progressive Party caused serious disunity
within the Movement. He participated in a national meeting
of the Wallace-for-President Committee and donated $100 to the
cause. The reaction within the Townsend clubs was instantaneous
and hostile and the doctor found it necessary to defend himself in the *Weekly* against charges that he had "sold out" the
Movement to Wallace.[37] Because of this criticism, he claimed,
the TNRP, Inc., had suffered a serious loss of revenue which
was crippling its operations; some clubs had ceased contributing
funds altogether. His own $100 contribution to the Wallace
party, he pleaded, did not constitute an endorsement, but was
intended as a challenge to the Democrats and Republicans who
would receive identical amounts for similar promises. Since both
parties had always rejected the plan, he felt there was no hope
of realizing its enactment through their ranks. He had submitted
the plan to supporters of the third party, he declared, and he
was gratified with their resolution urging a vote on the plan

as well as minimum retirement annuities of $100 a month to all citizens over sixty years of age.

The Wallace managers were not prepared to forfeit the co-operation of the aged in the Townsend Movement as a result of the pension leader's equivocation. They released the follow-ing statement which they claimed was written by Dr. Townsend while at the Chicago meeting of the National Wallace-for-President Committee on April 11, 1948:

Since Henry A. Wallace has had the initiative and courage to pro-pose a new political alignment . . . free from the domination of the great financial interests . . . I believe it to be the course of wisdom . . . to support with all our political strength the new party of which he is the leader.[38]

At the 1948 national convention of Townsend clubs, the pen-sion leader adopted an aggressive stand in favor of the Progres-sive Party, although he did not press openly for an official en-dorsement.[39] He announced his faith in the new party and affirmed his intention to help its presidential ticket. If Wallace were a Russian Communist as opponents charged, Dr. Townsend defiantly informed the delegates, then he, too, was a Communist, for he believed in public ownership of the mines, railroads and the banking system!

The Townsend Plan, in addition to a proposal for minimum pensions of $100 a month, was submitted to the Democratic, Republican and Progressive conventions. The platform commit-tee of the Progressive Party, before which the pension leader and his son appeared, refused to grant the concrete commitment for the plan which they demanded.[40] According to Robert C. Townsend, neither Wallace nor Glen Taylor, who were friendly to the doctor, were present, and the Communist element con-trolling the committee did not even treat them civilly; the two pension leaders left, determined not to support the new party.[41]

Anxious to retain whatever Townsend support was possible, the Progressive Party leaders wrote the following compromise into their platform:

We recognize the service which the Townsend Plan has performed in bringing to national attention the tragic plight of the senior citizens of America, and we condemn the bipartisan conspiracy in Congress over the past ten years against providing adequate old-age pensions.

We pledge our active support for a national old-age pension of $100 a month to all persons at 60 years of age, based on right and not on a pauperizing need basis.[42]

In 1936 and 1940, Dr. Townsend had endorsed Republican presidential candidates who had not promised a fraction as much. Nevertheless, the Townsend Movement remained neutral throughout the remainder of the 1948 campaign. The Progressive Party was much too radical for the aged members of the Townsend Movement to accept. The pension promoter must have realized this for Wallace was given no further support by Dr. Townsend. As for the other presidential candidates in 1948, only the Vegetarian Party's nominee, Dr. John Maxwell, a trustee of the Townsend Foundation, advocated the plan in his campaign! Dr. Townsend's commitment to the third-party technique was irrepressible, however, and, in 1949, the Ninth National Convention of Townsend Clubs was prevailed upon to vote for the establishment of a national third party.

III   THE TOWNSEND PARTY OF CALIFORNIA

From 1938 to 1942, a Townsend Party, officially sponsored by the Townsend Movement and operated under its name, competed in the state of California. A sufficient number of voters (32,970) registered as members of the new party in 1938 to qualify it under state law, and an organizational apparatus was established including a newspaper, *The New Era News*. The restricted nature of the party's appeal and the narrowness of its political base were evident from its initial platform: four points on the Townsend Plan plus recommendations for protecting American goods from foreign competition, reducing governmental bureaucracy, and including the public as a party to all labor disputes.[43] Its platform contained little relating to state politics or which could be enacted through the state government.

If it were seriously intended to be a party committed to seeking office and establishing firm loyalties, the strategy adopted by its managers with regard to candidates was a self-defeating one. The party's candidates in its first election included a Republican for governor, a Democrat for United States senator, and Republicans, Democrats and a few registered Townsend Party members for the United States House of Representatives. With major party candidates cross-filing on the Townsend Party ticket and the pension leaders anxious to procure the nomination for favored candidates in their party's primary, Townsendites were discouraged from developing an allegiance and voting loyalty to their own party.

The Townsend Party secured its highest registration and greatest number of votes in 1938.[44] However the 117,083 votes polled by its nominee for lieutenant-governor were insignificant in comparison with those of the Democratic-Progressive candidate who received 1,296,395 and the Republican for whom 1,159,967 votes were cast. For attorney-general, the Townsend candidate received 231,914 votes as against 1,542,847 cast for the Republican-Democratic-Progressive candidate, Earl Warren. Although a Townsend candidate was the only alternative to Warren listed on the ballot, the Townsend nominee was surpassed by a write-in who polled twice as many votes as he. Townsendite Sheridan Downey was elected United States senator on the Democratic-Progressive-Townsend tickets in 1938, but he was also the avowed candidate of the powerful "Ham and Eggs" pension group. On the other hand, support from Townsend clubs failed to save Republican Governor Frank F. Merriam from defeat by his Democratic opponent.[45]

A number of Townsend Party nominees in 1938–42 were elected, but solely because they were registered Democrats or Republicans who had also captured the major party primaries. With one exception, and he lost, candidates for Congress running under the Townsend designation alone or in combination with another minor party received very few votes. In two contests where candidates ran as nominees of both a major party and the Townsend Party, their opponents were elected; the Townsend label was no great asset. And in 1942, Townsend candidates seeking the two assembly and one state senate seat from Orange County were overwhelmingly defeated by their major party opponents.

According to the California Townsend organizer in 1950, the Townsend Party had been established primarily to place Townsend candidates in congressional elections and to influence congressmen to sign the discharge petition in the House of Representatives.[46] However, Townsend Party candidates participated in congressional elections against friends as well as enemies! Incumbent Congressman H. Jerry Voorhis (D), Thomas F. Ford (R–D) and Charles Kramer (D–Prog.), who had served on Townsend steering committees or had signed discharge petitions, were opposed in 1938 by candidates whom the leaders sponsored in their Townsend Party primary. Opponents of the first two congressmen gave them only minor competition, but Kramer's Republican-Townsend Party opponent polled 44,808 votes. Con-

TABLE XVI

TOWNSEND PARTY CANDIDATES COMPETE IN CONGRESSIONAL ELECTIONS,
CALIFORNIA, 1938–42

1938			1942		
Congressional District	Party	Total Votes	Congressional District	Party	Total Votes
1	Democratic-Republican	73,636	13	Republican	38,577
				Democratic	33,060
	Townsend	43,320		Townsend	6,306
11	Republican	68,712	15	Republican-	
	Democratic	59,993		Democratic	88,798
	Townsend	12,713		Townsend-	
12	Democratic	75,003		Prohibition	10,185
	Republican	40,457	20	Republican	62,628
	Townsend	7,903		Democratic	55,479
13	Democratic-Progressive	96,258		Prohibition	6,864
	Republican-Townsend	44,808		Townsend	3,537
16	Republican-Democratic	97,407			
	Townsend	16,045			
	Progressive	6,643			
17	Democratic	56,513			
	Republican	26,891			
	Townsend	8,870			
	Progressive	3,774			
19	Democratic	75,819			
	Republican-Townsend	66,402			

gressman Kramer retaliated by voting against the Townsend bill in 1939.

The Townsend Party in California was inaugurated as the first in a series of new state parties throughout the country. None of the others was ever organized, however. In California, the stronghold of the Movement, no candidate campaigning on the Townsend Party ticket alone ever captured state or national office. Registration declined sharply to 14,318 in 1940, and 8,689 in 1942. And failure in 1942 to obtain the minimum votes for remaining a legal party eliminated the Townsend Party thereafter from the ballot.

Perhaps the most noteworthy aspect of the Townsend Party stratagem was the action taken after 1942 to prevent its reestablishment. "It seemed obvious," wrote the *Weekly*'s editor, "that a party bearing Dr. Townsend's name might easily be subverted from its original purpose and through political manipulations—might even come to stand for something totally opposed to the aims and purposes of Townsendites."[47]

Aside from a general lack of interest among the aged and the party's ineffectiveness, herein lay the crux of the matter. The pressure organization feared to compete any more as a state party, apprehensive that its own instrument might, in a public primary, be subverted from its purpose, leadership and control. All activities on behalf of the party were discontinued and efforts to resurrect it were strongly discouraged.[48]

IV CLASSICAL MANEUVERING BETWEEN STATE PARTIES

The conciliatory statements issued by the Republican presidential candidate in 1936 and the vice-presidential nominee in 1940 revealed a degree of flexibility within the party system. Although they never accepted the plan or any of its features, their cautious feelers indicated that their party was prepared to bargain under the assumption that the Townsendites controlled votes vital to a Republican victory. Townsend experience in maneuvering between the Republican and Democratic parties in California and Massachusetts substantiates the general proposition that in the field of party politics the pressure group is most successful when it is considered to occupy a balance of power between the major parties.

In 1934, widespread Townsend support was given California's Republican Governor Frank F. Merriam whose reelection was seriously threatened by the Democratic nominee, Upton Sinclair. Although the Republicans had for many years been the dominant party in the state a swiftly rising Democratic tide portended defeat for them in 1934. In 1932 Roosevelt had captured traditionally Republican California, and Upton Sinclair, the Democratic gubernatorial candidate in 1934, threatened to repeat this feat. A dynamic individual with an imaginative program to End Poverty In California, Sinclair controlled an extensive network of EPIC clubs throughout the state. Democratic registration in 1934 for the first time exceeded the Republican registration, and the August primaries were even more ominous har-

bingers of a possible Democratic victory. Sinclair secured the
Democratic nomination with 435,220 votes in his party's primary
as against the 346,320 votes cast for Governor Merriam in the
Republican primary.[49] A comparison of the total votes cast in
both parties' primaries revealed a thin Democratic margin of
26,051 votes.

Whereas the first Townsend Club had been organized as late
as August 17, 1934, by October 1, 108 clubs had been chartered
in California, and by the middle of that month 200 clubs were
reported holding meetings throughout the state. Hundreds of
thousands of Californians were reported to have signed petitions
urging Congress to enact the plan. With Townsend membership
booming and clubs expanding, the allegiance and votes of this
new group were solicited by the Republican Party for its candidates. "The proposed Townsend plan is recommended for careful study by the Federal Government," was the skillfully drawn
plank in the 1934 platform of the California Republican Party.[50]

Campaigning in San Francisco in October, 1934, Republican
Governor Merriam urged a national program of pensions for
the aged, pointing out that 300,000 Southern Californians had
petitioned Congress on behalf of the Townsend Plan which had
been recommended to the federal government in his party's
platform.[51] And in a major radio address, a few days before the
election, he took care to reiterate that he had recommended the
plan to the attention of the national government. Merriam's
forces advertised lavishly in the official organ of the Townsend
Movement, one full-page advertisement ending as follows:

> Sinclair IS NOT for the Townsend Plan.
> Merriam IS FOR the Townsend Plan.
> GOVERNOR MERRIAM IS FOR THE TOWNSEND OLD-AGE
> PENSIONS PLAN.[52]

Although Sinclair publicly opposed the plan, his lieutenants
also felt it advisable to insert in the Townsend magazine an advertisement to the effect that the Democratic nominee favored
adequate old-age pensions on a national scale. An effort was apparently made, moreover, by Sheridan Downey, Sinclair's running mate and subsequently an important Townsend leader, to
reconcile the views of Dr. Townsend and Sinclair by bringing
the two together.[53] From the outset, however, Dr. Townsend had
been antagonistic to Sinclair, whom he labeled in private cor-
respondence in July as "our very greatest menace,"[54] and whose

EPIC plan he ridiculed as unworkable. The doctor's personal preference was to work through the Republican Party.

Many elements undoubtedly entered into Merriam's election, his winning margin exceeding 259,000, but Dr. Townsend claimed primary credit for the victory. Upton Sinclair certainly considered Townsend votes a material factor in his defeat as is evident from his account of the campaign:

> Impossible to imagine a greater instance of hypocrisy than Frank Merriam's coming out for the Townsend Plan. Of course, it cost him nothing; for it is avowedly a Federal plan, and he could grin and leave it to the poor victims to appeal to Roosevelt and to Congress. And meanwhile he would have the votes!
>
> I, too, needed those votes. How easy for me, when the proposal first came before the public, to say yea, of course I favored it; pay the old people pensions. . . . How they would have flocked around me—the million people who have signed Townsend petitions all over the State of California!
>
> Acting Governor Merriam got the extra votes which he needed, and now is Governor Elect. . . .[55]

Governor Merriam also must have deemed the Townsend votes crucial to his election. He persuaded a predominantly Republican state legislature in 1935 to adopt two petitions, one urging Congress to study the plan, and the second which actually memorialized Congress to incorporate the principles and objectives of the Townsend Plan into national law.[56] H. R. 3977, the most radical legislative version of the plan, was deliberately included in the second resolution in order, as the governor stated, to "avoid any misunderstanding as to the intention of the authors of the resolution and of the Legislature."[57] While the second resolution won easy acceptance in the lower house of the state legislature, the governor had to exert his executive and party leadership together with maximum Townsend pressure in order to induce a very reluctant Senate to endorse the Townsend Plan.

In 1936, a presidential year, the California Republican platform again recommended a careful study and fair hearing for the Townsend Plan. That year the Republican-controlled Assembly also memorialized Congress on behalf of the Townsend Movement which was under attack by a House investigating committee. And when Merriam sought reelection in 1938, he secured an outright endorsement from Dr. Townsend.

The close association in 1938 between the conservative Repub-

lican Party of Massachusetts and the Townsendites further ex-
emplifies this pattern of politics.[58] Townsend state leaders in
Massachusetts wrote a special plank for the Republican state
platform in return for which club members were encouraged to
vote for the Republican gubernatorial candidate.

Determined to regain power in the state government from
which they had been isolated since 1931, the Republicans had
undertaken a survey of the 1936 election in which they had lost
the key gubernatorial seat by a mere 28,000 votes. It disclosed
that the Union Party candidate, William H. McMasters, who
had received 68,467 votes, may have been responsible for the
loss of critically important Republican votes. By 1938 McMasters
had become a prominent Townsend leader. He conducted a
radio program which provided him with a state-wide propaganda
medium and his mail reflected a large response from small, predominantly Republican communities.

With Dr. Townsend's expressed permission, McMasters filed
in the Republican primary for governor.[59] He also filed on an
independent ticket, the Townsend Recovery Plan. Although
Leverett Saltonstall captured the Republican primary with 323,-
000 votes, the party's leadership was disturbed by McMasters'
strength in their primary; he had run second with 48,133 votes.
Since McMasters was also an independent Townsend candidate
in the final election, Republicans were confronted with a serious
possibility that the very candidate who had diverted crucial votes
from them in 1936 might attract enough votes in 1938 to defeat
their candidate again.

An agreement was arranged, therefore, whereby Republicans
would incorporate into their platform a Townsend plank in
return for which McMasters would support their candidates for
state office. According to McMasters, he drafted the following
resolution which the Republican state convention adopted
unanimously:

> Realizing that there are millions of thinking citizens throughout the
> Nation who have studied into and believe in the principles of the
> Townsend . . . plan as embodied in the bill . . . H. R. 4199 . . . *we
> pledge the entire Republican delegation in the Congress to a full dis-
> cussion at the earliest possible moment.*[60]

A subsequent paragraph in the platform disclaimed any commitment to the plan itself, but stated that it deserved consideration. McMasters admitted receiving approximately $2,000

from the Republicans for radio time used by him to endorse both Leverett Saltonstall and the Townsend Plan. Although it was impossible to remove McMasters' name from the final ballot, he succeeded in restricting his vote to a few thousand; the Republican candidate was safely elected. And in 1939, the Massachusetts General Court, under Republican direction, memorialized Congress to consider the Townsend Plan.[61]

State Politics: From a National Townsend Plan to State Townsend Plans

Initially all Townsend political activity centered on the plan as defined in national terms. Commencing in 1942–43 a reorientation in strategy occurred. While the national plan remained the goal to which efforts were directed in Congress, increasing emphasis was devoted toward enacting state Townsend plans and toward liberalizing the social security system through piecemeal reform within the states. This transition from a preoccupation with the national plan to the immediate ameliorization of the aged on the state level involved a basic shift in pressure technique.

I   STATE POLITICS AND THE NATIONAL TOWNSEND PLAN

In concentrating upon a single objective, the enactment of their national plan, the Townsend leaders subordinated all state politics to that purpose. The Republican parties of California and Massachusetts successfully made their deals with the state and national Townsend leaders by adopting platforms which urged Congress to study and consider the plan. The 1936 platform of the Republican Party in New Mexico which actually endorsed "the old-age revolving pension principles" did so within the context of national legislative action.[62] Candidates on all levels of state politics were judged by their attitude toward influencing Congress to adopt this course of action. An Oregon state legislator was in fact forced into a recall election and defeated by the Lane County Townsendites who claimed that he had violated his promise to vote for a state memorial to Congress on the subject of the plan.[63]

Townsend pressure on the state level was applied principally toward securing resolutions from legislatures which memorialized Congress to study, consider and enact the plan. Twenty-two state legislatures, in most cases both houses, petitioned Congress in behalf of the Townsend Plan and the Townsend Movement; at least seventeen repeated their memorials. Undoubtedly such petitions represented effective employment of the pressure technique. If state legislatures and local politicians in immediate contact with pension sentiment responded readily, then congressmen from such states were under obvious pressure to consider the political significance of this action.

TABLE XVII

STATE LEGISLATIVE MEMORIALS TO CONGRESS ON
BEHALF OF THE TOWNSEND PLAN, 1934–1952*

States	1934	1935	1936	1937	1938	1939	1940	1941	1943	1944	1945	1947
Far West												
Ariz.	1						1	1				
Calif.		2	1							1		
Colo.		1				1						
Idaho		1				1						
Mont.		1		1		1		1				
Nev.		1										
Ore.		1		1	1	1						
Wash.				1								
Wyo.						2						1
Midwest												
Ill.						1		1				
Ind.						1			1			
Mich.					1	1						
Minn.			1	1					1			
N. D.	1			1		1		1	1			
S. D.						1		1	1			
Wisc.						1		1	1			
Northeast												
Mass.					1	1		1				
N. H.						1		1				
South												
Ark.									1			
Fla.						1		1			1	
Ga.						1						
Okla.				1								

* See (Townsend) *Weekly,* 1935–52; *Congressional Record,* 76th Cong., 1st Sess. March 21, 1939, 3073–74.

The significance of the adoption of such petitions by state legislatures should however not be overemphasized. Of course, their actions reflected the assessment by state politicians of Townsend strength. At the same time, through this simple device of memorializing Congress, local politicos could easily placate the pressure group by shifting to the national government responsibility for enacting the plan. Once Townsendites sought to capitalize upon such state legislative action to secure the adoption of pension reforms on a state rather than the national level, the response from the legislators and the major parties was not as sympathetic.

II   THE ELECTORATE VOTES ON STATE TOWNSEND PLANS

Thwarted nationally, Townsend leaders redirected their efforts toward obtaining substantive reforms upon the state level—the enactment of state Townsend plans and the liberalization of old-age assistance programs. Although Townsendites entered the state sphere of politics rather belatedly, they discovered therein two advantages which had escaped them on the national level of pressure politics and in the field of party politics. The "initiative" enabled the pressure group to appeal directly to the electorate for a vote on the Townsend Plan and thus to circumvent both the state legislature and the political parties. In addition, the pension advocates discovered common ground upon which to cooperate with other interest groups.

Official attention was not directed toward enacting state Townsend plans until 1943. Prior to that time attempts to adopt the plan on the state level had been bitterly opposed by the national leadership as undermining the cause of the plan in Congress. It was contended, also, that only on a national scale could the plan operate effectively, and that local plans would paralyze business in the states which adopted them. Dr. Townsend campaigned personally in 1938 to defeat an Oregon initiative, placed upon the ballot by state Townsend leaders, which provided for a 2 per cent transaction tax, proceeds to be pro rated among qualified citizens sixty-five years and older on the basis of right. Townsend National Headquarters urged its Oregon members to vote against this initiative. In 1939, after the Welfare Committee of the Florida Senate had approved a $30-a-month Townsend bill, including a 3 per cent transaction tax and the compulsory spending feature, Dr. Townsend actively contributed to its defeat.[64] And National Headquarters boasted that its opposition

was principally responsible for defeating a North Dakota initiative which proposed granting $40-a-month pensions on the
basis of a gross income tax.[65]

In 1943 the Townsend leadership reversed itself completely
and campaigned for the adoption of state plans. Behind this
move lay a complex of organizational and political factors. Local
pension organizations, competing with the Townsend National
Recovery Plan, Inc., for allegiance and financial support from
the aged, promised immediate results on the state level. A very
liberal old-age pension plan had earlier been written into the
Colorado state constitution by a state pension organization
among whose prominent leaders were former Townsendites. And
the "Ham and Eggs," "$30-Every-Thursday" scheme had polled
over 900,000 votes in California. The TNRP, Inc., on the other
hand, had suffered a sharp decline in strength, its membership
having shrunk from 646,864 in 1940 to 297,610 in 1942, its income from $349,253 to $247,620.

Not only had other pension movements carved out a profitable role in state politics, but the Townsend record itself pre-
saged success in this field. An officially sponsored initiative favoring a national Townsend constitutional amendment had been
approved in 1938 by Oregon voters, 183,781 to 149,711.[66] An
initiative law sponsored by the Idaho clubs, in 1942, which
increased old-age assistance payments and provided free medical-
hospital care was approved by a tremendous majority, 75,090 to
35,344.[67]

In 1943, the Idaho legislature repealed this initiative law. The
Townsendites carried the issue to the state supreme court, but
the right of the legislature to repeal an initiative statute voted
by the people was approved. This latter action was one of the
principal reasons for the decision in 1943–44 to seek initiative
constitutional amendments.

Townsend clubs in Arizona, California, Oregon and Washington secured sufficient signatures from their electorates in
1944 to place on the ballot initiatives incorporating the fundamentals of the plan.[68] Except for the Washington measure which
was of a statutory nature, the initiatives sought to amend the
state constitutions to provide minimum monthly annuities of
$60 to all citizens sixty years of age and over as well as to the
blind and totally disabled. Although $60 a month was not an
extravagant sum, it was considerably higher than the average
old-age assistance payments in these states as well as the average

family benefit payments under the Old Age Survivors Insurance program in the United States. The compulsory spending provision of the Townsend Plan was to be suspended until six months after hostilities had ceased. Pensions were to be granted as a matter of right and pensioners required to abstain from gainful employment. A 3 per cent gross income tax was the sole financing device.

The California measure repealed the state sales tax and authorized a legislative appropriation of 20 per cent of the revenues from the income tax for the support of the public schools which had been dependent upon the former tax. The Oregon initiative prohibited any future enactment of a general retail sales tax. All four legislatures were empowered by the initiatives to lower the age and residence requirements for old-age assistance and to extend the benefits of the initiatives to widows with minor children and to partially disabled citizens.

Dr. Townsend and Sherman Bainbridge, editor of the *Weekly* and a former "Ham and Eggs" leader, personally directed the campaign in the Far West. In addition, national officers and organizers from other states were assigned to this region to assist them. A network of thirty-five radio stations was utilized in the four states to carry the Townsend message. Club members employed sound trucks, distributed hundreds of thousands of leaflets, and solicited house-to-house for votes. From July, 1943, to November, 1944, the campaign cost the Townsend forces more than $139,000.[69]

A significant feature of the campaign was the cooperation received for the first time in Townsend election politics from labor and other groups. Organized labor was confronted in a number of states with highly restrictive "Right to Work" initiatives sponsored by business and farmer organizations. Under the stimulus of self-interest, Townsendites and labor unions joined in an informal alliance. The president of the Arizona A. F. of L. campaigned with Dr. Townsend throughout the four states on a joint speaking tour, and the convention of the Arizona A. F. of L. endorsed the Townsend initiative. Unions from the C. I. O. and the Railway Brotherhoods cooperated as well. In California and in the other states, similar support was given although on a smaller scale. Some railway unions and county labor councils also contributed financially to the Townsend campaign. In turn, the Townsend leadership publicly condemned the anti-union proposals, and Townsend clubs supported labor's campaign, even to mailing union literature with their own.

Seeking to ally itself with other interest groups, the California Townsend Council endorsed a Veterans of Foreign Wars' proposal for rehabilitation loans and the state Grange's position on limiting Central Valley farms to 160 acres. The Washington Townsend Council endeavored to elicit Farmers Union support, while special attention in Arizona and California was directed toward securing the Negro vote.

The opposition to the Townsend initiatives was organized primarily by business and conservative groups who, ironically, were joined by the Communist press. Especially active in the drive to prevent the adoption of the state Townsend plans were the Chamber of Commerce and the Associated Farmers of California, the Washington Taxpayers' Association and a special "Committee Against the Unlimited Gross Income Tax" supported heavily by business, mining and farming interests of Arizona. They claimed that adoption of the Townsend initiatives would adversely affect school funds, curtail jobs, restrict business and bankrupt the state governments. The Townsendites in-

TABLE XVIII

POPULAR VOTE, TOWNSEND AND RELATED INITIATIVES, 1944*

State	Initiative	Yes	No
California	No. 11 (Townsend Plan)	1,017,924	2,089,102
California	No. 12 (Right to Work)	1,304,418	1,893,589
Washington	No. 158	184,405	437,502
Oregon	No. 316	180,691	219,981
Arizona	No. 100	22,698	77,693

* State of Arizona, Secretary of State, *Official Canvass of General Election Returns, November 7, 1944* (single sheet, unnumbered, November 27, 1944); State of Washington, Secretary of State, *Abstract of Votes . . . General Election, November 7, 1944* (Olympia, n.d.), p. 45; State of California, Secretary of State, *Statement of Vote, General Election, November 7, 1944* (Sacramento, 1944), p. 29; State of Oregon, Secretary of State, *Abstract of Votes . . . November, 1944 . . .* (looseleaf, unnumbered, 1944).

dignantly charged that department-store employees were compelled to distribute anti-Townsend leaflets to their customers, that banks sent such propaganda to their depositors and that the movie industry had produced special ten-minute trailers which urged citizens to vote against the pension initiatives.

Although the Townsend initiatives attracted a respectable vote, they were decisively defeated. Only in Oregon was the margin of defeat less than two to one. Pension leaders blamed their defeat upon the determined opposition of the press and the open hostility of the business community. Also, the labor movement had disappointed them. Instead of the "yes" votes on California Proposition No. 11 (the plan) approximating the "no" votes for No. 12 (the right to work proposal), the former fell short by 875,665 votes. Yet in the excitement of the 1943–44 state campaigns as well as the then current discharge petition drive in Congress, the income of the Townsend National Recovery Plan, Inc., rose for the first time since 1940 to $255,681 in 1943 and $373,695 in 1944; membership declines were restricted to 25,827 in 1943 and 2,150 in 1944.

A Townsend Plan initiative was again placed on the ballot in Oregon in 1946. Although similar to the previous initiative, it proposed a maximum pension of $100 rather than a minimum of $60, the compulsory spending provision was made mandatory, and the tax exemptions of $100 a month were permitted all individuals and businesses. Initiative No. 314, or the "Oregon Pension Plan and Business Builders' Act," was rejected 244,960 to 86,374, an even greater defeat than that of 1944.[70] Its interests not threatened in the election, labor furnished only minor assistance to the Townsendites, while business and industrial interests campaigned as aggressively against the initiative as they had in 1944.

The California clubs proposed in 1948 a new initiative providing for minimum monthly pensions of $60 at age sixty and incorporating provisions aimed at eliciting support from the blind, the disabled, labor unions, school teachers and farmers! It sought also to facilitate recourse to the initiative process by reducing the required number of signatures for initiative petitions. Having obtained 347,000 signatures on their petitions, Townsendites were dismayed to discover that some solicitors had falsely obtained signatures thus disqualifying their initiative. So strong was the pension sentiment in California at the time, however, that voters adopted an initiative sponsored by a rival state pension group which increased payments to the aged and the blind, lowered the eligibility age and liberalized old-age assistance requirements.

In 1948, an Oregon Townsend initiative amendment providing for minimum pensions of $50 a month, eliminating the state lien law and granting free medical care was approved by the voters, 313,212 to 172,531.[71] Washington clubs cooperated with the Washington Pension Union and the Aid to Dependent Children Union in securing the enactment of an initiative increasing aid to the aged, the blind and dependent children, abolishing lien and relative responsibility laws for the aged and providing additional medical benefits.[72] Arizona Townsendites worked closely with labor and minority liberal groups through the Arizona Legislative League, but were defeated in their efforts in 1950 to enact an initiative which authorized $75-a-month pensions to aged persons sixty years and older, prohibited the means tests and permitted a work allowance for retired pensioners.[73] Townsend leaders opposed California and Massachusetts initiatives sponsored by rival groups that year which proposed increasing old-age benefits through the legalization of gambling.

The initiative proved to be an excellent strategic tool through which Townsend and other pension groups were able to compel public consideration of the pension issue by a number of state electorates. In their concern for immediate social legislation, the Townsend clubs were able to develop cooperative alliances with labor, farmer, veteran and other interest groups on the state level which they had never achieved in the national political arena. Although no state Townsend Plan was ever adopted by any electorate, Townsend agitation for a lower pension age, increased benefits and the removal of relative responsibility clauses and lien laws undoubtedly helped contribute to the steady improvement of old-age assistance programs in a number of states.

CHAPTER IX

THE TOWNSEND MOVEMENT AND PENSION POLITICS: AN EVALUATION

Any evaluation of the Townsend Movement must explore, at the minimum, three questions, answers to which may also provide insights into the American political process. What accounted for the failure of the Townsend Movement? Not only did it fail to realize its avowed goal, but it ceased to function as a principal instrument for organizing and articulating the aspirations of the increasing millions of Americans entering into "old age." What significant alterations in public policy, public attitudes and political institutions have emerged as a result of the impact of the Townsend Movement upon our society? And finally, what are the prospects for continued or renewed pension politics on the part of the aged as a separate political force?

Why the Townsend Movement Failed

A comparison of the Townsend Movement with the more successful prohibitionist movement embodied in the Anti-Saloon League[1] may fruitfully initiate a consideration of these questions. During the 1930's the Townsend Movement was, indeed, often portrayed as another Anti-Saloon League. To impress politicians as well as the general public with the potentials inherent in the pension movement, alarmed commentators warned that experienced Anti-Saloon League leaders were engaged in its behalf. Of more significance for the purpose of this evaluation, both constituted popular mass movements employing direct political action to secure the adoption of their panaceas. While the abolition of the saloon and the consumption of liquor were primarily moral reforms and the establishment of revolving pensions was an economic one, both proposals were characterized by moral as well as economic features.

The effect of ameliorative governmental reform upon the political behavior of the two movements was intimately linked to the nature of their proposals. Legislation which the League secured in no way inhibited the activities of the prohibitionists, but in fact served to spur the League to greater efforts. On the other hand, the pension legislation adopted by the national government severely circumscribed the area of success for the Townsend Movement.

Although the Anti-Saloon League rejected any compromise with its ultimate goal, it espoused a variety of proposals at different political levels: local option, state prohibition, and national restrictions upon the interstate shipment of liquor. Whatever reform was enacted did not appease the prohibitionists, but represented positive steps toward the attainment of their ultimate goal. Piecemeal success indicated that additional governmental action was both possible and necessary. For the primary drive of the church elements and their allies lay in denying, once and for all, any opportunity for God's children to be tempted by the evils of liquor.

As long as saloons existed and the sale and indulgence in liquor were possible, prohibitionists were inspired rather than placated by partial reform. The League sought no direct benefits for its own members, but rather it endeavored to deny certain privileges to others. Its members could not be pacified, therefore, nor its ultimate solution undermined by compromise legislation incorporating portions of its program. National prohibition, alone, could fulfill the League's ambition.

With the enactment of the Social Security Act, the basic validity of the Townsend Plan was undermined and a wedge driven between the Movement and the great mass of its potential supporters, the aged and those already approaching this stage in life. As promulgated by its proponents, the Townsend Plan constituted an absolute solution, the sole remedy for America's ills. Without the enactment and operation of all its features—compulsory spending, a special tax, bountiful pensions and retirement at sixty—the plan could not operate, recovery was impossible, and the aged were precluded from securing any meaningful protection. Compromise or gradual reform was impossible since the definition of the goal and the means necessary for its achievement were in essence identical. Such a commitment restricted the possible area for political maneuver and proved fatal for the Townsend Movement once remedial legislation began ministering to the wants of the old people.

As the initial reform in the field of national old-age pensions,[2] the Social Security Act, not the Townsend Plan, established the dominant pattern for the American social security system. The Democratic Party, which controlled the national government almost continuously from 1932 to 1953, claimed credit for proposing and enacting this system of security. It could not tolerate a repudiation of a program so vital to its popular image. Nor could the Republican Party officially adopt the Townsend Plan as an acceptable alternative to the Social Security Act. Many Republicans may have flirted with the Townsend Movement because of political expediency, but the plan, itself, was much too radical a proposal. The Social Security Act was, moreover, very popular. Hence, the opposition party, also, was compelled to adopt the Social Security Act to survive politically. Not only was the Townsend Plan effectively blocked in Congress, therefore, but all additional reforms were channeled into the existing social security framework.

Club members were increasingly frustrated by the impossibility of enacting their plan. At the same time, the benefits they and their fellows derived from the Social Security Act underlined the fact that old-age security was accessible through other means than the Townsend Plan. Townsend leaders attacked the Social Security Act as un-Christian and niggardly, and the small average old-age insurance as well as assistance benefits testified to the accuracy of the latter charge. Nevertheless, the payments moved steadily upwards and club members received a regular income under one or the other of the two Social Security Act programs, and sometimes under both.

Economic change also dulled the appeal of the Townsend Plan whereas it made no impression whatsoever upon the drive for prohibition. The Townsend Movement arose primarily as a depression phenomenon, reflecting both the accelerated dislocation of old people within the society during a period of drastic crisis as well as the absence of any significant political adjustment. The tempestuous, uncertain times of the thirties encouraged a sympathetic response from the general population for whom economic insecurity also posed immediate and personal problems. With improved economic conditions, proposals for radical improvisations encountered a less congenial atmosphere. As a deep-rooted moral issue, prohibition, on the other hand, transcended the economic; the Anti-Saloon League was largely impervious to economic conditions.

The Townsend Movement operated under an imposing handicap in that death and infirmity rates among its members ranked considerably higher than in political groups not centering upon the aged. Yet instead of replenishing or expanding its ranks, the Townsend Movement suffered a radical and continuous contraction in membership at the very time that both the number and percentage of aged within the population were steadily increasing.[3] In commenting upon the loss of enthusiasm and the decreased participation on the part of the aged under the Townsend banner, Dr. Townsend, in 1948, conceded that the national movement had reached a point in its development ". . . . where we must find support from groups other than the aged."[4] Since they were already receiving aid, he contended, the aged were afraid to demand further benefits; they had become inactive and were no longer crusaders as in the early days of the Movement.

Organizationally as well as politically, the Anti-Saloon League and the Townsend Movement were ostensibly similar. Pressure politics constituted their principal tool—intervention in the election of legislators and the legislative process, the influencing of party policy and the use of direct action through initiatives and referenda. Both movements were also characterized by highly centralized control, actual governing power residing in the hands of a few men. A closer scrutiny of organizational structure and political behavior, however, reveals sharp contradictions underlying those similarities.

A principal difference lay in their types of leadership, ownership and control. Centralization within the League did not signify identification with or ownership and domination by one or two individuals. The League was a multi-organizational body representing many churches and temperance societies. Although centralized in operation, it was federal in structure. Its board of directors was composed of representatives from each state League in which local organizations were affiliated. The directors chose the executive committee or actual governing body which, in turn, appointed the various superintendents in charge of organization, lobbying and publications. The national leaders were ultimately responsible to representatives of the local Leagues who chose them. Consequently, the Anti-Saloon League escaped the problems associated with one-man operation and identification.[5] At each level of organization there existed legitimate and independent checks upon its administrative and executive officers.

The League commanded, moreover, invaluable strength in the independently organized groups of which it was composed. They provided it with a respectable status in the community, one its enemies could not destroy. At the same time, the League was able to draw upon influential leaders within the community. Conservatives, liberals, businessmen, laborers, people of all ages were members of a church or were willing to be associated with the aims of the League.

The Townsend Movement was seriously weakened by its own organizational structure. Plan and Movement were so identified with Dr. Townsend in name, origin, ownership and control that they became virtually synonymous.[6] The personal shortcomings of the leader were tremendously over-magnified in their effect upon the pension movement. Public disclosure before a special congressional investigating committee that the founder and co-founder of the Movement had benefited financially from it and had misled the membership as to their roles within the Movement undermined faith and confidence in the plan as well as in the leadership. While it is true that various state superintendents of the Anti-Saloon League were also exposed for misconduct or corruption, they did not comprise the national leadership nor was the League or the concept of prohibition identified exclusively with such individuals.

The Townsend corporate structure was such that any difference of opinion on policy was inevitably equated by National Headquarters with a personal attack upon Dr. Townsend's judgment and leadership. This militated against peaceful compromises and an orderly resolution of internal tensions and problems. Consequently, the Townsend Movement was severely shaken by periodic rebellions and secessions. At least six such major crises occurred in the period 1934–54, two of which seriously threatened the very existence of the Movement: the revolt in 1937 over the doctor's insistence that defeat of President Roosevelt's court reform proposal take precedence over the enactment of the Townsend Plan, and the bitter struggle in

1945–46 by the national council (representing the clubs) to exercise its control over the entire Movement.

These revolts and schisms weakened membership allegiance, dried up financial support and separated from the Townsend Movement both individual clubs and membership at large. Whereas virtually all of the dissenters initially retained an identification with the Townsend Plan, their creation of separate pension organizations eventually compelled them to espouse, in self-justification, different solutions. Such organizations competed with the Townsend Movement for the allegiance and support of the aged on state and national levels.

In contrast with the League, few if any prominent leaders on the community level or the national scene associated themselves with the Townsend Plan, which never, therefore, acquired the proper trappings of respectability and legitimacy. Nor did the Movement succeed in eliciting cooperation from organized groups in society except in its "initiative" drives. Only on the state level and after the Townsend Movement had declined precipitously in membership and power were *ad hoc* alliances entered into on a *quid pro quo* basis with labor unions and farm organizations.

Professor Peter Odegard attributes the transformation of prohibition sentiment and pressure into effective political action to four features of the Anti-Saloon League: centralization, singleness of purpose, avoidance of third parties, and reliance on the Protestant Church. Centralization of authority existed within both movements, but the decentralized Townsend endorsement procedure, operative in 1936 and since 1942, militated against the best interests of the pension movement. Singleness of purpose enabled the League to avoid issues which would have engendered internal dissension and interfered with its successful use of pressure techniques. Aside from women's suffrage, the League refused to espouse controversial proposals pertaining to child labor, free silver and the League of Nations which were urged upon it by many members. The Townsend Movement, on the other hand, floundered upon bitterly divisive issues which the founder insisted upon advocating.

The Prohibition Party was not the instrument of the League which, in fact, never identified itself with any third party. A third party was in reality a political cul-de-sac, a point well recognized by the brewers who heaped abuse upon the Anti-

Saloon League while at the same time praising and financing the Prohibition Party.

Dr. Townsend found it difficult to resist the allure of the third-party tactic. His endorsement of Lemke and the Union Party in 1936 aroused considerable resentment among many of his followers and rebounded to the Movement's disadvantage. A serious division within the Townsend ranks was only narrowly avoided in 1948 when the leaders of the Progressive Party balked at incorporating the plan in their platform. And on the state level, an independent Townsend Party in California was inaugurated which failed completely. Nevertheless, the Townsend leadership remained enamored with the third-party position.

The power of an unorthodox group intent upon writing public policy is inextricably associated with its ability to operate as a political machine. Both in election politics and in lobbying, two important facets of the pressure technique, the Anti-Saloon League and the Townsend Movement differed radically. Odegard contends that the adoption of the Eighteenth Amendment and state local option laws could never have been achieved unless the League had demonstrated to politicians that it controlled substantial votes which could determine election results. An endorsement policy whereby support was granted only those whose records clearly indicated a "dry" sentiment or whose promises were definite insured the League that its candidates, once elected, would invariably cooperate with it. The League refused to reendorse its renegades and as a rule it succeeded in defeating them. Every means of engineering the political demise of its "wet" opponents was employed.

The political strength which the Townsend Movement mobilized was largely dissipated through a disorganized endorsement policy and inept lobbying. Congressional supporters were often ignored in their candidacy for reelection while their opponents were frequently endorsed. Individuals not seriously contending for office were recommended, thereby depriving the Movement of an opportunity to exert its strength in numerous elections. Endorsements were granted on the most general type of promises, resulting in an inadequate mobilization of support within Congress. The pension movement proved incapable, moreover, of curtailing the political careers of its principal congressional opponents as well as its renegades.

When the pension leaders did appear before Congress, backed in 1935 by a tremendous demand for the plan and in 1939 by the relevancy of the Townsend issue in the 1938 elections, the strength that had been generated was almost totally nullified by singularly incompetent lobbying. Their first appearance can be excused as due to inexperience with congressional politics. No such explanation can be extended their 1939 performance. The Townsend bills were poorly constructed and their irresponsible nature became immediately apparent. Not only were their proponents ill-prepared to defend them, but the pressure group leaders did not effectively coordinate their efforts with those of their congressional supporters. Both in 1935 and in 1939, the bills were repudiated by some of their sponsors as well as by experts summoned to testify in their behalf.

The Anti-Saloon League's proposals were, of course, much more simple and less technical than the plan. Yet they were as bitterly attacked and ridiculed. Prohibition leaders, however, marshalled not merely votes but astute strategy and careful planning behind their legislative efforts.

Additional differences characterized the political behavior of the two movements. The first stemmed from their organizational-geographical bases. Congressional enactment of substantive legislation invariably requires the combination of sufficient votes from the various sections of the country. Through the Protestant Church, prohibition became an indigenous and politically potent movement in every region of the United States. Especially powerful in the South, the League was strongly entrenched in all regions; only in the large cities did it encounter great opposition. The composition of the Townsend forces in Congress reflected the great disparity between the geographical distribution of Townsend clubs and the holders of political power in that institution. Townsend legislative strength was proportionately greatest in the Far West, the region with the smallest representation in the House of Representatives. The plan drew only insignificant support from the South, and failed to penetrate the East sufficiently.

Before attempting to secure its objective through a national constitutional amendment, the League had concentrated upon reforms at the state and local levels wherein lay its primary strength. It did not have to enter into its major test of power until after many years of growth. Consequently, its leaders accumulated political experience and its membership was encouraged by frequent successes. The Townsend Movement was compelled to enter the congressional arena almost immediately

—after it had been in existence only a little more than a year. Although rebuffed at the national level, the leadership campaigned against any attempt to initiate local Townsend plans in those states where Townsend clubs were most active. Only after the Movement's strength and popularity had faded did Townsend leaders first seek victory for the plan on the state level.

In the concrete and vivid symbols of "evil" embodied in the saloon, the bottle of liquor and the drunkard, the League possessed invaluable assets. In the everyday presence of these symbols, church members and their associates in the prohibitionist movement hardened their ranks. Townsendites, on the other hand, were favored with no concrete or personal enemies which were inherently "evil," or on whom the old folks could project their fears or hatreds. Old age, itself, could not be attacked, only the inequities associated therewith. But whom to blame? The Townsend leaders did seek to establish in the minds of their followers a set of "devils," the economic system and economists. However, these were too impersonal and nebulous. Wall Street and big business were downgraded in the Townsend demonology since the pension prophet, himself, had proclaimed President Franklin D. Roosevelt, the Democratic Party, and the Social Security Act to be the principal enemies. It was difficult if not impossible to so stigmatize the New Deal and its leaders in the face of their program of humanitarian and social reform. The absence of a recognizable, acceptable set of enemies to the pension movement, itself, or to the aged, in general, deprived the Townsend Movement of vital unifying forces which might otherwise have served as deterrents to disorganization.[7]

The Influence of the Townsend Movement

The old-age provisions of the Social Security Act, that keystone of the welfare state, memorialize the impact of the Townsend Movement upon national public policy. Agitation for the Townsend Plan greatly accelerated the time schedule for the appearance of a national old-age security program. In crystalizing an overwhelming public clamor for action, the Townsend Movement afforded that program tremendous popular support, the political overtones of which neither the President nor the Congress could ignore. And the very inception of old-age insurance payments at a date earlier than that scheduled in the Social Security Act represented, in good part, a political response to the pressure generated by the Townsend and other pension movements. Initial increases in federal contributions to old-age assistance programs as well as the liberalization of these programs by certain state governments, particularly in the Far West, are also attributable to this pressure.

The Townsend Movement did more to dramatize the plight of the aged than any other force in American life. An entire generation of Americans was made intensely aware, for the first time, of the social problems associated with old age. The Townsend Movement contributed also to the shaping of a public opinion favorable to the concepts that old-age protection was a matter of right, not charity or need; that benefits should be ample, not niggardly; that their provision was properly the responsibility of government; and that pensions were indispensable to the stability of the national economy as well as to the dignity of the individual.

The Townsend Movement fashioned an articulate self-consciousness among many of the aged members of our population. It represented a new element in American politics, for with the exception of the very transitory Pope movement in 1933 the aged as such had not participated in the political arena. Now for the first time the polity was confronted by the special demands of the aged on a scale comparable in magnitude to that of the more traditional interest groups. Hence the plurality of American society was expanded and became thereby more complex.

The heritage of the Townsend Movement is ascertainable also in many of the other old-age pension movements which arose on the state and national levels. Some of these movements represented direct offshoots of the Townsend Movement. Among them were the National Annuity League which successfully amended the Colorado state constitution in the interests of the aged pensioner, the General Welfare Federation of America, Inc., the American Pension Union, Inc., and the McMasters' group in Massachusetts. While others were independent in origin, their genesis is to be found, in part, at least, in the potential revealed by Townsend successes in organizing the aged: the Washington Pension Union, the "Ham and Eggs" movement and the McLain movement in California. Many of these pension groups displayed a marked similarity to the Townsend Movement in the patterns of their leadership and their organization.

Two aspects of major party politics deserve to be considered

in a discussion of the influences of the Townsend Movement—
the close political relationship between this pension movement
and many Republican Party politicians, and the adoption of
campaign tactics by both major parties which focus on the
"senior citizen." In the years 1934–44, when the Townsendites
were the most active, a number of Republican leaders—candidates for the presidency and vice-presidency as well as congressmen, governors and state legislators—deliberately cultivated
Townsend endorsements and votes. In the election of 1938,
which marked the first surge of Republican strength in Congress
since 1928, the demand for improved old-age pensions became
a major political issue, and many Republicans identified their
campaigns with that of the Townsend Movement.

Such a pattern of Republican–Townsend associations would
appear to be incongruous in view of the ninety-six to one vote
for recommitting the social security bill cast by Republicans in
the House of Representatives, in 1935, and also the conservative
nature of their party. Republicans, however, were the "out" or
minority party in the national government. Moreover, they had
lost control of or were threatened with defeat in a number of
states. The Townsendites also were an "out" group, blocked in
Congress by the Democratic Administration and by Democratic
majorities. Since the pension issue apparently generated votes,
Republicans entered into a variety of arrangements with the
Townsend forces.

Social security was too popular an issue for the Republicans
to permit it to be monopolized by the majority party, despite
the Republican opposition in the House of Representatives in
1935. Association with the Townsend pension forces afforded
many Republicans a viable position from which to attack the
Democratic program as inadequate and improperly financed. At
the same time it facilitated their identification with the social
security concept for the aged, central to the new politics of the
welfare era. As a result of their Townsend experience, many
Republican politicians were able to assimilate more easily into
their ideological framework the concept of a national pension
system.

Both major political parties have adopted as an integral element in their campaigning an image of the aged which the
Townsend Movement helped create. It is now an accepted political postulate that many old people will respond to appeals
addressed to their special interests and role as aged. Hence in

the congressional campaign of 1958, the Republican National Committee sought to organize a number of senior citizens clubs. And in the 1960 presidential campaign, the Democratic National Committee established a special division, Senior Citizens for Kennedy and Johnson, with Congressman Aime J. Forand as its national chairman.[8]

It remains to be demonstrated whether political parties can, as did the pension movements, elicit support from the aged by fashioning special campaign drives in terms of their aims and interests. What is significant, however, is that neither major party now feels that it can afford not to proceed upon this assumption! The operating principle of the pension movement has been absorbed into the politics of the major political parties.

It is true that today the Townsend Movement is an insignificant force, its few remaining clubs isolated from the great body of the aged and its proposals virtually unknown to the general population. While the Townsend Movement may have never achieved its goal, adoption of the Townsend Plan, the imprint of the Townsend Movement is recognizable in features of our public policy, the configuration of public opinion and in the tactics and forms of politics. As long as old age continues to pose difficult socio-economic problems for our society which become converted into issues of politics and public policy, the long-range effects of the Townsend Movement will be manifest.

Prospects for Future Old-Age Politics in the United States

Does America face the prospect of a war of generations, old versus young, as was envisaged in 1951 by the economist for the American Medical Association?[9] Certainly many forces which have aggravated old-age insecurity are still operative today. In 1960, among persons sixty-five and over, 67 per cent resided in urban areas. The proportion receiving earnings from employment had declined to 24.2 per cent, representing, in part, a further reduction in employment opportunities for older people. And fewer than one in four persons sixty years and older had as much as $2,000 cash income while more than one-half had less than $1,000! At the same time, those sixty-five and over had increased by 150 per cent since 1930, numbering 16.6 million or 9.2 per cent of the population in 1960. While the total population grew by only 18.5 per cent in the decade from 1950 to 1960, the aged increased by nearly 35 per cent, and the oldest group, those aged 85 and over, increased by more than 60 per cent to number approximately 929,000.

Since the aged will comprise an ever increasing proportion of the eligible voters in the United States for a long time to come —they constituted 15.4 per cent of the population twenty-one years and older in 1960 as against only 9.1 per cent in 1930— what does this portend for social security politics? Old people have special problems arising out of their social, economic and physical conditions. Will the aged again resort in large numbers to independent political action? Robert J. Havighurst has warned that if this group should ever form a solid political bloc, it could secure almost anything it might demand from government.[10] Old-age movements of the depression decade, Ewan Clague has contended, were in their political infancy in comparison to the pension movements of the future.[11]

On the basis of this study of the Townsend Movement and corollary pension movements, the author feels that such pessimistic hypotheses are largely unwarranted. They reflect a lack of awareness that socio-political conditions have been so altered as to inhibit old-age politics comparable to that of the depression decade.

The major political parties have incorporated into their politics a positive attitude toward the social security system. One need only refer to the party platforms or to the public positions of Republican and Democratic leaders to comprehend the popularity of social security as a political issue. On the same day that Republican President Dwight D. Eisenhower labeled the Tennessee Valley Authority an example of "creeping socialism," he praised the social security system and called for its expansion. During the Eisenhower Administration in Washington, improvements in benefits and extensions in coverage were written into the Social Security Act. And a significant expansion and liberalization in the O. A. S. I. program was secured by President John F. Kennedy in the first six months of his Democratic Administration in 1961.

The American people have enthusiastically accepted the socialization of risk for old age and death as well as unemployment. A political party would seriously penalize itself if it failed to reflect this sentiment. It can be expected, therefore, that the extension and liberalization of the present old-age insurance and assistance programs will continue to be championed by the major parties. Their leadership in expanding protection for the aged preempts that position which special pension movements had for a brief period monopolized.

An aggressive, influential labor movement is now, as compared with the pre-depression era, intimately involved in politics to protect itself and advance the socio-economic position of its members. Adequate pensions for the aged constitute a primary objective in labor's program of social reform. It was largely the economic espousal of pensions by organized labor, and not independent political action by the aged, which compelled a reconsideration of social security legislation by the national government in 1950. The brief success of George H. McLain's pension group in the California election of 1948 was attributable, in part, to a favorable climate of public opinion generated by labor's agitation across the table of collective bargaining for improved old-age security.

The social security system today protects millions of workers and their families. The latest extensions have included all but a very small minority of the self-employed and other groups previously excluded. The addition of survivors' and disability insurance as well as the lowering of the eligibility age have improved its coverage and benefits. Old-age assistance, a joint federal-state project, is operative in all the states. Consequently, an ever improving system of protection removes much of the economic incentive that stimulated old people to participate in pension movements. It is unlikely that their predicament can ever again approximate the desperation and hopelessness which prevailed in the 1930's. In addition, a growing concern today on the part of private as well as public organizations with the socio-psychological needs of older people promises to help further reduce the isolation in which many find themselves. The existence of Golden Age clubs and similar organizations testify to the attempts by many communities to provide appropriate programs and units wherein old people can participate in meaningful and satisfying activities.

To imply that independent political action on the part of the aged may henceforth be dismissed is as unwarranted as to suggest that it will increase in gravity. Old-age pension movements will continue to agitate American politics. Viewed in proper perspective, however, their political significance can be evaluated as minor only.

National and state pension organizations remain active today, although they encompass only a very slight fraction of the nation's aged population. In some of these organizations clubs furnish a warm social environment for the old—opportunities for friendship, marriage, and a sense of belonging as well as avenues for leadership and status. Participation provides meaningful activity, enabling elderly people to feel that they still retain a voice in society. Other pension organizations provide assistance to old people in obtaining their benefits under the complicated old-age assistance programs. A major element in the appeal of the California Institute of Social Welfare, the McLain movement, has been its successful efforts to mediate between the aged and the complex, impersonal aspects inherent in the administration of this system. Organized groups of occupationally homogeneous pensioners have also begun to make their appearance and to lobby actively in the interests of their members.[12]

Certain states will undoubtedly continue to be active loci of pension politics. Revivals of old-age politics can be expected wherever a high concentration of aged is accompanied by a tradition of political unorthodoxy, the availability of the initiative or referendum for independent action, and disorganization within the major parties. Such conditions are particularly characteristic of some of our Western states. On the other hand, Florida, parts of New England and of the Midwest, which have had strong concentrations of Townsend clubs as well as local pension movements, may also anticipate some activity.

Our social security system lends itself to continued pension politics since old-age assistance focuses pressure upon state parties and legislatures. As long as old-age assistance is inadequate and needs tests, relative responsibility clauses and other restrictions are imposed by state legislatures, discontent will be generated among the aged. The legislation enacted by Congress in 1960 which provided for health protection for old persons through the assistance program, as defined by the state legislatures and administered by state social welfare agencies, may therefore provide a stimulus for state and perhaps even national pension movements. Indeed, pension movements have already deemed it imperative to press for improved medical benefits for the aged. The problem of maintaining health is a particularly acute one for old people as was indicated as early as 1952 by the report of the President's Commission on the Health Needs of the Nation.[13] The 1960 political debate over adding old-age health protection to the insurance provisions of the Social Security Act reflected the sensitivity of the major political parties to this issue.

The action of Golden Age clubs and similar organizations in which old people participate may presage their increasing involvement in the political arena.

It has already been amply demonstrated that in the event of an economic recession, old-age insurance benefits will not be reduced. The major party leaders are well aware of the popular support behind social security. In addition, insurance benefits are conceived of today as counter-cyclical devices, built-in stabilizers which inhibit the precipitous nature of a recession. Old-age assistance programs are more exposed to restriction by state legislatures. Any such action, however, would presage a resurgence of independent politics in certain states. If inflation is again permitted to cut sharply into the real income of the aged, aggressive pension politics can be expected on the part of pension groups and labor unions. On the whole, however, there are little prospects in the United States for the reemergence of extensive old-age politics through special pension movements of the aged.

NOTES

NOTES TO CHAPTER ONE (Pages 17–27)

1. Helen F. Hohman, *Old Age in Sweden, A Program of Social Security* (Washington, 1940), p. 15.

2. For an historical analysis of forces leading to the adoption of Great Britain's Old Age Pension Law of 1908 see Francois Lafitte, *Britain's Way to Social Security* (London, 1945), pp. 10–11; Karl de Schweinitz, *England's Road to Social Security, From . . . 1349 to . . . 1942* (Philadelphia, 1943), chapters 16–18; Arnold T. Wilson and G. S. MacKay, *Old Age Pensions, An Historical and Critical Study* (London, 1941), chapters 2–4.

3. Leslie L. Lipson, *The Politics of Equality, New Zealand's Adventures in Democracy* (Chicago, 1948), p. 209.

4. Abraham Epstein, *The Challenge of the Aged* (New York, 1928), p. 299.

5. Socialt Tidsskrift, ed., *Social Denmark, A Survey of the Danish Social Legislation* (Copenhagen, 1945), p. 34.

6. Joseph K. Folsom, "Old Age as a Sociological Problem," *American Journal of Orthopsychiatry*, 10 (January, 1940), 33; T. Lynn Smith, "The Aged in Rural Society," in Milton Derber, ed., *The Aged and Society* (Champaign, 1950), pp. 51–52.

7. Talcott Parsons, *Essays in Sociological Theory, Pure and Applied* (Glencoe, 1949), p. 230.

8. Smith, *op. cit.,* pp. 43–48.

9. Parsons, *op. cit.,* p. 231.

10. U. S. Department of Labor, Bureau of Labor Statistics, *Employment and Economic Status of Older Men and Women* (Bulletin No. 1092, Washington, May, 1952), 17.

11. Maurice Leven, Harold G. Moulton and Clark Warburton, *America's Capacity to Consume* (Washington, 1934), pp. 54, 96.

12. Ewan Clague, "The Aging Population and Programs of Security," *The Milbank Memorial Fund Quarterly*, 18 (October, 1940), 346.

13. Epstein, *The Challenge of the Aged,* pp. 52, 118.

14. Abraham Epstein, *Insecurity: A Challenge to America* (3rd. revised edit., New York, 1936), p. 500; Committee on Economic Security, *Report to the President* (Washington, 1935), 24.

15. U. S. Department of Labor, Bureau of Labor Statistics, *op. cit.,* 17.

16. *Hearings before the Committee on Labor on H. R. 1623, etc.,* U. S. House of Representatives, 73rd Cong., 2nd Sess. (Washington, 1934), 47–176.

17. Earl Warren, "California's Biggest Headache," in David Farrelly and Ivan Hinderaker, ed., *The Politics of California* (New York, 1951), p. 6.

18. Winston W. Crouch and Dean E. McHenry, *California Government, Politics and Administration* (revised edit., Berkeley, 1949), p. 66.

NOTES TO CHAPTER TWO (Pages 28–46)

1. OARP, Ltd., Townsend National Radio Division, *Townsend Talk,* August 26, 1936 (No. 26-C: Official Series).

2. See the reinterpretation of the American political tradition drawn by the historian, Richard Hofstadter, *The American Political Tradition And The Men Who Made It* (New York, 1949), pp. vii-x.

3. This is not to imply that Edward Bellamy, the International Workers of the World, or the Utopian and Marxist Socialists were not within the American radical tradition. Measured by their impact upon Congress, state legislatures and the major political parties or by rallying widespread mass support, they did not compare in political significance with the more conservative forces in American radicalism.

4. *The Folklore of Capitalism* (New Haven, 1937), pp. 2–4.

5. V. O. Key, Jr., *Political Parties and Pressure Groups* (1st edit., New York, 1942), p. 66.

6. Quoted in Richard Milne, *That Man Townsend* (Long Beach, 1935), p. 2.

7. Robert O. Foote, "Pensions for all at 60, an Idea from the West," New York *Times,* September 16, 1934, IX.

8. Russell Owen, "Townsend Talks of his Plan and Hopes," New York *Times Magazine,* December 29, 1935, 3.

9. Dr. Francis E. Townsend, *New Horizons,* edited by Jesse G. Murray (Chicago, 1943). In 1952, describing the genesis of the plan, Dr. Townsend again failed to mention the "old-women-garbage-can" story. *Townsend National Weekly,* May 17, 1952.

10. Bruce Barton, "How to Fix Everything," *Vanity Fair,* 36 (August, 1931), 31, 70; Richard L. Neuberger and Kelley Loe, *An Army of the Aged* (Caldwell, 1936), pp. 50–53.

11. Luther Whiteman and Samuel L. Lewis, *Glory Roads, The Psychological State of California* (New York, 1936), p. 66. Text of a plan,

copyrighted August 7, 1931, by Mr. C. Stewart McCord, may be found in *Hearings before the Select Committee Investigating Old Age Pension Organizations pursuant to H. Res. 443,* U. S. House of Representatives, 74th Cong., 2nd Sess. (Washington, 1936), vol. 1, 758–64.

12. Dr. Townsend estimated the number of eligible pensioners to total between 15 and 20 million although the 1930 census reported only 10.3 million people over sixty years of age. In a copy of this original letter reprinted in his autobiography, Townsend *op. cit.,* pp. 137–40, the number was altered to read between 9 and 12 million.

13. *Ibid.,* pp. 141–42.

14. Neuberger and Loe, *op. cit.,* p. 58, asserted that one of the original features of the plan was the printing of two billions of "new currency" to initiate the fund. There is no evidence in the original letter or pamphlets to substantiate this conclusion. Although on the whole the plan did not concern itself with the question of funds for the initial payment of pensions, and only incidental attention seems to have been given it, where it was mentioned in Townsend literature, either a loan, bonds or a direct congressional appropriation was recommended. In OARP, Ltd., *Questions and Answers* (Long Beach, n.d.), p. 15, Robert E. Clements, the "co-founder" of the Townsend Movement, offered the following answer: "The Government . . . has on hand several billions of your money and who has a better right to borrow it for 30 days than you to whom it belongs?"

15. Townsend, *op. cit.,* pp. 137–40. An illustration of the fabrication characterizing Townsend literature is to be found also in "The Letter That Launched the Townsend Plan," *Townsend National Weekly,* March 22, 1952. While this copy of the letter does contain the $150 figure, the original sales tax provision has been abstracted and replaced with a "gross income tax," a feature first embodied in the plan in 1939. For probably the first time in many years, Dr. Townsend admitted in 1954 that his plan had originally started with a national sales tax. *Townsend National Weekly,* January 30, 1954.

16. OARP, Ltd., *Old Age Revolving Pensions, a National Plan . . . Proposed by Dr. F. E. Townsend* (presumably 1st edit., Long Beach, 1934), p. 10.

17. Samuel M. Dick, *$200 Per Month In Action* (3rd edit., Watertown, 1935).

18. Dr. F. E. Townsend, "Introduction," in Sheridan Downey, *Why I Believe in the Townsend Plan* (Sacramento, 1936), p. 11.

19. Owen, *op. cit.,* p. 15.

20. Richard Milne, *That Man Townsend* (Long Beach, 1935), p. 27.

21. *Ibid.,* p. 28.

22. Dr. Francis E. Townsend, *The Townsend National Recovery Plan, New Reference Book* (2nd edit., Chicago, 1941), p. 6. In the *Townsend National Weekly,* November 9, 1946, Dr. F. E. Townsend

was quoted as follows: "Actually it was not for $200 that I asked, this was a figure put in my mouth by newspaper reporters—but I never bothered to deny it. . . . But that figure, $200 a month, had drama, and I let it stand without denial."

23. OARP, Ltd., *Old Age Revolving Pensions, A National Plan . . . Proposed by Dr. F. E. Townsend* (presumably 1st edit., Long Beach, 1934), p. 9.

24. OARP, Ltd., *Speaker's Manual* (Los Angeles, 1935), "Suggestions to Speakers." [Looseleaf, unnumbered]

25. The source to which the Townsendites finally attributed their figure was an estimate advanced by Dr. E. A. Goldenweiser, Director of Research and Statistics, Federal Reserve Board. *Hearings before the Committee on Ways and Means on H.R. 1, etc.,* U. S. House of Representatives, 72nd Cong., 1st Sess. (Washington, 1932), 741. The " . . . total volume of transactions . . . in 1929 was about twelve hundred billions of dollars, and it decreased by 1931 to six hundred billions. . . . "

26. There is a marked similarity between these and the four psychological factors Hadley Cantril views as central to the Townsend Plan's success: (1) It satisfies need; (2) It is simple enough to be understood; (3) It fits into old norms; (4) It preserves or enhances self-regard. Hadley Cantril, *The Psychology of Social Movements* (New York, 1941), pp. 201–9. However, it is the opinion of this writer that in elaborating upon his four factors, Professor Cantril overlooked and understressed aspects of the plan that were crucial to its success.

27. See Pendleton Herring, *The Politics of Democracy* (New York, 1940), pp. 314–17, 319, for his discussion of this problem in regard to the prohibition and women's suffrage movements.

28. Stuart Chase, "Our Capacity to Produce," *Harper's Magazine,* 170 (February, 1935), 344. See also his "On the Paradox of Plenty," *The New Republic,* 73 (January 18, 1933), 258–60.

29. John Maynard Keynes, "The World's Economic Outlook," *The Atlantic Monthly,* 149 (May, 1932), 525.

30. Quoted in Arthur Dahlberg, *Recovery Plans* (Monograph No. 25, Temporary National Economic Committee, Washington, 1940), p. 13, n. 2.

31. Irving Fisher, "The Stamped Scrip Plan," *The New Republic,* 73 (December 21, 1932), 163–64. The Townsend plans, after January 1, 1935, provided a penalty for not spending the monthly annuity or for spending it illegally.

32. Owen, *op. cit.,* p. 15.

33. *Hearings before the Committee on Ways and Means on H.R. 4120,* U. S. House of Representatives, 74th Cong., 1st Sess. (Washington, 1935), 680.

34. Townsend, "Introduction," In Downey, *op. cit.,* p. 9.

35. OARP, Ltd., *The Townsend Plan* (presumably 1st edit., Wash-

ington, 1935), p. 7. A sample speech prepared for Townsend speakers gave assurances that the plan would curb radicalism and destroy the growth of communism at its source. OARP, Ltd., *Speaker's Manual*, "Sample Speech No. 2." Although in a 1947 editorial Dr. Townsend rejected the free enterprise profit system as "freedom to rob legally" and as an unworkable system, this was a personal expression and did not concern the plan. *Townsend National Weekly*, February 15, 1947.

36. National Resources Committee, *Consumer Incomes in the United States: Their Distribution in 1935–1936* (Washington, 1938), pp. 2–3.

37. See M. J. Bonn's conclusion that the plan was in direct line with American frontier psychology. "The Making of a National State," *The Political Quarterly*, 8 (October-December, 1937), 589. "The monetary conceptions embodied in . . . Dr. Townsend's plan was but the corollary of the national land policy. . . . The issue of unlimited fiduciary money was always the ideal of the frontier, which depended upon an unlimited supply of free land. Since its exhaustion, the need for free money is even greater."

38. Ruth S. Cavan and Associates, *Personal Adjustment in Old Age* (Chicago, 1949).

NOTES TO CHAPTER THREE (Pages 47–85)

1. See Richard L. Neuberger and Kelley Loe, *An Army of the Aged* (Caldwell, 1936), Chapter I, "Townsend Meeting Tonight"; Duncan Aikman, "Townsendism; Old Time Religion," New York *Times Magazine*, March 8, 1936, 5, 25; Lewis Nordyke, "Report to the Editor; Old Age in Our Town," *Saturday Evening Post*, 216 (November 20, 1943), 6; Harry T. Moore, "Just Folks in Utopia," *The New Republic*, 85 (November 13, 1935), 9–10. Observations about Townsendites and their club activities are also based upon a perusal of the Townsend *Weekly*, 1935–54 and interviews with a number of state organizers who had been in direct contact with the clubs since 1934.

2. Based on a poll conducted by the *Weekly*, 2,500 Townsendites responding, *Townsend National Weekly*, February 14, 1953.

3. *Hearings before the Select Committee Investigating Old Age Pension Organizations pursuant to H. Res. 443,* 74th Cong., 2nd Sess. (Washington, 1936), vol. 1, 208.

4. Tolan's figures cited in *National Townsend Weekly*, May 25, 1936. This publication has appeared under three different names: *Official Townsend Weekly,* January-July, 1935; *National Townsend Weekly,* July, 1935-October, 1936; *Townsend National Weekly,* October, 1936 to 1958. Hereafter it will be referred to as the *Weekly* unless the full title is called for.

5. Outside of the Far West and some states in the Midwest, only Pennsylvania, Florida and a few New England states were reported in

1934 to have had strong Townsend organizations. See "OARP Branch Offices," *The Modern Crusader,* 1 (September 29, 1934), 14–15.

6. Mary Conyngton, "Extent and Distribution of Old Age Dependency in the United States," *Monthly Labor Review,* 38 (January, 1934), 6.

7. V. O. Key, Jr., *Southern Politics in State and Nation* (New York, 1949), p. 5.

8. See Stuart N. Lake, "If Money . . . ," *Saturday Evening Post,* 207 (May 11, 1935), 12–13, 121–27.

9. One reason fewer Townsend clubs were organized in Utah than in New Mexico, Arizona, Wyoming, or Idaho, with comparable or smaller numbers of aged, may have been the expressed opposition of the head of the Mormon Church who attacked the plan as contrary to church teachings. See New York *Times,* October 3, 1936.

10. See Dr. Francis E. Townsend, *New Horizons,* edited by Jesse G. Murray (Chicago, 1943), pp. 135–36.

11. *Ibid.,* p. 52.

12. *Ibid.,* p. 95.

13. *Ibid.,* pp. 95–97.

14. *Ibid.,* p. 95

15. *Ibid.,* pp. 142–43.

16. Interview with Robert C. Townsend, Cleveland, Ohio, January, 1950.

17. Dr. Townsend remained an active titular leader until his death in 1960.

18. Detailed information concerning organization in the first two years of the Townsend Movement is to be found in *Hearings before the Select Committee Investigating Old Age Pension Organizations,* 74:2, vol. 1 and 2; *Hearings before the Committee on Finance on S. 1130,* 74th Cong., 1st Sess. (Washington, 1935), 1042–66 *passim;* Richard Milne, *That Man Townsend* (Long Beach, 1935). Information relating to the later years is drawn from the *Weekly* and such special sources as are cited.

19. California law required three incorporators. The doctor's brother constituted the third incorporator although he never assumed an active role in the Movement. He resigned almost immediately as executive officer and director.

20. *Hearings before the Select Committee Investigating Old Age Pension Organizations,* 74:2, vol. 1, 26.

21. The number of voting delegates, aside from Honor and Visiting Delegates, was always a large one: 1936–11,866; 1941–4,528; 1947–1,782.

22. *Hearings before the Select Committee Investigating Old Age Pension Organizations,* 74:2, vol. 1, 367. [Italics added]

23. *Ibid.,* 163–64.

24. *Official Townsend Weekly*, May 13, 1935.

25. *Idem*. This was to prove particularly embarrassing to Dr. Townsend when it was disclosed at the congressional investigation in 1936 that thousands of dollars had been divided between the two partners in dividends of which the clubs were never informed.

26. *Official Townsend Weekly*, May 13, 1935; May 27, 1935.

27. *National Townsend Weekly*, July 27, 1936; New York *Times*, July 15, 1936.

28. *Townsend National Weekly*, November 29, 1941; December 30, 1944.

29. Although some information pertaining to council meetings was reproduced in the *Weekly*, the latter is a poor source since much of what transpired was not publicly printed. This writer has relied almost entirely upon the "Minutes of the Meetings of the National Council, TNRP, Inc.," May 21-23, 1945; August 27-29, 1945; October 26-27, 1945; November 8-9, 1945, and May 22-24, 1946, which are found, in bound mimeographed form, at Townsend National Headquarters, and upon interviews with some of the participants.

30. Interview with one of the founder's most loyal and trusted advisers, Harrison N. Hiles, Secretary, The Townsend Plan, Inc., Cleveland, Ohio, January, 1950.

31. See his editorial entitled "The Press and the National Council," *Townsend National Weekly*, September 22, 1945.

32. His speech is not contained in the "Minutes of the National Council." A copy may be found at Townsend National Headquarters entitled "Address by Dr. Townsend to the National Council and Board of Directors Meeting, TNRP, Inc., May 22, 1946," on which is noted: ". . . by agreement expunged from the records."

33. Interview with Robert C. Townsend, Cleveland, Ohio, January, 1950.

34. Interview with H. N. Hiles, secretary of the corporation, Cleveland, Ohio, January, 1950. They had "stupidly" informed him, he contended, of their intention to force the doctor's resignation.

35. Seventh Convention of the Townsend Clubs, *Proceedings* (Washington, 1947), p. 167.

36. The Townsend Plan, Inc., *Townsend Club Manual* (Cleveland, 1948), Article XII, p. 18.

37. *National Townsend Weekly*, April 16, 1936; *Townsend National Weekly*, April 5, 1937. Loans of $10 or more from individual Townsendites had already been initiated when the Securities and Exchange Commission condemned the entire venture. *Townsend National Weekly*, April 26, 1937.

38. One individual donated $1,000 and nine contributors, including Dr. Townsend, $500 each. *Townsend National Weekly*, April 26, 1947.

39. Cited in Twentieth Century Fund, The Committee on Old Age Security, *The Townsend Crusade* (New York, 1936), p. 14.

40. Hadley Cantril, *The Psychology of Social Movements* (New York, 1941), pp. 191–93.

41. See *Townsend National Weekly,* July 19, 1941, and Townsend Youth Association membership book records, Townsend National Headquarters.

42. See two special pamphlets: Willis Owen, *Making Money for the Merchant* (Chicago, 1937); Dr. F. E. Townsend, *A Message to the Businessmen of America* (Chicago, n.d.).

43. "Threat of Pension Pressure Groups," *Tax Policy,* 7 (November, 1939), 6–7.

44. *Townsend National Weekly,* January 17, 1942.

NOTES TO CHAPTER FOUR (Pages 86–100)

1. Except for a very minor incident in the House of Representatives in January, the Townsend bill did not play any role in Congress in 1936. The Townsend forces were too preoccupied with meeting a congressional attack upon their Movement, seeking to determine the outcome of the presidential election, and coping with major organizational crises in their own ranks to concern themselves with legislative politics in behalf of a Townsend bill.

2. "I don't care what you think of Townsend, but you've got to admit he did some job. He dramatized the situation of the aged." Harry Hopkins, in a speech delivered before a Conference on Unemployment and Education. New York *Times,* May 16, 1937.

3. Frances Perkins, *The Roosevelt I Knew* (New York, 1946), pp. 278–79.

4. New York *Times,* November 15, 1934.

5. Quoted in Perkins, *op. cit.,* p. 294.

6. *Official Townsend Weekly,* March 18, 1935.

7. See New York *Times,* December 22, 1934; *Time Magazine,* 25 (January 14, 1935), 14.

8. Letter from Frank Peterson to Robert E. Clements, January 20, 1935, *Hearings before the Select Committee Investigating Old Age Pension Organizations pursuant to H. Res. 443,* U. S. House of Representatives, 74th Cong., 2nd Sess. (Washington, 1936), vol. 1, 873.

9. See President's Committee on Economic Security, *Report to the President* (Washington, 1935); H.R. 4120, 74th Cong., 1st Sess.

10. Perkins, *op. cit.,* pp. 279, 281. "He always regarded the Social Security Act as the cornerstone of his administration and, I think, took greater satisfaction from it than from anything else he achieved on the domestic front." *Ibid.,* p. 301.

11. To a nephew, Roosevelt wrote that the Townsend Plan would

bankrupt the government. Franklin D. Roosevelt to James Davis, March 9, 1935, Franklin D. Roosevelt Library.

12. New York *Times*, January 18, 1935.

13. *Hearings before the Committee on Ways and Means on H.R. 4120*, U. S. House of Representatives, 74th Cong., 1st. Sess. (Washington, 1935), 111.

14. *Ibid.*, 678–79 for text of Townsend bill H.R. 3977.

15. *Ibid.*, 678, 680–82.

16. *Ibid.*, 1124. [Italics added]

17. *Hearings before the Committee on Finance on S. 1130*, United States Senate, 74th Cong., 1st Sess. (Washington, 1935), 1243–47. See *Ibid.*, 1015–51, 1061–66 for Dr. Townsend's testimony.

18. George Burnham, Henry E. Stubbs and John H. Tolan from California; Martin F. Smith from Washington.

19. Revealed in a speech by John H. Heoppel (Calif. D.), *Congressional Record*, 74th Cong., 2nd Sess., April 2, 1935, 4883–84.

20. McGroarty introduced H.R. 7154 on April 1, 1935. Its text may be found in the *Congressional Record*, 74th Cong., 1st Sess., 5888–90.

21. The political reason for this new provision was openly admitted in a Townsend editorial which proclaimed that it would win more support from Southern congressmen since it answered their objections. *Official Townsend Weekly*, April 8, 1935.

22. *Congressional Record*, 74:1, 588–90 for text.

23. Only thirty minutes were allotted for debate on the bill before it came up for a vote. Intermittent speeches, however, were delivered between April 11–18, 1935.

24. *Congressional Record*, 74:1, 5958. An unsuccessful discharge petition was later filed on H.R. 7154. In January, 1936, the bill was again offered for a vote but was ruled out of order as "new legislation" because it was presented as an amendment to an appropriation bill. *Congressional Record*, 74:2, 964.

NOTES TO CHAPTER FIVE (Pages 101–124)

1. See Buel W. Patch, "Agitation for Pension and Scrip Schemes," *Editorial Research Reports*, 2 (October 1, 1938), 228–30; George E. Anderson, "A Pension Planner's Carnival," *Banking*, 31 (January, 1939), 27.

2. New York *Times*, August 16, 1938.

3. See Table XIII for the names and voting records of these representatives on the Townsend bill in 1939.

4. From an address Hopkins delivered at Grinnell College, quoted in Robert E. Sherwood, *Roosevelt and Hopkins, an Intimate History* (1st ed.; New York, 1948), p. 20.

5. See the recommendations embodied in the President's message

including those submitted by the Social Security Board and by the Advisory Committee on Social Security. *Hearings before the Committee on Ways and Means relative to the Social Security Act Amendments of 1939,* U. S. House of Representatives, 76th Cong., 1st Sess. (Washington, 1939), vol. 1, 1–25. In 1937 and again in 1938 a special Advisory Committee on Social Security, established jointly by the Social Security Board and the Senate's Finance Committee, had suggested to Congress a number of important amendments to the Social Security Act.

6. In a book written prior to congressional reexamination of the social security question, Maxwell S. Stewart pointed out that "Pressure from the Townsendites may lead Congress to consider raising the maximum federal contribution to the state old-age pension plans from the present $15 per person to $20 or even $30 a month. . . . " He felt it unlikely that Congress would do so since the Social Security Board flatly opposed this proposal. *Social Security* (Rev. edit., New York, 1939), p. 294.

7. Numerous observers at the time were quick to point this out. See "Congress Looks at Social Security," *Congressional Digest,* 18 (May, 1939), 133; "The Week," *The New Republic,* 100 (August 16, 1939), 30. See also remarks by Senator Pat Harrison (Miss. D) during the Senate debate on the social security amendments, *Congressional Record,* 76th Cong., 1st Sess., July 11, 1939, 8830.

8. To the indignation of Chairman Robert L. Doughton and others, Dr. Townsend had assured his followers that the advance from bill number H.R. 7154 to bill number H.R. 2 represented considerable Townsend progress. See *Hearings relative to the Social Security Act Amendments of 1939,* 76:1, vol. 1, 94. For text of H.R. 2, see *Ibid.,* 282–88.

9. "The support of these large and influential groups will help materially in getting the bill through Congress. . . . " TNRP, Inc., *General Welfare Act of 1937* (Chicago, 1937), p. 31.

10. *Hearings relative to the Social Security Act Amendments of 1939,* 76:1, vol. 1, 107.

11. Slichter did not agree with his fellow economists that prices would increase since he felt there was no reason to believe demand would be raised in the slightest. Dewhurst estimated that prices of consumer goods would increase 5–10 per cent or more. *Ibid.,* 793, 879.

12. Statement by Matthew Woll, *Hearings relative to the Social Security Act Amendments of 1939,* 76:1, vol. 2, 1351.

13. *Hearings relative to the Social Security Act Amendments of 1939,* 76:1, vol. 1, 519.

14. *Ibid.,* 544.

15. *Ibid.,* 548.

16. See Arthur Krock's analysis of this maneuver in New York *Times,*

May 25, 1939. After the Republican congressional gains in 1938, Majority Leader Sam Rayburn had declared that he was determined to force these new representatives to vote on the Townsend Plan through the public process of a roll call. Bertram M. Gross is completely mistaken in his assertion that a Townsend discharge petition " . . . forced members of the Ways and Means Committee to counter with an unfavorable report on the Townsend bill." *The Legislative Struggle, A Study in Social Combat* (New York, 1953), p. 332. No discharge petition was filed in 1939, and the bill was reported without any recommendation.

17. *Congressional Record,* 76:1, May 31, 1939, 6363.

18. *House Report 690,* 76th Cong., 1st Sess., May 25, 1939.

19. *Congressional Record,* 76:1, 6360.

20. After conferring with House leaders, the Rules Committee, which had at first refused to act upon the bill, reluctantly gave it a rule for debate and vote. New York *Times,* May 26, 1939.

21. *Congressional Record,* 76:1, 6359.

22. *Ibid.,* 6367.

23. Arizona—1, California—6, Colorado—1, Florida—4, Idaho—1, Indiana—1, Iowa—1, Kansas—1, Maine—3, Montana—1, New Hampshire—1, North Dakota—2, Ohio—5, Oklahoma—1, Oregon—3, Pennsylvania—1, South Dakota—2, Washington—2, Wisconsin—6. The debate is to be found in *Congressional Record,* 76:1, 6367–6463, 6518–24.

24. A total of eighteen congressmen from fourteen states spoke against the bill: California—1, Illinois—1, Kentucky—1, Louisiana—1, Massachusetts—2, Michigan—2, Missouri—1, New York—1, North Carolina—1, Ohio—2, Oklahoma—2, Tennessee—1, Virginia—1, Wisconsin—1.

25. *Congressional Record,* 76:1, 6521. Jeffery denied all such allegations. See *Townsend National Weekly,* June 23, 1939. The Townsend press claimed that in 1938 Dirksen had committed himself on the Townsend Plan in the following signed statement. ". . . I favor and will support and promote the principles embodied in H. R. 4199 . . . the General Welfare Act, or a similar measure." *Idem.*

26. *Congressional Record,* 76:1, 6524–25.

27. For the way the Townsend-endorsed congressmen divided on the vote, see Table XIII.

28. Farley's radio address is to be found in *Congressional Record, Appendix,* 76th Cong., 1st Sess., June 21, 1939, 2763.

29. *Hearings before the Committee on Finance on H. R. 6635,* United States Senate, 76th Cong., 1st Sess. (Washington, 1939).

30. *Ibid.,* 484.

31. New York *Times,* July 8, 1939, *Townsend National Weekly,* August 25, 1939.

32. See *Townsend National Weekly,* August 25, 1939, and *Congressional Record,* 76:1, 9010–23.

33. *National Townsend Weekly,* July 27, 1936.

34. In February, 1939, Hendricks introduced H. Jt. Res. 186 proposing an amendment to the Constitution relating to old-age assistance. He and Brewster introduced similar resolutions in April: H. Jt. Res. 269 and H. Jt. Res. 270.

35. *Senate Report 704,* 76th Cong., 1st Sess., June 30, 1939.

36. In Townsend literature and in speeches on the floor of Congress, it was asserted that 90 per cent of the workers and 95 per cent of the farmers would thereby be exempt from the tax.

37. *Hearings before the Special Committee to Investigate the Old Age Pension System pursuant to S. Res. 129,* United States Senate, 77th Cong., 1st Sess. (Washington, 1941), Part I.

38. *Hearings before the Committee on Ways and Means on Social Security Legislation,* U. S. House of Representatives, 79th Cong., 2nd Sess. (Washington, 1946), Part 6, 743–55.

39. *Hearings before the Committee on Ways and Means on H. R. 2892 and Other Bills,* U. S. House of Representatives, 81st Cong., 1st Sess. (Washington, 1949), Part 1; *Hearings before the Committee on Finance on H. R. 6000,* United States Senate, 81st Cong., 2nd Sess. (Washington, 1950), Part 2.

40. *Congressional Record,* 79th Cong., 2nd Sess., July 30, 1946, 10427, 10429–39.

41. Speech by Representative Abe Murdock· (Utah, D) before representatives of the American Pension Clubs of Illinois and Indiana on May 25, 1947. See *Congressional Record, Appendix,* 80th Cong., 1st Sess., May 27, 1947, A 2510.

NOTES TO CHAPTER SIX (Pages 125–155)

1. V. O. Key, Jr., *Political Parties and Pressure Groups* (1st edit., New York, 1942), pp. 212-13.

2. O. A. R. P., Ltd., *Townsend Club Manual* (Washington, 1935), p. 13.

3. Figures obtained from a comparison of recommended candidates contained in the *Townsend National Weekly* for November, 1936, and United States Congress, Clerk of the House of Representatives, *Statistics of the Presidential and Congressional Election of November 7, 1936* (Washington, 1936).

4. TNRP, Inc., *Townsend Club Manual* (Chicago, 1938), pp. 17–18.

5. Interview with Robert C. Townsend, Boston, Mass., September 9, 1951. The younger Townsend had worked closely with Jeffery.

6. *Congressional Record, Appendix,* 76th Cong., 1st Sess., May 31, 1939, 2339.

7. After leaving the Townsend Movement, Jeffery became an assistant to Republican Senator Ralph O. Brewster (Maine) and served for

a time as executive secretary to the Republican Senatorial Campaign Committee from which he resigned in 1951. He then became a staff member of the Republican Congressional Campaign Committee.

8. *Hearings before the Committee on Ways and Means relative to the Social Security Act Amendments of 1939*, U. S. House of Representatives, 76th Cong., 1st Sess. (Washington, 1939), vol. 1, 445-50, 656-57.

9. *Townsend National Weekly*, January 27, 1940.

10. A statement declaring that $144.47 was collected and spent by the Townsend National Voters League was filed by its treasurer, R. J. Webb, in a letter, dated January 1, 1941, to the Clerk of the U. S. House of Representatives, Townsend National Headquarters.

11. *Townsend National Weekly*, July 25, 1942.

12. *Townsend National Weekly*, October 31, 1942.

13. New York *Times*, June 17, 1936.

14. *National Townsend Weekly*, February 3, 1936.

15. There are no official records as to who such representatives were, the only compilation being the Honor Roll printed in the *Official Townsend Weekly*, June 3, 1935, which contained the names of *fifty-nine* instead of fifty-six. In answering a Townsend questionnaire as to their attitude toward the plan, nine congressmen whose names were not on the Honor Roll reported that they, too, had voted for the bill. *Townsend National Weekly*, December 30, 1935.

16. *Townsend National Weekly*, August 29, 1938.

17. New York *Times*, February 21, 1936.

18. New York *Times*, August 10, 1936. See also article by Harris G. Sims, "Andrews' Victory Surprises Florida," New York *Times*, August 16, 1936, IV.

19. New York *Times*, August 16, 1936, IV. Sims suggested that additional factors played a role in Andrews' victory: a poor turnout, lethargy among Carlton's friends, Andrews' advocacy of cross-channel ship competition.

20. New York *Times*, August 13, 1936.

21. See, in particular, *Townsend National Weekly*, June 30, 1939. News about the Trailblazers may be found in the *Weekly* from June through November, 1939.

22. Details of the Washington lobbying campaign of 1935 are to be found in the *Hearings before the Select Committee Investigating Old Age Pension Organizations pursuant to H. Res. 443*, U. S. House of Representatives, 74th Cong., 2nd Sess. (Washington, 1936), vol. 1, 146, *passim*.

23. Although The Townsend Plan, Inc., filed under the national lobbying act financial statements of large sums, the expenses ascribed to the Washington office have always been small: 1939—$12,082; 1952—

$22,063. Data obtained from the financial reports of the Townsend pressure organization.

24. *Congressional Record*, 74th Cong., 2nd Sess., February 19, 1936, 2355.

25. *National Townsend Weekly*, January 6, 1936.

26. *Congressional Record*, 75th Cong., 3rd Sess., March 24, 1938, 4057.

27. See Dr. Townsend's and Congressman McGroarty's explanations in *Hearings before the Select Committee Investigating Old Age Pension Organizations*, 74:2, vol. 1, 703–8, 785–86. See also *Congressional Record*, 74:2, 8756–58.

28. Sheridan Downey, *Why I Believe in the Townsend Plan* (Sacramento, 1936), pp. 10–11.

29. See telegram from Clements to Dr. Townsend, February 11, 1936, in *Hearings before the Select Committee Investigating Old Age Pension Organizations*, 74:2, vol. 1, 196.

30. See the testimony of Dr. Townsend and Congressman Sheppard on this conflict in *Hearings relative to the Social Security Act Amendments of 1939*, 76:1, vol. 1, 93–94, 646–48. For Congressman Crosby's version of this meeting see *Congressional Record, Appendix*, 75th Cong., 1st Sess., August 21, 1937, 2274–75.

31. *Townsend National Weekly*, May 31, 1937.

32. In a letter to a club secretary in Kansas, Dr. Townsend acknowledged having said that the court issue ". . . was infinitely more important to us than anything else before the public." *Townsend National Weekly*, July 5, 1937.

33. Legislative Representative Arthur L. Johnson's letters of resignation, including one refusing Dr. Townsend's plea to reconsider, are to be found in the *Congressional Record, Appendix*, 75th Cong., 1st Sess., 1537–38. The allegedly "shady" character referred to was one Blair Coan, who was accused of being connected with "Harry Daugherty and . . . the Ohio gang in the Harding administration."

34. *Congressional Record, Appendix*, 76:1, 2365.

35. See the speeches of Everett M. Dirksen (Ill., R), Dewey Short (Mo., R), Harry N. Routzohn (Ohio, R), Earl C. Michener (Mich., R), Hamilton Fish (N. Y., R), W. Sterling Cole (N. Y., R), Edward H. Rees (Kan., R) and John M. Vorys (Ohio, R). Most of them insisted that they had merely promised to secure consideration for the bill, not to vote for it; a few claimed that the bill was not in the best interests of the Townsendites.

36. Floyd M. Riddick, *The United States Congress: Organization and Procedure* (Washington, 1949), pp. 256–57.

37. *Townsend National Weekly*, December 16, 1944. That the discharge petition ever contained 217 valid signatures at one time was disputed by Congressman Earl C. Michener (Mich., R). He claimed

that the Townsend leaders had personally informed him that their petition had never lacked the one necessary signature to bring the total to 218. *Congressional Record, Appendix*, 78th Cong., 2nd Sess., December 18, 1944, A 4848. He admitted to 213 signatures, and since four had withdrawn, it is possible that 217 did sign but that not all were on the petition at the same time.

38. This total is arrived at by comparing the endorsement-election list of 1942 with the names of the 217 printed in the *Townsend National Weekly*, 1943–44. The thirteen were: J. William Fulbright (Ark., D), Karl M. LeCompte (Iowa, R), Ulysses S. Guyer (Kan., R), Paul H. Maloney (La., D), A. Leonard Allen (La., D), Fred L. Crawford (Mich., R), Clinton D. Anderson (N. M., D), James A. O'Leary (N. Y., D), Joseph A. Gavagan (N. Y., D), Jay La Fevre (N. Y., R), Herman P. Eberharter (Pa., D), Aime J. Forand (R. I., D), and Thaddeus F. B. Wasielewski (Wisc., D). Gavagan resigned from Congress in December, 1943, and O'Leary died in March, 1944.

39. A Townsend-sponsored constitutional amendment was favorably reported in 1940 by the Senate Committee on Judiciary. Two endorsed senators on the committee, Patrick A. McCarran (Nev., D) and Alexander Wiley (Wisc., R), voted for its recommendation, whereas Borah, who had been endorsed in 1936, opposed it. This resolution called for an amendment allowing the national government to tax its citizens for revenue to pay old-age pensions.

40. Sheridan Downey, *Why I Believe in the Townsend Plan* (Sacramento, 1936); *Pensions or Penury?* (New York, 1939); *Highways to Prosperity* (Chicago, 1940).

41. Congressman Hull delivered his attack upon Knutson in a speech before a Wisconsin Townsend Club, *Townsend National Weekly*, October 4, 1947.

42. *Townsend National Weekly*, October 25, 1947.

43. *Hearings before the Committee on Finance on H. R. 6000*, United States Senate, 81st Cong., 2nd Sess. (Washington, 1950), Part II, 677.

44. *Townsend National Weekly*, June 21, 1941.

45. See letter from Dr. Townsend to Southern congressmen in *Congressional Record, Appendix*, 78th Cong., 1st Sess., May 21, 1943, A 2547–A 2548.

NOTES TO CHAPTER SEVEN (Pages 156–168)

1. Official Bulletins No. 66 and 68, December 27, 1935 and January 10, 1936, Townsend National Headquarters.

2. See *National Townsend Weekly*, May 27, 1935, and November 4, 1935.

3. For details of this campaign see New York *Times*, November 20,

1935, through December 22, 1935. See also *Hearings before the Select Committee Investigating Old Age Pension Organizations pursuant to H. Res. 443*, U. S. House of Representatives, 74th Cong., 2nd Sess. (Washington, 1936), vol. 1, 145, 152–55.

4. New York *Times*, November 20, 1935; November 24, 1935.

5. New York *Times*, December 17, 1935.

6. New York *Times*, December 18, 1935.

7. Text in *Hearings before the Select Committee Investigating Old Age Pension Organizations*, 74:2, vol. 1, 1–2.

8. It is significant that the economic criticism of the plan was undertaken by non-political bodies in 1936: National Industrial Conference Board, *The Townsend Scheme* (N. I. C. B. Studies 219, New York, 1936); Tax Policy League, *The Townsend Plan Analyzed* (New York, 1936); *The Economic Meaning of the Townsend Plan, a University of Chicago round table . . .*, edited by H. D. Gideonse (Public Policy Pamphlet No. 20, Chicago, 1936); The Twentieth Century Fund, Committee on Old Age Security, *The Townsend Crusade* (New York, 1936).

9. See *Hearings before the Committee on Labor on H. R. 1623, etc.*, U. S. House of Representatives, 73rd Cong., 2nd Sess. (Washington, 1934), 47–176.

10. Richard L. Neuberger, "The Townsend Plan Exposed," *The Nation*, 141 (October 30, 1935), 505–7; Richard L. Neuberger and Kelley Loe, *An Army of the Aged* (Caldwell, 1936), Chapter IX, "Revolt!"

11. Edwin E. Witte to Merrill G. Murray, Director of the Unemployment Compensation Division, Social Security Board, December 13, 1935, Franklin D. Roosevelt Library.

12. Two other hypotheses regarding the cause of the investigation must be rejected. Luther Whiteman and Samuel L. Lewis find its genesis in a personal attack by Clements upon Congressman Percy L. Gassaway (Okla., D) during a radio debate. "The Honor of Congress was now at stake." *Glory Roads, The Psychological State of California* (New York, 1936), p. 118. This suggestion is naïve and far-fetched. A misconception of a more serious nature credits the Gallup Poll with responsibility for the inception of the investigation. Charles W. Smith claims that once the poll revealed Townsend strength as over-inflated, only 3.8 per cent of the public favoring the plan, Congress felt it had nothing to fear and, therefore, launched the investigation. *Public opinion in a Democracy: A Study in American Politics* (New York, 1939), pp. 413–14. Unfortunately, a desire to prove that polls constitute an antidote for pressure politics has led to an unwarranted assumption of fact. George Gallup and Saul F. Rae in their *The Pulse of Democracy* (New York, 1940), p. 147, are too cautious and circumspect in their story to advance such an assertion.

13. New York *Times*, January 30 ,1936.

14. New York *Times,* February 13, 1936.

15. Text in *Hearings before the Select Committee Investigating Old Age Pension Organizations,* 74:2, vol. 2, 1060.

16. New York *Times,* February 13, 1936.

17. Neuberger and Loe, *op. cit.,* p. 288, claim the reverse, that Clements was obviously eager to give testimony damaging to Dr. Townsend. The record does not bear this out. In my opinion, Clements, perhaps unwittingly, was one of the doctor's best witnesses. Perhaps because whatever applied to the doctor, held true for himself since Clements had been responsible for organizational affairs.

18. *Hearings before the Select Committee Investigating Old Age Pension Organizations,* 74:2, vol. 1, 457.

19. For the exact statement he intended to read see Dr. Francis E. Townsend, *New Horizons,* edited by Jesse G. Murray (Chicago, 1943), p. 202.

20. *Congressional Record,* 74th Cong., 2nd Sess., 8219–23.

21. New York *Times,* February 21–22, 1936.

22. *National Townsend Weekly,* March 23, 1936.

23. *National Townsend Weekly,* May 25, 1936. Although the *Weekly* ascribed to Tolan the statement that fifty new affidavits were being received each day, the number of clubs so responding was never again reported.

24. See dispatch by Richard L. Neuberger, "Townsend Dimes Fall Off," New York *Times,* April 12, 1936, IV.

NOTES TO CHAPTER EIGHT (Pages 169–198)

1. See letter from M. H. McIntyre, Assistant to the President, to Dr. F. E. Townsend, December 18, 1934, informing the doctor that an interview with the President could not be arranged, and suggesting that he see the Secretary of Labor (Franklin D. Roosevelt Library). The doctor had written to the President on December 17, 1934.

2. *Official Townsend Weekly,* February 4, 1935.

3. Stanley High to Stephan Early, August 25, 1935 (Franklin D. Roosevelt Library).

4. See telegram, dated October 21, 1935, from Congressman Martin F. Smith (Wash., D) to James E. Farley expressing anxiety over this situation. See also letter, dated January 15, 1936, from the Comptroller of the Treasury to the White House suggesting the importance of an immediate meeting between Dr. Townsend and the President (Franklin D. Roosevelt Library).

5. *National Townsend Weekly,* June 12, 1936.

6. Herbert Harris, "That Third Party," *Current History,* 45 (October, 1936), 83.

7. New York *Times,* May 31, 1936; June 2, 1936.

8. See *National Townsend Weekly*, June 29, 1936; New York *Times*, June 23, 1936. Dr. Townsend did not repudiate Smith until after the two had parted in November, 1936.

9. *National Townsend Weekly*, June 15, 1936.

10. New York *Times*, June 20, 1936.

11. See his radio lecture of December 22, 1935. Reverend Charles E. Coughlin, *The Townsend Plan* (Royal Oak, 1935), p. 2.

12. See New York *Times*, July 14, 1936; July 15, 1936.

13. *Congressional Record*, 75th Cong., 3rd Sess., March 24, 1938, 4052. For a description of the convention see the issue devoted entirely to its proceedings, *National Townsend Weekly*, July 27, 1936. It contains no mention of such a proposal. On the other hand it excludes Gomer Smith's controversial speech, so that this issue is not the most accurate source for the convention's proceedings. See, therefore, New York *Times*, July 16–20, 1936 and articles by Frank R. Kent in the Baltimore *Sun*, July 15–17, 1936.

14. New York *Times*, July 24, 1936.

15. New York *Times*, August 14, 1936; September 22, 1936.

16. *Literary Digest*, 122 (August 22, 1936), 5.

17. *National Townsend Weekly*, October 19, 1936.

18. In particular see their joint statement in the New York *Times*, July 26, 1936, as well as the New York *Times* and the *Weekly*, September through October, 1936.

19. New York *Times*, October 8, 1936; October 11, 1936, IV.

20. New York *Times*, October 11, 1936, IV.

21. Text is in *Townsend National Weekly*, November 2, 1936; New York *Times*, November 3, 1936.

22. New York *Times*, October 18–22, 1936.

23. New York *Times*, August 16, 1936, IV.

24. *Townsend National Weekly*, July 20, 1940. The official vote on the resolution was 12,000 to 3. A somewhat more tempestuous meeting was pictured in the New York *Times*, July 5, 1940.

25. *Townsend National Weekly*, August 17, 1940; New York *Times*, August 30, 1940. Attachés of the senator's office disclaimed any intention on the part of McNary to endorse the plan.

26. *National Townsend Weekly*, June 22, 1936.

27. New York *Times*, June 26, 1936. Since Senator Lewis B. Schwellenbach failed to attend the meeting of the Democratic Resolutions Committee, the Washington delegation's resolution was never presented. The Washington and Colorado delegations to the Prohibition Party Convention also came with Townsend planks, support for which was indicated by the chairman of the California delegation. New York *Times*, May 5, 1936.

28. *Townsend National Weekly*, July 13, 1940.

29. *Townsend National Weekly*, June 26, 1943.

30. *Official Townsend Weekly*, May 6, 1935.

31. Dr. Townsend to Robert E. Clements, September 4, 1935, *Hearings before the Select Committee Investigating Old Age Pension Organizations pursuant to H. Res. 443*, U. S. House of Representatives, 74th Cong., 2nd Sess. (Washington, 1936), vol. 1, 596–97.

32. See Congressmen McGroarty's and Gomer Smith's versions of these episodes in *Congressional Record*, 74th Cong., 2nd Sess., June 2, 1936, 8756–58, *Congressional Record*, 75:3, March 24, 1938, 4052–53.

33. See *National Townsend Weekly*, December 23, 1935.

34. *National Townsend Weekly*, September 4, 1936. [Italics added].

35. *Townsend National Weekly*, November 16, 1940.

36. Letter, dated March 9, 1943, from Dr. Townsend to S. Bainbridge, editor, *Townsend National Weekly*, Townsend National Headquarters. Their first step, he informed his editor, was to "round up" a dozen national leaders and induce them to call a convention at which a party could be organized.

37. *Townsend National Weekly*, April 24, 1948.

38. Baltimore *Sun*, April 28, 1948, quoted in the *Congressional Record, Appendix*, 80th Cong., 2nd Sess., April 30, 1948, A 2632.

39. According to one news report, which remains unverifiable in terms of official Townsend records, Dr. Townsend came to the convention prepared to urge the clubs to commit themselves to Wallace, but his resolution never got beyond the Townsend National Council. See the Washington *Post*, June 6, 1948. For the official transcript of the convention see Eighth Convention of Townsend Clubs, *Proceedings* (Washington, 1948).

40. See *Townsend National Weekly*, July 31, 1948; New York *Times*, July 23, 1948.

41. Interview with Robert C. Townsend in February, 1950, Cleveland, Ohio.

42. Progressive Party, *Freedom and Abundance, The Platform of the Progressive Party* (New York, 1948), p. 16.

43. *Townsend National Weekly*, October 3, 1938.

44. California data obtained from State of California, Secretary of State, *Statement of Vote, General Elections* for years 1938, 1940, 1942 and from the United States Congress, Clerk of the House of Representatives, *Statistics of the Congressional Election of November 8, 1938* (Washington, 1938), pp. 2–3.

45. For some unexplained reason, the Townsend Party label was not listed after Merriam's name on the official *Statement of Vote*, although he secured the most votes in the Townsend primary.

46. Interview with John C. Cuneo, August, 1950, Los Angeles, California.

47. *Townsend National Weekly*, January 9, 1943.

48. In a special bulletin to the California Townsend Clubs, dated

on May 8, 1943, Dr. Townsend insisted that the Townsend Party had interfered with the pressure organization's activities. Clubs were requested to abstain from any further Townsend Party activity. Bulletin at Townsend National Headquarters.

49. State of California, Secretary of State, *Statement of Vote at Primary Election . . . August 28, 1934 . . .* (Sacramento, 1934), pp. 5–6.

50. Los Angeles *Times,* September 21, 1934.

51. Los Angeles *Times,* October 24, 1934.

52. *The Modern Crusader,* 1 (October 17, 1934), 16. At this date the journal was titled, "Official Organ of the O. A. R. P., Ltd."

53. Joseph Alsop and Robert Kintner, "Merchandising Miracles; Sheridan Downey and the Pension Business," *The Saturday Evening Post,* 212 (September 16, 1939), 86.

54. Letter from F. E. Townsend to Mr. A. R. White, Alhambra, California, July 19, 1934. *Hearings before the Select Committee Investigating Old Age Pension Organizations,* 74:2, vol. 1, 484.

55. Upton Sinclair, *I, Candidate for Governor: and How I Got Licked* (New York, 1935), pp. 97–98.

56. California, Assembly, *Journal of the Assembly,* 51st Sess. (Sacramento, 1935), vol. 1, 163–65, 707, 862–66. California, Senate, *Journal of the Senate,* 51st Sess. (Sacramento, 1935), 168–69, 183, 475, 567–72.

57. California, Assembly, *Journal of the Assembly,* vol. 1, 861.

58. See testimony by William H. McMasters and Dr. Townsend in *Hearings before the Committee on Ways and Means relative to the Social Security Act Amendments of 1939,* U.S. House of Representatives, 76th Cong., 1st Sess. (Washington, 1939), vol. 1, 313–44, 612–14, 618. Details of Republican strategy are derived from an interview in March, 1951, Boston, Massachusetts, with a Republican who occupied a position within the inner circles of party leadership at the time of the Republican-Townsend agreement. His request for anonymity must be honored.

59. Although Dr. Townsend later disclaimed any endorsement of McMasters, he had addressed a letter to the Ballot Law Commission of Massachusetts on July 29, 1938 which contained the following: "The use of the words 'Townsend Recovery Plan' by William H. McMasters, in his campaign for Governor in the Republican primary or on election day, meets with my approval." Cited in *Hearings relative to the Social Security Act Amendments of 1939,* 76:1, vol. 1, 612–13.

60. *Ibid.,* 323. [Italics added]

61. See *Congressional Record,* 76th Cong., 1st Sess., April 13, 1939, 4181.

62. Albuquerque *Tribune,* August 19, 1936.

63. New York *Times,* March 10, 1935, IV; March 21, 1935.

64. New York *Times,* May 10, 1939; May 17, 1939. *Townsend National Weekly,* June 2, 1939.

65. *Townsend National Weekly,* October 6, 1939. All the clubs had been instructed to campaign against the measure.

66. State of Oregon, Secretary of State, *Abstract of Votes . . . November, 1938 . . .* (looseleaf, unnumbered, 1938).

67. State of Idaho, Secretary of State, *Twenty-sixth Biennial Report of the Secretary of State of Idaho* (Boise, 1942), "Abstract of Votes . . ." (Unnumbered attachment).

68. According to the *Townsend National Weekly,* August 5, 1944, the following number of signatures had been obtained: Arizona—22,000; California—290,000; Oregon—38,000; Washington—71,000. See *Townsend National Weekly,* August 26, 1944, for the features of the four initiatives.

69. Figures from TNRP, Inc., financial records, 1943 and 1944. More than $108,000 was spent in California alone of which $39,046 was donated locally and over $69,000 was contributed by the national organization.

70. State of Oregon, Secretary of State, *Abstract of Votes . . . November, 1946 . . .* (looseleaf, unnumbered, 1946).

71. State of Oregon, Secretary of State, *Abstract of Votes . . . November, 1948* (single sheet, unnumbered, 1948).

72. State of Washington, Secretary of State, *Abstract of Votes . . . State-General Election, November 2, 1948* (Olympia, 1948), 2. The vote was 420,751 to 352,642 on Initiative No. 172. The Townsend leaders opposed a more liberal initiative sponsored by the Washington Pension Union in 1950 which was defeated.

73. State of Arizona, Secretary of State, *Official Canvass of Vote on Initiative and Referendum Measures, General Election, November 7, 1950* (single sheet, unnumbered, 1950).

NOTES TO CHAPTER NINE (Pages 199–214)

1. For a fascinating study of the League, see Peter H. Odegard, *Pressure Politics, The Story of the Anti-Saloon League* (New York, 1928). I have relied upon this source as a basis for drawing comparisons between the League and the Townsend Movement.

2. The Railroad Retirement Act of 1934 had required railroads to contribute to a pension fund for their superannuated employees. It subsequently was invalidated by the Supreme Court in 1935.

3. Townsend claims of more than 12,000 clubs, during the 1950's, constituted typical pressure group exaggeration. For a much more realistic picture of paid membership and club strength see Tables I and II in Chapter Three.

4. *Townsend National Weekly,* April 24, 1948.

5. Not all multi-group organizations avoid these problems. Note the problems arising from an identification of Philip Randolph with the

National Council for a Permanent FEPC. Louis C. Kesselman, *The Social Politics of FEPC* (Chapel Hill, 1948), pp. 35–37.

6. Virtually the same relationship holds true for George McLain and his California pension movement which operates under the title, the California Institute of Social Welfare. The organizational and political liabilities inherent in their arrangement are explored in the study by Frank A. Pinner, Paul Jacobs and Philip Selznick, *Old Age and Political Behavior, A Case Study* (Berkeley, 1959).

7. In contrast, the "perceived enemies" of the aged members of the McLain movement in California emerged not merely as a result of internal propaganda, but because the latter coincided with and shaped preexisting political beliefs and images of distrust. The set of four "enemies" eliciting the highest number of such designations from the old age assistance recipients in and outside the McLain movement were: Chamber of Commerce, State Senator Fred Weybret, big business, and boards of supervisors. *Ibid.*, pp. 169–76.

8. See Blue Carstenson and James O'Brien, "Report to the National Chairman of Senior Citizens for Kennedy . . . An Evaluation of the Senior Citizens for Kennedy Campaign Effort" (presumably Washington, D.C., ca. 1961), 7 pp., [mimeographed].

9. Frank G. Dickinson, "Economic Aspects of the Aging of Our Population," in T. Lynn Smith, ed., *Problems of America's Aging Population* (Gainesville, 1951), pp. 79–82.

10. Robert J. Havighurst, "Old Age—An American Problem," *Journal of Gerontology*, 4 (October, 1949), 299.

11. Ewan Clague, "The Aging Population and Programs of Security," *The Milbank Memorial Fund Quarterly*, 18 (October, 1940), 347–48.

12. Clark Tibbitts, "Politics of Aging: Pressure For Change" (Washington, D.C., 1960), 2–3 [typescript], paper delivered before the Fifth International Congress of Gerontology, August, 1960.

13. The President's Commission on the Health Needs of the Nation, *Building America's Health, Findings and Recommendations, A Report to the President* (Washington, 1952), vol. 1, 71–72.

BIBLIOGRAPHY

BOOKS

Arnold, Thurman W. *The Folklore of Capitalism*. New Haven: Yale University Press, 1937.

Bates, Ernest, and Williams, Alan. *American Hurly-Burly*. New York: Robert M. McBridge & Co., 1937.

Bond, Floyd A., *et al. Our Needy Aged: A California Study of a National Problem*. New York: Henry Holt & Co., 1954.

Burns, James M. *Congress on Trial*. New York: Harper & Brothers, 1949.

Cantril, Hadley. *The Psychology of Social Movements*. New York: John Wiley & Sons, 1941.

Cavan, Ruth S., and Associates. *Personal Adjustment in Old Age*. Chicago: Science Research Associates, Inc., 1949.

Cleland, Robert Glass. *California in Our Time, 1900–1940*. New York: Alfred A. Knopf, 1947.

Coyle, David Cushman. *Age Without Fear*. Washington: National Home Library Foundation, 1937.

Crouch, Winston W., and McHenry, Dean E. *California Government, Politics, and Administration*. Revised edit. Berkeley: University of California Press, 1949.

de Schweinitz, Karl. *England's Road to Social Security, From . . . 1349 to . . . 1942*. Philadelphia: University of Pennsylvania Press, 1943.

Dorman, Morgan J. *Age Before Booty; an explanation of the Townsend plan*. New York: G. P. Putnam's Sons, 1936.

Douglas, Paul H. *Social Security in the United States; an analysis and an appraisal of the Federal social security act*. New York: McGraw-Hill Book Co., 1936.

Downey, Sheridan. *Highways to Prosperity*. Chicago: Townsend National Weekly, Inc., 1940.

———. *Pensions and Penury*. New York: Harper & Brothers, 1939.

237

———. *Why I Believe in the Townsend Plan.* Sacramento: Sheridan Downey Publishing Co., 1936.

Epstein, Abraham. *Insecurity: A Challenge to America.* 3rd revised edit. New York: Random House, 1936.

———. *The Challenge of the Aged.* New York: The Vanguard Press, 1928.

Farrelly, David and Hinderaker, Ivan. (ed.) *The Politics of California.* New York: Ronald Press Co., 1951.

Gallup, George, and Rae, Saul F. *The Pulse of Democracy.* New York: Simon & Schuster, 1940.

Gross, Bertram M. *The Legislative Struggle; A Study in Social Combat.* New York: McGraw-Hill Book Co., 1953.

Herring, Pendleton. *The Politics of Democracy.* New York: Rinehart & Co., 1940.

Hofstadter, Richard. *The American Political Tradition and the Men Who Made It.* New York: Alfred A. Knopf, 1949.

Hohman, Helen F. *Old Age In Sweden, A Program of Social Security.* Washington: Government Printing Office, 1940.

Industrial Relations Research Association. *The Aged and Society.* Champaign, Illinois: Industrial Relations Research Association, 1950.

Kent, Frank R. *Without Grease; political behavior, 1934–1936, and a blueprint for America's most vital presidential election.* New York: Wm. Morrow & Co., 1936.

Kesselman, Louis C. *The Social Politics of FEPC: A Study in Reform Pressure Movements.* Chapel Hill: University of North Carolina Press, 1948.

Key, V. O., Jr. *Political Parties and Pressure Groups.* New York: Thomas Y. Crowell Co., 1942.

———. *Southern Politics in State and Nation.* New York: Alfred A. Knopf, 1949.

Lafitte, Francois. *Britain's Way to Social Security.* London: Pilot Press, 1945.

Leven, Maurice, Moulton, Harold G., and Warburton, Clark. *America's Capacity to Consume.* Washington: The Brookings Institution, 1934.

Lipson, Leslie. *The Politics of Equality, New Zealand's Adventures in Democracy.* Chicago: The University of Chicago Press, 1948.

Myers, Margaret G. *Monetary Proposals for Social Reform.* New York: Columbia University Press, 1940.

Neuberger, Richard L., and Loe, Kelley. *An Army of the Aged.* Caldwell: The Caxton Printers, Ltd., 1936.

Odegard, Peter. *Pressure Politics: The Story of the Anti-Saloon League.* New York: Columbia University Press, 1928.

Parsons, Talcott. *Essays in Sociological Theory, Pure and Applied.* Glencoe: The Free Press, 1949.

Perkins, Francis. *The Roosevelt I Knew.* New York: The Viking Press, 1946.

Pinner, Frank A., Jacobs, Paul, and Selznick, Philip. *Old Age and Political Behavior, A Case Study.* Berkeley: University of California Press, 1959.

Pollak, Otto. *Social Adjustments in Old Age.* New York: Social Science Research Council, 1948.

Riddick, Floyd M. *The United States Congress; Organization and Procedure.* Washington: National Capitol Publishers, Inc., 1949.

Roosevelt, Nicholas. *The Townsend Plan; Taxing for Sixty.* New York: Doubleday, 1936.

Schattschneider, E. E. *Party Government.* New York: Farrar & Rinehart, Inc., 1942.

Sinclair, Upton. *I, Candidate For Governor; and How I Got Licked.* New York: Farrar & Rinehart, Inc., 1935.

Smith, Charles W., Jr. *Public Opinion in a Democracy; A Study in American Politics.* New York: Prentice-Hall, Inc., 1939.

Socialt Tidsskrift (ed.). *Social Denmark, A Survey of the Danish Social Legislation.* Copenhagen: Socialt Tidsskrift, 1945.

Stewart, Maxwell S. *Social Security.* New York: W. W. Norton & Co., 1939 (revised).

The Unofficial Observer. *American Messiahs.* New York: Simon & Schuster, 1935.

Townsend, Dr. Francis E. *New Horizons.* Edited by Jesse G. Murray. Chicago: J. L. Stewart Publishing Co., 1943.

Truman, David B. *The Governmental Process.* New York: Alfred A. Knopf, 1951.

Twentieth Century Fund. Committee on Old Age Security. *The Townsend Crusade.* New York: Twentieth Century Fund, Inc., 1936.

Wecter, Dixon. *The Age of the Great Depression, 1929–1941.* New York: Macmillan Co., 1948.

Wells, H. G. *The New America, The New World.* New York: Macmillan Co., 1935.

Whiteman, Luther, and Lewis, Samuel L. *Glory Roads, The Psychological State of California.* New York: Thomas Y. Crowell Co., 1936.

Wilson, Sir Arnold T., M.P., and MacKay, G. S. *Old Age Pensions: an historical and critical study.* London: Oxford University Press, 1941.

Wright, David McCord. *The Creation of Purchasing Power; A Study in the Problem of Economic Stabilization.* Cambridge: Harvard University Press, 1942.

PERIODICAL ARTICLES

Aikman, Duncan. "Lemke's New Party, and Three Key Men," New York *Times Magazine,* July 26, 1936, 6–7, 18.

———. "Townsendism: Old Time Religion," New York *Times Magazine,* March 8, 1936, 5, 25.

Alsop, Joseph W., Jr., and Kintner, Robert E. "Merchandizing Miracles: Sheridan Downey and the Pension Business," *The Saturday Evening Post,* 212, September 16, 1939, 5–7, 85–90.

Anderson, George E. "A Pension Planner's Carnival," *Banking,* 31, January, 1939, 27.

Barton, Bruce. "How to Fix Everything," *Vanity Fair,* 36, August, 1931, 31, 70.

Bliven, Bruce. "The Midwestern Messiah," *The New Republic,* 86, May 6, 1936, 365.

Bonn, M. J. "The Making of a National State," *The Political Quarterly,* 8, October-December, 1937, 587–96.

Chase, Stuart. "On the Paradox of Plenty," *The New Republic,* 73, January 18, 1933, 258–60.

———. "Our Capacity to Produce," *Harpers,* 170, February, 1934, 343–52.

Clague, Ewan. "The Aging Population and Programs of Security," *The Milbank Memorial Fund Quarterly,* 18, October, 1940, 345–58.

Clapper, Raymond. "Middle Age Money-Go-Round," *Survey Graphic,* 27, November, 1938, 533–37.

"Congress Looks At Social Security," *Congressional Digest,* 18, May, 1939, 133.

Conyngton, Mary. "Extent and Distribution of Old Age Dependency in the United States," *Monthly Labor Review,* 38, January, 1934, 1–10.

Crowell, Chester T. "The Townsend Plan—A Challenge to Congress," *The American Mercury,* 34, April, 1935, 456–60.

Fisher, Irving. "The Stamped Scrip Plan," *The New Republic,* 73, December 21, 1932, 163–64.

Folsom, Joseph K. "Old Age as a Sociological Problem," *American Journal of Orthopsychiatry,* 10, January, 1940, 30–39.

Harris, Herbert. "Dr. Townsend's Marching Soldiers," *Current History,* 43, February, 1936, 455–62.

———. "That Third Party," *Current History,* 45, October, 1936, 76–92.

Havighurst, Robert J. "Old Age—An American Problem," *Journal of Gerontology,* 4, October 1949, 298–304.

"Health Needs of the Nation's Aging," *Geriatrics,* 8, February, 1953, 102–4.

Johnson, Rudolph. "Colorado Old Age Pensions," *The Nation,* 147, October 22, 1938, 436.

Keynes, John Maynard. "The World's Economic Outlook," *The Atlantic Monthly*, 149, May, 1932, 521–26.

Lake, Stuart N. "If Money, Survey of Townsend Plan Promotion in San Diego," *The Saturday Evening Post*, 207, May 11, 1935, 12–13, 121–27.

MacWilliams, Carey. "Ham and Eggs," *The New Republic*, 100, October 25, 1939, 331–33.

——. "Pension Politics in California, II. Who Shall Represent the Aged?" *The Nation*, 169, October 1, 1949, 320–22.

McKee, Oliver, Jr. "The Townsend Plan," *Commonweal*, 23, February 7, 1936, 399–401.

Mechem, John L. "Did Townsend Win in Michigan?" *Review of Reviews*, 93, March, 1936, 45, 74.

Menefee, Selden C. "Old Folks Go Union," *Survey Mid-Monthly*, 74, January, 1938, 9–10.

Messinger, Sheldon L. "Organizational Transformation: A Case Study of a Declining Social Movement," *American Sociological Review*, 20, January, 1955, 3–10.

Miller, Alvin J. "Colorado's Experience: A Warning to States Where Townsendites Are Gaining," *Annalist: a magazine of finance, commerce and economics*, 52, September 28, 1938, 430.

Millikin, Seymour J. "$200 a Month at Sixty," *Forum*, 92, December, 1934, 326–29.

Moore, Harry T. "Just Folks in Utopia," *The New Republic*, 85, November 13, 1935, 9–11.

Neuberger, Richard L. "The Old People's Crusade," *Harpers*, 172, March, 1936, 426–38.

——. "The Townsend Plan Exposed," *The Nation*, 141, October 30, 1935, 505–7.

——. "Townsend Racket: New Phase," *The Nation*, 147, September 17, 1938, 259–60.

Nordyke, Lewis. "Report to the Editor; Old Age in Our Town," *The Saturday Evening Post*, 216, November 20, 1943, 6.

Owen, Russell. "Townsend Talks of his Plan and Hopes," New York *Times Magazine*, December 29, 1935, 3, 15.

Patch, Buel W. "Agitation for Pension and Scrip Schemes," *Editorial Research Reports*, 2, October 1, 1938, 227–44.

Peterson, Frank. "Concerning the Townsend Plan," *The New Republic*, 81, January 23, 1935, 305–6.

Richberg, Donald R. "The Townsend Delusion," *Review of Reviews*, 93, February, 1936, 24–27.

Roosevelt, Nicholas, and Townsend, Dr. Francis E. "Townsend Pensions: Sense or Nonsense? A Debate," *Forum*, 95, May, 1936, 282–87.

Schnapper, M. B. "Gold Bricks for the Aged," *The Nation*, 140, January 9, 1935, 43–44.

Silva, Louis. "The Townsendites and the Economists," *The New Republic*, 98, March 15, 1939, 168.

Swing, Raymond Gram. "Dr. Townsend Solves It All," *The Nation*, 140, March 6, 1935, 268–70.

Thomas, Norman. "The Townsend Plan and Cough Drops," *Vital Speeches*, 2, September 1, 1936, 275–78.

"Threat of Pension Pressure Groups," *Tax Policy*, 7, November, 1939, 1–7.

"Townsend's $200 a Month," *The New Republic*, 81, December 19, 1934, 153–54.

Ward, Paul W. "How Strong is the Townsend Plan?" *The Nation*, 142, January 8, 1936, 37–38.

"The Week," *The New Republic*, 100, August 16, 1939, 30.

White, Elwyn B. "One Man's Meat," *Harpers*, 179, October, 1939, 553–56.

"The Wrong Way to Start a New Party," *The New Republic*, 87, July 29, 1936, 338–39.

PAMPHLETS AND MISCELLANEOUS

Bittleman, Alexander. *The Townsend Plan; What it is and what it is not.* New York: Workers Library Publishers, 1936.

Carstenson, Blue and O'Brien, James. "Report to the National Chairman of Senior Citizens for Kennedy . . . An Evaluation of the Senior Citizens for Kennedy Campaign Effort." Presumably Washington, D.C., ca. 1961. [mimeographed].

Coughlin, Reverend Charles E. *The Townsend Plan.* Lecture, December 22, 1935. Royal Oak: The Radio League of the Little Flower, 1935.

Dick, Samuel M. *$200 a Month in Action.* 3rd edit. Watertown: Leroy S. Eaton, 1935.

The Economic Meaning of the Townsend Plan; a University of Chicago round table . . . Public Policy Pamphlet No. 20. Chicago: The University of Chicago Press, 1936.

Lindsay, Arthur G. "The Washington State Old Age Pension Union, A Political Pressure Group." Unpublished Masters Thesis. Seattle: University of Washington, 1940.

Miller, H. B. M. *The Answer: A Complete Analysis of the Plan.* 2nd edit. San Francisco: Miles & Scott, Inc., 1935.

Millikin, William V. B. *Sermon on the Townsend Plan.* Ft. Lauderdale, Florida: V. B. William Millikin, n.d.

Milne, Richard. *That Man Townsend.* Long Beach: Prosperity Publishing Co., 1935.

National Industrial Conference Board, Inc. *The Townsend Scheme.* Studies, No. 129. New York: National Industrial Conference Board, Inc., 1936.

Progressive Party. *Freedom and Abundance, The Platform of the Progressive Party.* New York: Progressive Party, 1948.

Tax Policy League. *The Townsend Plan Analyzed.* New York: Tax Policy League, 1936.

Thompson, Harry H. *A Common Sense Analysis of the Townsend Plan.* Kansas City: Harry H. Thompson, 1936.

Tibbitts, Clark. "Politics of Aging: Pressure for Change." Washington, D.C., 1960. Paper delivered before the Fifth International Congress of Gerontology, August, 1960. [Typescript].

West, George E. *The Spot-Light of Truth on the Townsend Plan.* Revised edit. Chicago: P. W. Treloar, 1936.

GOVERNMENT SOURCES (UNITED STATES)

House of Representatives

Committee on Labor. *Hearings on H. R. 1623, etc.* 73rd Cong., 2nd Sess., 1934.

Committee on Ways and Means. *Hearings on H. R. 1, etc.* 72nd Cong., 1st Sess., 1932.

———. *Hearings on H. R. 4120.* 74th Cong., 1st Sess., 1935.

———. *Hearings relative to the Social Security Act Amendments of 1939.* 76th Cong., 1st Sess., Vol. 1, 2, and 3, 1939.

Committee on Ways and Means. *House Report No. 690.* 76th Cong., 1st Sess., May 25, 1939.

———. *Hearings on Social Security Legislation.* 79th Cong., 2nd Sess., Part 6, 1946.

———. *Hearings on Bills referred to the Committee.* 80th Cong., 1st Sess., 1947.

———. *Hearings on H.R. 2892 and Other Bills.* 81st Cong., 1st Sess., Part 1, 1949.

Select Committee Investigating Old Age Pension Organizations pursuant to H. Res. 443. *Hearings.* 74th Cong., 2nd Sess., Vol. 1 and 2, 1936.

Senate

Committee on Finance. *Hearings on S. 1130.* 74th Cong., 1st Sess., 1935.

———. *Hearings on H. R. 6635,* 76th Cong., 1st Sess., 1939.

———. *Hearings on H.R. 5417.* 77th Cong., 1st Sess., 1941.

———. *Hearings on S. 1932.* 77th Cong., 1st Sess., 1941.

———. *Hearings on H. R. 7378,* 77th Cong., 2nd Sess., 1942.

———. *Hearings on H.R. 6000.* 81st Cong., 2nd Sess., Part 2, 1950.

Committee on the Judiciary. *Senate Report No. 704.* 76th Cong., 1st Sess., June 30, 1939.

Special Committee to Investigate the Old Age Pension System pursuant to S. Res. 129. *Hearings.* 77th Cong., 1st Sess., Part 1, 1941.

Special Committee to Investigate Unemployment and Relief pursuant to S. Res. 37. *Hearings.* 75th Cong., 3rd Sess., Vol. 1 and 2, 1938.

Miscellaneous

President's Committee on Economic Security. *Report to the President.* Washington: Government Printing Office, 1935.

———. *Supplement to Report to the President.* Washington: Government Printing Office, 1935.

President's Commission on the Health Needs of the Nation. *Building America's Health, Findings and Recommendations, A Report to the President.* Washington: Government Printing Office, 1952.

Congressional Record. 61st through 82nd Congress.

Dahlberg, Arthur. *Recovery Plans.* Monograph No. 25. Temporary National Economic Committee. Washington: Government Printing Office, 1940.

The National Archives. The Franklin D. Roosevelt Library, Hyde Park, New York. Files on the Townsend Plan.

National Resources Committee. *Consumer Incomes in the United States: Their Distribution in 1935–1936.* Washington: Government Printing Office, 1938.

United States Congress. Clerk of the House of Representatives. *Statistics of Congressional Elections* for the years 1936–1952. Washington: Government Printing Office.

United States Department of Commerce. Bureau of the Census. Fifteenth through eighteenth *Census of the United States,* 1930 through 1960. *Population.* Vol. 2. Washington: Government Printing Office.

United States Department of Labor, Bureau of Labor Statistics. *Employment and Economic Status of Older Men and Women.* (Bulletin No. 1092), Washington: Government Printing Office, 1952.

GOVERNMENT SOURCES (State)

State of Arizona. Secretary of State. *Official Canvass of General Election Returns, November 7, 1944.* Single sheet, unnumbered, 1944.

———. Secretary of State. *Official Canvass of Vote on Initiative and Referendum Measures, General Election, November 7, 1950.* Single sheet, unnumbered, 1950.

State of California. Secretary of State. *Statement of Vote, General Elections* for the years 1938, 1940, 1942. Sacramento, California.

———. Secretary of State. *Statement of Vote at Primary Election . . . August 28, 1934. . . .* Sacramento, California.

————. Assembly. *Journal of the Assembly, 51st. Sess.* Vol. 1. Sacramento, California, 1935.

————. Senate. *Journal of the Senate, 51st Sess.* Sacramento, California, 1935.

State of Idaho. Secretary of State. *Twenty-sixth Biennial Report of the Secretary of State of Idaho.* "Abstract of Votes...." Boise, 1942.

State of Massachusetts. Secretary of the Commonwealth. *Election Statistics* for the years 1936, 1938. Boston: State Printers, 1937, 1939.

State of Oregon. Secretary of State. *Abstract of Votes* . . . . for years 1938–1950. Single sheet, unnumbered.

State of Washington. Secretary of State. *Abstract of Votes* .... for years 1944–1950. Olympia, Washington.

TOWNSEND SOURCES

Pamphlets

Brinton, J. W. *The Townsend Plan, National Recovery Program, Ready Reference.* 2nd edit. illustrated. Chicago: OARP, Ltd., 1936.

————. *The Townsend National Recovery Plan.* 3rd edit. revised. Chicago: The Townsend National Weekly, 1936.

Old Age Revolving Pensions, Ltd. *Old Age Revolving Pensions, A National Plan. . . . Proposed by Dr. F. E. Townsend.* (At least 3 editions.) Long Beach: OARP, Ltd., 1934.

————. *Questions and Answers.* Long Beach: OARP, Ltd., n.d.

————. *The Townsend Plan.* (At least 2 editions.) New York and Washington: OARP, Ltd., 1935.

————. *The Townsend Pension Bill Before Congress.* Townsend Booklet No. 2. Los Angeles: OARP, Ltd., 1935.

Owen, Willis. *Making Money for the Merchant.* Chicago: The Townsend National Weekly, 1937.

Townsend, Dr. Francis E. Series of pamphlets. Chicago: Townsend National Weekly, Inc., n.d.
  "The American Farmer"
  "The American Workingman"
  "Dollars and Sense"
  "Insurance for All"
  "The Land and The Market"
  "The Market! The Market! The Market!"
  "A Message to the Businessmen of America"
  "A Message to the Physicians of America"
  "National Insurance for All"
  "Questions and Answers"
  "They Said It Couldn't Be Done"
  "Use the Machines of America"

"Where Is the Money Coming From?"

———. *The Townsend National Recovery Plan, New Reference Book.* 2nd edit. Chicago: Dr. Francis E. Townsend, 1941.

Townsend National Recovery Plan, Inc. *General Welfare Act of 1937.* Chicago: TNRP, Inc., 1937.

Townsend National Weekly, Inc. *33 Questions and Answers.* Chicago: Townsend National Weekly, Inc., 1938.

———. *Townsend Youth Association Manual.* Chicago: Townsend National Weekly, Inc., 1940.

The Townsend Plan, Inc. *The Townsend Legionnaire, A Business Insurance Program.* Cleveland: The Townsend Plan, Inc., n.d. (approximately 1950).

———. *The Truth About the Townsend Plan.* Cleveland: The Townsend Plan, Inc., n.d. (approximately 1950).

———. *Why I Am for the Townsend Plan.* Cleveland: The Townsend Plan, Inc., n.d. (approximately 1950).

Leaflets

Old Age Revolving Pensions, Ltd. *A National Movement for Permanent Recovery.* (Four editions from 1934 to 1935. No dates indicated but dates are ascertainable from contents of material.) OARP, Ltd.

———. *Old Age Revolving Pensions, A National Plan.* Long Beach: OARP, Ltd., n.d.

Townsend leaflets from all Townsend corporations, 1934–1950. (Approximate dates listed.)

"The A-B-C of Social Security for You" (1948–50)

"An Honest Dollar for America's Aged Unemployables" (1950)

"Buying Power, The Quest of the Hour" (1937)

"Cheating Yourself!" (1935)

"Face the Facts . . . Mr. Business Man. . . ." (1939)

"Heads Up America! With . . . The Townsend Plan" (1939)

"How You Can Retire on $156 a Month for the Rest of Your Life" (1949–50)

"Insurance Bargain! The Townsend Program" (1951)

"Knowledge from a Loaf of Bread" (1939)

"The $ixty Four Dollar Question Answered" (1948–50)

"The Townsend National Recovery Plan, Inc. What is It?" (1947)

"A Young Man's Viewpoint of the Townsend Plan" (1950)

General Publications and Records

Donaldson, Dr. John. "Memorandum on H.R. 1649." Donaldson Report Supplement, *Townsend National Weekly,* February 19, 1944, A-1 to A-16.

Financial Records (different Townsend corporations)

Prosperity Publishing Co., 1935–1936
Old Age Revolving Pensions, Ltd., 1934–1936
Townsend National Recovery Plan, Inc., 1937–1947
Townsend National Weekly, Inc., 1937–1953
The Townsend Plan, Inc., 1948–1953
Townsend Foundation, 1941–1952

Magazines and Newspapers

The Modern Crusader, June 7, 1934-January 5, 1935.
Official Townsend Weekly, January 21, 1935-July 22, 1935.
National Townsend Weekly, July 29, 1935-October 12, 1936.
Townsend National Weekly, October 19, 1936-May 31, 1958.
Townsend Plan National Courier, June 7, 1958.

Minutes of the Board of Directors and of the "Members" of the different corporations.

Townsend National Weekly, Inc., 1938–1949
Townsend National Recovery Plan, Inc., 1938–1947 (Includes Minutes of Meetings of National Council, 1945–1946).
The Townsend Plan, Inc., 1948–1949.
United Publishing Co., 1948–1949.

National Convention of Townsend Clubs. *Proceedings* for years 1938–1941, 1946–1953.
Old Age Revolving Pensions, Ltd., *Speakers' Manual,* Los Angeles: OARP, Ltd., 1935.
———. Townsend National Radio Division, *Townsend Talk,* Official Series, Chicago: OARP, Ltd., 1936.

Townsend Club Manuals

Old Age Revolving Pensions, Ltd., 1935–1936.
Townsend National Recovery Plan, Inc., 1937–1947.
The Townsend Plan, Inc., 1948–1950.

Interviews

Cuneo, John C. California State Townsend Organizer.
Eaton, Mrs. Edna L. New England Regional Townsend Organizer.
Elliott, John D. Statistician, (Townsend) Washington Legislative Bureau.
Ford, Mrs. J. A. Director, (Townsend) Washington Legislative Bureau.
Hiles, Harrison N. Secretary, The Townsend Plan, Inc.
Townsend, Dr. Francis E. President, The Townsend Plan, Inc.
Townsend, Robert C. Treasurer, The Townsend Plan, Inc.

INDEX

A

Aged, the: and absence of independent politics outside U.S., 17–20; impact upon, of Townsend Movement, 17, 25, 208; and membership in Townsend clubs, 51–55; new image of, in politics, 209–10; population, growth of, 21, 22, 210–11; and reasons for independent politics in U.S., 20–24; and special appeal of Townsend Plan, 46, 55–57

American Association for Labor Legislation, 22

American Association for Old Age Security, 22

American Association for Social Security, 92, 109, 118

American Commonwealth Federation, 182

American Farm Bureau Federation, 84, 118

American Federation of Labor, 22, 28, 109, 118

American Pension Clubs, 226 n41

American Pension Committee, Inc., 76

American Pension Union, Inc., 208

American Radicalism, 25, 29–30, 31, 44, 45, 216 n3

American Retail Federation, 109

An Army of the Aged, 34

Andrews, Sen. Charles O., 120, 136, 227 n19

Angell, Rep. Homer D., 117, 154

Anti-Saloon League, 32, 199–207, 235 n1

Arbuckle, F. A., 65

Argentina, 19

Arizona: and Townsend initiatives, 194–98 *passim*, 234 n68

Arizona Federation of Labor, 195

Arizona Legislative League, 198

Arnold, Thurman, 30

Associated Farmers of California, 196

B

Bailey, Sen. Josiah W., 119

Bainbridge, Sherman, 195

Barton, Bruce, 34

Bell, Rep. C. Jasper, 137, 159, 160, 161; (*See also* Select Committee to Investigate Old Age Pension Organizations)

Bender, Rep. George H., 117

Bismarck, Chancellor Otto von, 8

Black, Sen. Hugo L., 96

Blackely, Canon William, 18

Blanton, Rep. Thomas L., 159

Blatnik, Rep. John A., 154

Bonn, M. J., 219 n37

Booth, Charles, 18

Borah, Sen. William E., 135–36, 142, 229 n39

Bouma, Otis J., 112

Brewster, Cong. Ralph O., 114, 117, 151, 152, 225 n34, 226 n7

Brookings Institution, The, 21

Buck, Rep. Frank H., 114, 150

Burnham, Rep. George, 93

Butler, Rep. John C., 138

C

California: 103, 198; inception of Townsend Movement in, 25–27, 53; and Republican-Townsend cooperation in, 177, 187–89; and state Townsend Party, 184–87; 205; and Townsend initiatives, 194–98 *passim*, 234 n68, 235 n69; (*See also* Ham and Eggs; McLain Movement)

249

aged, 24; and California guber-
natorial campaign, 1934, 61, 142,
187–89
Slichter, Prof. S. H., 108, 109, 224
n11
Smith, Charles W., Jr., 230 n12
Smith, Rep. Clyde H., 117, 118
Smith, Rev. Gerald L. K., 60, 84,
140, 171–76 *passim*, 231 n8
Smith, Gomer, 65, 137, 174, 175, 178,
181, 232 n13
Smith, Rep. Joe L., 149
Smith. Sen. Margaret C., 124
Smith, Rep. Martin F., 114, 117, 123,
174, 231 n4
Social Democrats (*See* Socialists)
Socialists: and pension legislation
outside U.S., 18–19; oppose Townsend Plan, 28
Social Security Act: 18, 100; attitudes
of Townsendites toward, 78, 207;
and future pension politics, 211–14
passim; impact upon of Townsend
Movement, 87–89, 105, 207–8, 224
n6; and major political parties,
89–90, 104, 105, 147, 201, 209, 211;
as obstacle to Townsend Plan, 89–
90, 124, 200–1; and pension politics of 1938, 86, 101–4, 105; and
President Roosevelt, 87–90, 104–5,
222 n10
Social Security Board, 105, 109
South: failure of Townsend Movement in, 53–55, 96; and opposition to Townsend bills, 155; Townsend efforts to placate, 107, 155,
223 n21
Stearns, Rep. Foster, 149
Stewart, Maxwell S., 224 n6
Sweden, 18

T

Taylor, Sen. Glen H., 124, 183
Technocracy, 26, 41–43 *passim*
Thomas, Sen. J. W. Elmer, 151
Thomas, Norman, 175
Thompson, "Big Bill," 28
Tolan, Rep. John H., 48, 161, 167,
231, n23
Townsend *Flash* (*See* Congress, Town-
send lobby in)

Townsend Foundation (*See* Townsend Movement, corporate structure)
Townsend, Dr. Francis E.: 25, 139;
appeals to labor movement, 85;
appeals to Southern congressmen,
155; appearance of, 60; attitude toward Townsend Movement, 63, 76,
166; attitude toward major parties,
54, 170, 179–81, 182; background
of, 32, 33, 58–62, 63; and Clements,
Robert E., 36, 38, 58, 64, 66–67,
71, 72, 141, 161–65 *passim*, 181–
82, 221 n25; and congressional supporters, 63, 140–43, 228 n32; in
contempt of Congress, 166–67, 231
n19; death of, 220 n17; and "democratic" club government, 73–77,
167, 221 n34; effect of success upon,
62–63; and election-endorsement
policy, 126–30 *passim*, 135, 136,
157; and finances of, 63, 66, 72,
78, 82; and free enterprise system,
218 n35; opposes F.D.R., 63, 126,
142, 143, 170–79 *passim*, 203, 231
n1, 231 n4; special role as leader,
58, 60, 61, 63, 69, 72–77 *passim*,
161, 170, 203; and state Townsend
plans, 193, 194; testifies before
Congress, 90, 93–96 *passim*, 98,
101, 114–15, 116, 119, 123, 124;
and third-party politics, 140, 141,
165, 170–78 *passim*, 180, 181–84,
187, 205, 233 n36, 233 n39, 233 n48,
234 n59; and Townsend Plan, features of, 35–40, 42, 44, 61, 94–96
passim, 98, 140–43 *passim*, 217 n15,
217 n22; and Townsend Plan, origin of, 32–36 *passim*, 216 n9, 217
n12 (*See also* Clements; Congress;
Coughlin; Landon; Roosevelt; Sinclair; Smith, Rev. G. L. K.; Social
Security Act)
Townsend Legion (*See* Townsend
Movement, auxiliary organizations)
Townsend Millions Clubs (*See* Townsend Movement, auxiliary organizations)
Townsend Movement: and aged
members, 26, 47–58, 66, 68, 77–78,
88, 136, 178, 182, 184, 194, 197,